I am from there, I am from here,
but I am neither there nor here.
I have two names which meet and part . . .
I have two languages, but I have long forgotten
which is the language of my dreams.

Maḥmūd Darwīsh,
*Edward Said: A Contrapuntal Reading*

To all those who dare to move,
braving the seas and the mountains,
the men and their borders.

And to my parents, who have stayed
but patiently put up with my daring move.

# Pomegranates
# & Artichokes

*A food journey from Iran to Italy*

SAGHAR SETAREH

Interlink Books

An imprint of Interlink Publishing Group, Inc.
Northampton, Massachusetts

# INTRODUCTION

I moved to Italy at the age of 22. Oblivious, insecure, but full of hope. From the moment my passport was stamped in Tehran's airport to the moment I finally got off the plane in the unbearably humid air of Rome, something kept repeating inside my head: "It's over." You might wonder whether I was fleeing something dreadful; a political persecution perhaps, a violent unrest involving guns and bombs, or a menacing family. But the reason I left Iran was far less dramatic: I was young, and I simply sought to write my life story elsewhere. Just like many other young people all over the world.

I had chosen Italy by pure chance. Although the funnier, slightly romanticized version of that story is that I ended up here as the indirect result of a bet I had made on the 2006 Italy vs Germany soccer game. At the time, I wasn't partial to Italy in any way, and I certainly didn't have a particular passion for food. Despite this, my arrival in Rome shaped some of the strongest culinary memories that I have to this day.

The very first night, together with some other students, I went to Tiberina Island on the Tiber River and opened a bottle of chilled white wine—something I had never tried before. Next, my first *pizza al taglio*, the very Roman one topped with potatoes. Then, my first mind-blowing *cappuccino e cornetto* for breakfast in a busy bar. Later, countless bottles of Peroni beer, and a short period of obsession with pork steaks. I had never eaten fresh pork before coming to Italy, and for a while it looked like I was determined to make up for my 22 years of pork-free life.

Years passed, terrifyingly quickly, and somewhere on the verge of turning 30, when the allure of cheap alcohol and late-night student parties had long withered, like many foreigners before me I found myself totally enchanted by Italian cooking and the lifestyle, opening my eyes for the first time to how food expresses culture, history, and economy.

Soon I found my lantern, my mirror, and my passion in food, lighting up not only my path to understanding Italy but also illuminating the reflection of my own Iranian culinary heritage. Like many immigrants before me, I came to know—and cherish—my homeland, by comparison with the new country.

The more I learned about Italy and its food, the more curious I found myself about Iranian food. As I dug into my memories and those of other people from the Middle East and the Mediterranean, the food of these places started to appear to me as a multilayered déjà vu of flavors. Going down this rabbit hole through travel and tasting, while tracing the red thread of common ingredients, I realized that you can draw a road map between the Iranian palate and the Italian one and back, using a whole spectrum of Middle Eastern and Mediterranean food.

Take the eggplant, for example. Brought to Italy by Arabs in the Middle Ages, it was initially mistrusted and disliked, just as it had been in the Levant in previous centuries. Today, many beloved

Italian dishes are based on eggplant—parmigiana (page 243), for example, an assembly of fried eggplant, tomato sauce, and cheese. In Turkey, there are many dishes with similar ingredients, including *Imam bayildi* (page 149), which is a fried eggplant stuffed with onion in tomato sauce. The eggplant is much loved all over the Levant—one of the most popular dishes of this region being *baba ghanoush* (page 130), a dip of charred eggplant flavored with garlic, tahini, and lemon. In Iran, too, eggplant are much loved, and one of the famous dishes there is *mirza ghasemi* (page 57), where the eggplant are again charred, then cooked with tomatoes and eggs.

These are very different dishes, of course, but what brings them together—apart from the deliciousness—are the ingredients and cooking methods that have migrated through these territories over centuries, appearing in different forms and with different condiments.

I went further, researching more similarities between dishes across these apparently distant lands and cultures. What I found entranced and surprised me. There are some dishes that have verifiable historical links, and others that are built around very similar ideas, even if no direct relation between them can be found. But most importantly, I found that ingredients, methods, and recipes have never abided by borders between nations and religions. They have allowed themselves to be transformed, transported, and exchanged at each encounter, with each migration.

This is essentially what *Pomegranates & Artichokes* is about: migrations. Of ingredients, of recipes and of stories—but most importantly, of the people who make them. Of a home that is no longer a solid, fixed space but is now an immense, fluid concept with undefined borders, free to wander and take new shapes, just as the eggplant dish takes different names as the condiments change.

The quest for home has followed me closely in the kitchen; at times I have cooked Iranian to put up a small resistance. In a world where everything from the weather to the language, the culture, every habit, tradition, and holiday was different, dinner had to be the same. Dinner meant reassurance. Dinner was who I am; deliciously different from the land I'm living in.

Other times, I have done the exact opposite. In my (almost desperate) attempt to fit in, I have cooked and eaten only the "new food." For those of us coming from the Middle East or the Balkans area to Italy, this isn't even drastically challenging. I have devoured the markets, asked for recipes, eaten at way more restaurants than I could afford, and cooked the food of my new home. I've tried my best to belong, constantly confronting who I have been, and who I was becoming with each new recipe I cooked.

My cooking, just as the languages I speak and the person that I am, is not bound to a national identity. There's a lot of Iran when I speak, when I think, and when I cook. But there's also a lot of Italy, in equal measure. It's often said the language you dream in is the predominant language of your brain. In the same way, one can say what you normally cook is your predominant cuisine. I can cook Iranian, Italian, and everything in between for a simple Tuesday lunch, the same way I can fit Persian, English, and Italian words into my morning conversation over a cup of coffee.

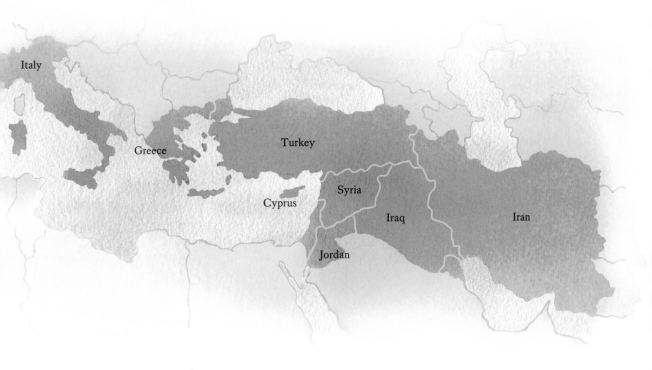

Consequently, this is also a book about identity. It is an audacious claim, to unapologetically declare the duality of my life as an immigrant. Neither nostalgic about the "exotic Persia," nor in search of "dolce vita" in Italy, but simply living and breathing both, and everything in between. Owning the reality of belonging to more than one culture, despite the efforts of those who would deny me it.

So, come with me on a culinary road trip that starts in Iran, then travels west through the Levant and Eastern Mediterranean, finally arriving in Italy, with ingredients, recipes, and stories as our guiding stars. By taking this journey together, I hope to highlight the similarities between the recipes and stories, rather than the differences. Please notice that by mentioning these similarities I'm not looking for the "origin" of the dishes or for who invented what first. This is not an academic endeavor but rather a quest to observe encounters, past and present, in search of shared humanity. The enthralling history of common roots between the food of these territories is a much wider matter, but for the sake of space and purpose I couldn't delve into all of them here.

I hope along the way in this journey you'll be as fascinated and surprised as I have been to see that what we believe to be "exotic and afar Persia," the "embattled" Middle East, the beautiful and familiar Mediterranean, and the adored and European Italy, share much more culinary heritage than you might expect.

Let us begin.

Iran

The question "Where are you from?" has punctured most days of my life,
and has been both innocuous and frightening.

Fatimah Asghar, "On Loneliness,"
*The Good Immigrant USA*


Only the sound of luggage cart wheels can be heard as we walk along the corridors that link Tehran's IKA airport arrivals section to passport control. The line isn't long, which is a relief, because it's after 2 a.m. and my terrible flight with the low-cost Turkish airline has left me very stiff. I give a jaunty hello to the officer who checks my passport. He greets me back, albeit with less enthusiasm. But he doesn't welcome me back to Iran.

Heading out of the airport, my brother asks if I want any coffee. No thanks. I'm anxious to eat and drink many things now that I'm in Iran—but airport coffee isn't one of them. That will be for when I'm back in Rome.

Coming from Europe, it's the vastness of Iran that first gets to you. The plains look endless, the land ancient. Despite the dark, I look out of the car windows to catch a glimpse of the high, gigantic mountains, a colossal presence always in one's field of vision, almost godlike. Mount Damavand, the True North of Tehran, capped with snow in the winter and rosy pink at dusk.

We're on our way to have *kalle pache* (*khash*), the broth of sheep's head and trotters, usually consumed in the very early hours of the morning, either before a hard day of work, or to soothe the hangover after a night of drinking contraband alcohol (perhaps in a small gathering of friends, perhaps in a large party, but always behind closed doors).

My father points out how the price of *kalle pache* has risen, like the cost of everything else in Iran. I get lost in the too many zeros of prices that are unrecognizably different each time I visit. I understand enough to realize that our tables are getting smaller and smaller in Iran; crippling economic sanctions from the West paired with incommensurable internal mismanagement and corruption have brought a nation, which happens to sit on one of the largest sources of oil and gas in the world, to starvation.

It's difficult to talk about Iran from any angle. I don't think at the moment any two Iranians in the world could agree on anything other than, perhaps, that *chelo kabab* represents the national dish of Iran. And indeed, is it Iran, or Persia?

The short story is that Iranians have called their country Iran for thousands of years, whereas Persia was the name used by the West. In 1935, the name of the country was officially changed to Iran—which is pronounced *ee-rān* by the way, not *eye-ran*—for all international purposes. But after the 1979 revolution and the establishment of the Islamic Republic, it became extremely inconvenient to be "Iranian," so many started presenting themselves as Persian. "Persia" evokes images of fluffy cats, expensive carpets, and the kingdoms of *One Thousand and One Nights*, whereas "Iran" was linked to a hostage crisis, extremism, revolution, and war.

This is problematic in several ways. First, there is no country called "Persia" on the map, just as there isn't one for the Roman, Ottoman, Han, or Aztec empires. But the main problem with referring to the culture of Iran as Persian (as opposed to Iranian), is that "Persians," as an ethnicity, are only one of many present in Iran, and only make up half the population. The remaining Iranians belong to other ethnicities, often with their own dialect or language. Referring to the culture of Iran as "Persian" alone is an act of erasure to all those beautiful ethnicities and regional differences which, together with the breathtaking natural beauty of Iran, make the country so extraordinarily diverse.

On the other hand, the Persian language, *Farsi*—the country's official language—is not limited to the current Iran. It is also the official language of Afghanistan and Tajikistan, although the legacy of old Persian culture extends beyond the neighboring countries. Just as everywhere else, modern borders don't define where a culture ends or begins.

Find the situation confusing? You're not alone. Trying to preserve our identity as a country with a very rich culture and a turbulent history, while grappling with modernity on one hand and a religious regime and decades of semi-isolation on the other, has left us "on a pendulum between self-veneration and self-deploration," to quote the multi-award-winning Iranian film director Asghar Farhadi. What we really want, though, apart from everything else, is an ounce of *normality*.

"Normality," this extraordinary privilege, has been taken away from us twice: once by the totalitarian regime that tries to police our lives (and that we've been incessantly fighting back), and once by Western media, with their perverted image of us, against which we have little means of fighting.

In my years out of Iran, too many times I've had strangers trying to get me to confirm their distorted view of my country, while impressing their Orientalist "knowledge" of Iran upon me. On the other hand, with the lack of multiple and diverse Iranian voices in the media, those few present have been burdened by the impossibility of representing an entire heterogeneous nation, and its large diaspora.

I have desperately and unfalteringly wanted to leave this place for good. And yet it's only here where people know how to properly pronounce my name, making it sound as poetic and astounding as it is—*cup of wine, star*.

A tinkling pop song can be heard from the car next to us. The young driver is snapping his fingers to the rhythm. Here, our limbs are ready to spring to dance, even first thing in the morning. Here, music is in our bones, and poetry is in our blood, and the aftertaste of saffron and roses lingers after every bite.

And that's how I know I am home.

# THE IRANIAN PANTRY

Most of the ingredients used in Iranian food are available from regular markets and stores, and those that aren't can usually be found in Middle Eastern and/or Indian grocery shops. Search for special Persian/Iranian stores online; you might be surprised to find one in your own town.

**Saffron:** Undoubtedly the most characteristic Iranian flavor. You need good-quality saffron to make Iranian dishes sing, and naturally, I'm biased toward Iranian saffron. There's a good chance any saffron you buy in any Middle Eastern store is Iranian, even if the brand says otherwise. Due to American sanctions on Iranian trade, saffron farmers have been suffering to the point of losing their family livelihoods, resulting in desperate measures to sell their "red gold," such as smuggling it to Afghanistan and even Europe, and selling it under non-Iranian labels. Read how to prepare saffron on page 18.

**Turmeric:** Sometimes known as the saffron of the poor, turmeric is the foundation of almost all Iranian dishes, usually listed together with salt and pepper in the ingredients of a recipe.

**Other spices:** Cinnamon, cardamom, ground rose petals, black cumin, and red and black pepper are common in many Iranian recipes.

**Damask rose:** As petals and as an essence (rosewater), this is an important ingredient in all of the Middle East (and beyond), but these dramatically beautiful and inebriatingly aromatic roses appear in more than just Iranian food; they feature in poetry and art, too. Everything you see, touch, and eat in Iran has an aftertaste of roses, even if not detectable at first bite.

**Dehydrated fruits:** In first place are barberries, known for the brightness they add to every dish with their sharp sourness and ruby red color, followed by dried apricots, prunes, dates, sour cherries, and more. Fruit, both dried and fresh, is essential in Iranian cooking.

**Nuts:** Iran is the world's largest producer of pistachios, so pistachios appear very often in Iranian dishes, savory and sweet. As with saffron, export rates have dropped dramatically in recent years due to crippling US sanctions, leaving thousands of pistachio farming families in near hunger. Walnuts and almonds are also important components of the Iranian pantry.

**Pomegranate molasses:** Sour condiments such as pomegranate molasses, plum molasses, and tamarind paste appear in many dishes around the country.

**Fresh herbs, galore:** By the kilo, of each type. However, the recipes in this book use only moderate amounts of herbs.

**Rice:** Has become a staple in Iranian cooking in the last couple of centuries. We grow excellent rice in the green regions of northern Iran, with long grains and a wonderful perfume. In its absence, a good-quality basmati rice will work as well.

**Bread:** Read more about it on page 28.

**Yogurt:** Read more about it on page 66.

# Golden onion

*Piaz dagh* | پیاز داغ

> Know that onion is the flavor of all that one cooks, and it is to all *khoresh* (stews)
> what is soul to the body. For a body without a soul is no more than a rock, or a log.
>
> Nadder Mirza Qajar (1883), *Karname-ye Khoresh* (کارنامه‌ی خورش)

I want to say fried onion is what *soffritto* is to Italian cooking, but that would be an understatement, since the Iranian *piaz dagh*—golden onion—appears in a greater variety of dishes, both as a foundation to build the dish upon, and as a garnish on top. The important characteristic of Iranian golden onion is that simply sweating and sautéing onions won't be enough. The onions need to be sliced (not diced), then fried in one layer in abundant hot oil for about 10 minutes, until they turn golden. You also need a neutral-flavored oil with a high smoke point, such as sunflower or peanut oil.

It's very handy to have golden onion on hand when you're cooking Iranian dishes (or any other recipes starting with onion), so making a bigger batch is a good solution. It takes some time to slice and fry all the onion, but it will keep in the fridge for a couple of days, and you can also freeze some (in one layer, that's the key).

The general rule of thumb is that one medium onion makes 1 tablespoon of fried golden onion. So if your recipe asks for 2 tablespoons of golden onion, it means you'll need to fry two onions with a dash of ground turmeric.

If your recipe starts with golden onion, such as the mutton braise with zucchini on page 91, fry your onion in the same pot you'll be cooking the rest of the dish in.

*Makes 2 tablespoons golden onion*

oil, for deep-frying
 (the quantity will depend
 on the size of your pan)
2 onions, halved, then sliced
 ¼ inch (5 mm) thick
¼ teaspoon ground turmeric

In a large pan suitable for frying, heat the oil over medium-high heat. Make sure the onion half-rings are separated from each other. When tiny bubbles appear in the oil, add one slice of onion to check the heat. If the oil around the onion bubbles and the onion comes to the surface, the oil is hot enough; otherwise, wait until this happens.

Usually, two sliced onions can be fried in two or three batches, in a 9 inch (23 cm) pan. If your pan is smaller, you should fry the onions in more batches. This is actually time-saving, contrary to what you may think, because one layer of onion fries more

*Continued ›*

«

quickly, and piled-up onions become soggy and take more time to become golden and crunchy.

Fry each batch over medium-high heat for 8–12 minutes, or until the onion has shrunk down and is completely golden. At the last moment for the first batch, add all the turmeric, stir around a bit, then with a slotted spoon transfer the onion to a large dish lined with paper towel. The onion will darken once removed from the pan, turning golden brown on the paper. Add another batch of onion to the pan and repeat. For this amount of onion, the turmeric added to the oil at the end of the first batch is enough. (If you're making more than this amount, add a dash more turmeric each second or third batch.) You can keep the frying oil for a week for frying up more golden onion, or to use in dishes where a hint of onion and turmeric would be welcome.

You can keep the golden onion in the fridge in an airtight container for 3–4 days, or freeze for up to 3 months. If using frozen golden onion, you won't need to thaw it—just break off a piece and add it to the hot pan. It will just take a little longer to cook as it thaws in the pan and the water evaporates.

# Saffron infusion

*Za'feran-e dam kardeh* | زعفران دم کرده

Saffron is probably the most iconic, defining flavor associated with Iranian cuisine. We pride ourselves on producing the best saffron in the world, although we are rarely recognized for doing so. This is partly due to lack of international marketing, and mostly to sanctions, forcing some Iranian-grown saffron to be exported to Spain, and somehow labeled there as "Spanish" saffron. But if you buy your saffron in any Middle Eastern shop around the world, chances are it has been cultivated in Iran, no matter what the label says.

The best saffron is farmed in Ghayenat, in the grand and ancient region of Khorasan in the north-east of current Iran. "Khorasan" means "where the sun rises," since it has always been Iran's most easterly area, even when it contained most of current Afghanistan and parts of Central Asia. Sunrise

*Continued ›*

is also when the delicate purple crocus flowers that yield the saffron threads must be picked—traditionally a job for teenage girls and young women. The vivid red thread-like stigmas, or strands, need to be carefully and swiftly picked out of the crocus flowers within a few hours of harvesting, and then packed. You can recognize high-quality saffron by its color: the threads or strands will all be deep ruby red, with no orange or yellow parts.

Infusing is the technique we use in Iran to prepare saffron for all our dishes, both savory and sweet. We call this infusing "brewing" in Persian—the same verb we use for preparing tea and steaming rice. I know there are other methods of preparing saffron as well, but please, whatever you do, don't use the saffron threads dry and on their own. It's unforgivably wasteful, because the spice's exquisite flavor and color are released much better when the threads are infused in warm water. It's also way too expensive to just sprinkle dry saffron threads on top of dishes, not to mention also a bit obnoxious—especially to those young hands that collected those flowers one morning at sunrise in the east of the world.

You can make a larger batch and keep the infusion in the fridge for up to 5 days—ready to add spoonfuls to your tea, or to drizzle over your eggs and pretty much every dish.

*Makes 3 tablespoons*
*saffron infusion*

½ teaspoon saffron threads,
    very loosely packed
a good pinch of sugar

Grind the saffron strands with the sugar in a small mortar. If you don't have a small mortar, you can put the saffron and sugar on a piece of parchment paper, fold all the sides so the powder won't escape, then grind with a jam jar or rolling pin until you have a very fine powder.

Bring a kettle of water to a boil, then let it sit for a few minutes. Tip the powder very gently into a small glass teacup, then gently pour 3 tablespoons of the hot water over it. (Never use boiling water, or you'll "kill" the saffron.) Cover the cup with a lid or saucer and let the mixture "brew" for at least 10 minutes without removing the lid, to release the color and aroma of the saffron. After this time your saffron infusion is ready to use.

If you make a larger batch, store the leftovers in a clean sealed jar in the fridge for 4–5 days. You can also make a refreshing drink called a *sharbat* (page 116) with any leftover saffron infusion, or add it to your regular cup of tea.

# Iranian rice

*Chelow* | چلو

Iranian rice is the pride and joy of contemporary Iranian cuisine—an art form perfected over many centuries. We fuss over our rice way more than Italians fuss over pasta; we just haven't been given the chance to tell the world how opinionated we are about it.

Different varieties of rice are grown in Iran, mainly in the green line in the north, sandwiched between the Caspian Sea and Alborz Mountains. The best-quality rice is fragrant and has long grains that don't break down easily and that lengthen nicely during cooking.

There are a couple of different techniques for cooking Iranian rice. The one I describe here is perhaps most commonly used, and although it may sound tedious with two cooking stages, including long, slow steaming, I believe it achieves the best result more easily.

Before cooking, the rice needs to be cleaned of small stones. It is then rinsed gently with cold water several times until the water is almost clear; the water will always remain a bit cloudy.

Where Iranian rice can't be found, basmati is an acceptable substitute. It's best for Iranian rice to be soaked in water overnight with a generous amount of salt, as this allows the rice grains to swell during cooking without breaking (a mark of good-quality rice is that it can withstand long soaking and cooking). For basmati rice, even an hour of soaking is enough, although 2–3 hours is better. Basmati also needs to be properly seasoned with salt, and this is best done during the soaking time.

There are two cooking stages. The first, parboiling, only takes a few minutes with the basmati I've been using in the West, although the cooking time varies based on the quality of rice, as well as the altitude of the region you're cooking in, as water takes longer to boil at higher elevations than at sea level.

After parboiling you drain the rice; if you want to prepare *tahdig*—the famous crust at the bottom of the pot of rice that everyone adores—you can make it at this stage. You can make *tahdig* in several ways: with rice alone; or you can add a few spoonfuls of yogurt and a dash of saffron infusion for a cakey *tahdig* quite similar to *tahchin* (page 72); or you can use slices of raw potato (my absolute favorite), or pieces of thin flatbread, such as lavash. A generous amount of oil is always required for the bottom of the pot. I suggest using a mixture of a neutral-flavored cooking oil and ghee (although you can skip the latter), and butter or ghee for the top. Olive oil is not a good choice for cooking Iranian rice as it is too strongly flavored.

The second stage of cooking is steaming (or what Iranians call "brewing"). If you steam the rice plain, without any condiments, then the rice is called *chelow*. If you layer the parboiled rice with a condiment or other ingredients (as you do with the *lubia polow* on page 48), it's a *polow* (pilaf).

*Continued ›*

«

*Serves 4–5*

**For soaking**
2 cups (350 g) Iranian or basmati-
    style long-grain rice
approximately ¼ cup (70 g)
    coarse salt

**For parboiling**
1 tablespoon vegetable oil

**For steaming**
1 tablespoon ghee (or half butter,
    half vegetable oil)

### SOAKING THE RICE

At least 2–3 hours before you want to serve the dish, gently rinse the rice with cold water, discarding the water. Do this at least three times. The water will always remain a bit cloudy, but rinsing removes the excess starch from the rice, which will make the rice fluffy once cooked, with each grain separated.

Add the rice to a large bowl, with enough water to cover the rice by at least 2 inches (5 cm). Add the salt and fold gently, possibly with your hand. Taste the water: it should be as salty as the sea. Don't worry if the water seems too salty—the rice absorbs the salt it needs, and any excess salt can be rinsed away after the first cooking (the parboiling stage).

Soak the rice for 2–3 hours, or at least 30 minutes. You can even soak the rice overnight.

### PARBOILING THE RICE

Bring a large pot of water to a boil. Add the vegetable oil. Discard most of the soaking water from the rice, without draining it completely, then gently add the rice and what's left of the soaking water to the boiling water. Do not stir the rice too much, or you'll break the grains. If needed, put the lid on to return the water to a boil as quickly as possible.

We want to partially cook the rice at this point; meaning the grains will swell, and the outer part of the grain should be soft, but a bit of a bite should remain in the center (similar to very al dente, if we were talking about pasta). The parboiling time varies depending on the quality of rice, and even the humidity of the region in which you live. This amount of rice would usually take 5–10 minutes to cook.

### DRAINING & RINSING THE RICE

Place a fine-meshed colander in your kitchen sink, then very gently and carefully drain the rice into the colander. Taste the rice. If it's too salty (it shouldn't be), run cold water over the rice for several minutes. Otherwise, run the cold tap water for only about 30 seconds, just to stop the cooking process.

### STEAMING (OR "BREWING") THE RICE

Up to this point, the rinsing, soaking, and parboiling steps are the same for all the Iranian rice recipes in this book. From here on the method changes slightly, based on what rice dish you're preparing, and what *tahdig* you're making for the crusty base of the rice dish.

In a large nonstick pot, bring 1 cup (250 ml) water to a boil, together with the ghee, which will melt. Set half of this oily water aside in a cup.

(If making rice with *tahdig*, place the *tahdig* of your choice—raw slices of potato or slices of flatbread—in one layer in the bottom of the pot, then follow the recipe for layering the rice and other ingredients into the pot. Otherwise, just proceed to the next step once the water and ghee have come to a boil.)

Very gently scatter the rice in the pot, without pressing down, to form a cone. If the rice needs salt, you can sprinkle some between each layer. With the end of a wooden spoon, poke a few holes into the mound of rice to let the steam rise from the bottom. Pour the reserved cup of oily water over the rice. Put the lid on and cook over high heat for 5–10 minutes, until the rice "sweats" and condensation forms under the lid, and you can hear the oil sizzle at the bottom of the pot.

Now wrap the lid in a clean folded tea towel, then place the lid on the pot, making sure it seals tightly. Cook the rice over the lowest possible heat for 45 minutes to 1½ hours; a heat diffuser is best here, especially if cooking on a gas burner. If all goes well, this recipe should give you the simple rice *tahdig*. Success at making good *tahdig* is a combination of experience, a good pot, lots of oil, and a bit of luck.

Use a skimmer or a slotted spoon to gently fluff and dish out the rice in a scattering movement. A flat serving spatula, cake server, or rice paddle also work well. The point is, use a flat or very shallow utensil, to avoid breaking the rice grains.

Any leftover rice can be reheated with a splash of water and perhaps a tiny amount of butter, ghee, or oil.

# *Nashta*, food to
# begin the day with

The word *nashta* literally means both without food (fasting), and the first meal that breaks the fast (breakfast). Breakfast in Iran can be both a scanty, hasty matter of a cup of tea and a *loghmeh* (mouthful) of flatbread and cheese, or a lavish spread of jams and eggs and cheese and butter, to name a few options.

The recipes in this chapter are inspired by Iranian breakfast dishes. Most of them can easily double up as quick lunches or weeknight dinners as well.

A few Iranian breakfasts deserve special mention, even if there isn't a recipe for them in this book: *kalleh pache*, also known as *khash*, the boiled head (including brain and tongue) and trotters of sheep, a dish we have in common with the Caucasus, Balkans, and the rest of the Middle East; *halim*, the wheat porridge with meat, served with sugar and cinnamon on top; and what we call an omelet, which is really eggs cooked in tomatoes (now commonly known as *shakshuka*).

# The typical Iranian breakfast platter

*Sobhaneh* | صبحانه

It all starts with bread.

Bread is such an important part of an Iranian breakfast that the utmost effort and love you can put into the meal is to visit a bakery early in the morning to get some fresh bread, still hot from the oven. In my early university years when my brother was still in high school, my father would "torment" us by coming back home with fresh bread at 8 a.m. on Fridays* and forcing us to get up for a lavish breakfast spread—when all we wanted in the world was to get an hour more of sleep. We would complain, nag, and curse, but we would sit at the table anyway to enjoy the meal. One could say we were spoiled. I say my father's only way of showing love was to share huge amounts of food.

The traditional bakeries of Iran—which are sadly disappearing in big cities—each specialize in one type of bread. It could be *sangak*, a very long flatbread cooked in an oven full of hot pebbles ("sangak" means "little pebble"); *lavash*, a very soft flatbread; *barbari*, a long, narrow leavened bread with large air bubbles inside; or *taftoon*, a small, round rustic flatbread. A lavish breakfast spread will have more than one type of fresh bread to choose from.

Jams also appear on the Iranian breakfast table—at least two types on a formal one—with sour cherry, strawberry, carrot, and orange zest among the favorites. Quince jam with cardamom pods, made in copper pots that turn the jam ruby red, is saved for more luxurious breakfasts as there's always so little of it, due to the short quince season. Other special Iranian jams are citron zest—bittersweet, with an intoxicatingly beautiful aroma—and rose petal jam, which is unexpectedly chewy.

Then of course there's butter, to spread on the hot bread before slathering on one of these jams or cheese—or, if you're lucky, the dairy delicacy known as *kaymak* (or *sarshir* in Persian, which translates to "top of the milk"), not unlike clotted cream. In fact, the luscious, creamy *sarshir* is obtained by simmering whole-fat milk for a long time until all the cream comes to the top. The cream is then set aside, and sometimes left to ferment slightly in some Central Asian and Caucasian cultures. *Sarshir* is best on warm bread with some honey; in its absence, thick (heavy) cream or clotted cream is served with honey on the side.

There's always cheese—the Iranian white cheese, which is very similar to feta and used to be sold in

---

* *Fridays are the weekend in Iran, much like Sundays are in the Western world. The Iranian week begins on Saturday.*

large metal cans full of brine. A little bowl of shelled walnuts with this salty white cheese is a match made in heaven. One of the most nutritious breakfasts or snacks that children in Iran take to school is a little lavash wrap spread with white cheese and scattered with walnut pieces.

As well as sweet bites such as *sarshir* and honey served with *sheermal* bread (page 33), Iranians also enjoy savory breakfasts: hard-boiled eggs, fried eggs, and eggs and tomato. The latter has sprung to fame in recent years under the name of *shakshuka*, but for us it has always been simply an "omelet," although it looks nothing like an actual omelet. Friday's breakfast table might also include sliced tomatoes and fresh, crunchy, aromatic cucumbers.

What follows is not a recipe, but rather an inspiration, for breakfast.

## Breakfast ideas

hot black tea
sugar to sweeten the tea
   (optional)
slices of your flatbread of choice
butter
at least one type of jam
*sarshir, kaymak*, clotted cream,
   or thick (heavy) cream
honey
Iranian white cheese
   or feta cheese
1 hard-boiled or fried
   egg per person
sliced tomatoes
a bowl of walnut halves
sliced cucumbers

Take a sip of hot black tea (or the bicolored tea on page 32), sweetened with sugar if desired. Tear off a small piece of bread, then spread it with some butter and jam. Try also the combinations of clotted cream and honey, butter, and cheese, or egg and tomato, cheese and walnuts or cucumber, and any other combination you can think of.

*Pictured on pages 30–31*

# My grandmother's bicolored tea

*Chai-e do rang* | چای دو رنگ

Ruby red on top, and crystal clear at the bottom, this little cup of tea appears on the breakfast table like a magic token straight from some fairyland. Or at least this is how I saw it when my grandmother used to make it for me and my cousins on Friday mornings, if we had stayed at her place the night before. She was not the type of grandmother who would coddle her grandchildren, but this was her little something special for us tiny ones back then.

What actually makes the miracle of this tea happen, though, is no fairy dust, but a ridiculous amount of sugar. In most parts of Iran, sweetened tea is drunk only for breakfast, and normally only a teaspoon or two of sugar is used; the many other teas during the day are drunk with a sugar lump or two, or none at all. Bicolored tea, however, requires at least 4 teaspoons of sugar per cup. (I should also say that Iranians believe in the healing powers of *nabāt*—crystallized sugar with a bit of saffron. Melted in tea or just hot water, it is advised for anyone with a stomachache or any other digestive problems. Don't laugh, because I should also tell you it does work!)

Bicolored tea is still a little treat from a fairyland, in the end, as it is only served once in a blue moon. So bring out your sugar bowl and your best teapot, and put the kettle on.

*Makes a scant 1 cup (200 ml)*

boiling hot water
4–5 teaspoons sugar
very strong black tea, the best
    quality you have, freshly
    brewed in a teapot

Fill your cup—preferably a glass teacup, so you can see the tea colors—three-quarters full with boiling hot water. Add the sugar and stir until all the sugar has completely dissolved. Wait a moment to watch the water stop swirling.

Hold a teaspoon facing upright over the middle of your cup. Very patiently and slowly pour the tea into the teaspoon, so the tea drizzles off the teaspoon into the cup, and stays suspended over the water. This will work better if your teapot is not too close to the teaspoon, but the teaspoon is close to the surface of the hot water in the cup. Continue until the teacup is filled.

You will see that the layer of hot water saturated with sugar in the bottom of the teacup has remained transparent, and the colored tea has settled on top. Serve with a teaspoon on the side to stir before drinking.

# A milky bread

*Naan-e sheermal* | نان شیرمال

Enghelab Street in downtown Tehran is always busy and bustling with people from all walks of life, but never as much as around 5 p.m., when university students, workers, and employees alike, tired from the day's work and weary of the traffic and pollution, spend the last of their energies winning the race of getting a cab, bus, or the metro to finally take them home. The "Revolution Road" is home to many universities, among which the University of Tehran is one of Iran's best and largest. The street was renamed after the 1979 revolution from Shah Reza—the name of the father of Iran's last Shah—to Enghelab, which means revolution. If the battered asphalt and blackened building walls along this long street could talk, they'd speak of many turmoils and unrests, with students at the heart of them, of tear gas and gunshots and bloodshed, but they'd also tell you a lesser-told story: one about the street food of Tehran.

*Continued ›*

«

Enghelab Street is not famous for historical literary cafés like the ones in Naderi Street, a few blocks down. All along this long street are little sandwich shops and eateries selling something cheap and delicious, mostly to take away. I was raised to eat only homemade food, and was instructed to never eat at such places by my mom (who's still skeptical of all street foods—a shame). I grew out of it— thank God—when I went to Art and Architecture university, located on a cross street of Enghelab Street. My university years were filled to the brim with the best—and absolute worst—street foods that could be found in the neighborhood around us. I wasn't a great fan of the sandwiches on Enghelab Street (a little skepticism here actually didn't hurt), but on chilly winter evenings I did especially love the hot bowls of *aash* (thick soups of noodles, herbs, and beans) and *haleem* (wheat porridge with pounded meat, served with sugar and cinnamon)—or the occasional hot *piroshki*, one of the many culinary souvenirs of the Russians and Armenians that Iranians love so much we have adopted them as our own.

One of my greatest disappointments with the street food of Enghelab Street came one afternoon when I bought a loaf of *sheermal*. I was craving something bready and a little sweet for the journey home, and I felt nostalgic for the buttery, soft, and fragrant *sheermal* my grandmother baked when I was a child. But ladies and gentlemen, that dry, plasticky, flavorless thing that was sold to me was not by any account a proper *sheermal*, despite its many regional and family variations.

So I took a page from my street-food-wary mom's book and decided to bake my own *sheermal* at home. I could always get my post-lesson sweet snacks at my beloved France Pastry, a classic meeting place since 1965, sipping a hot mug of tea and biting into a freshly baked Danish pastry, perched on a stool, watching through its picture windows the people and cars bustling by along busy Enghelab Street.

*Makes 2 loaves*

1 cup (250 ml) milk
2 teaspoons (7 g) active-dry yeast
¼ cup (50 g) sugar
7 tablespoons (100 g) butter, melted
2½ cups (300 g) all-purpose flour, plus extra for dusting
1¾ cups (200 g) whole wheat flour
1 egg
1½ teaspoons saffron infusion (page 18)
1½ teaspoons salt
nigella seeds, sesame seeds, or flaxseeds, to garnish

Heat the milk in a small pot until it's lukewarm but not hot. Dissolve the yeast and sugar in the milk. Cover and set aside for 5–10 minutes to activate the yeast. If, after this time, there's no foam, discard the mixture and start again.

Reserve 1 teaspoon of the melted butter and add the rest to a large bowl with the two flours, egg, saffron infusion, and salt, mixing well with a wooden spoon. Now work in the yeast and milk mixture and, once everything comes together, start kneading the dough with your hands (*sheer* means "milk" and *mal* means "rubbing," so rub that milk dough). The final result should be a slightly sticky dough. Different flours in different temperatures absorb liquid differently, so if the dough is too wet, add a little flour; if it's too dry, add a splash of milk.

*Continued ›*

«

**For the egg wash**
2 tablespoons melted butter
1½ teaspoons saffron infusion
   (page 18)
1 egg, lightly beaten
a splash of milk

Knead the dough for 5–10 minutes in the bowl or on a work surface. Use some of the reserved melted butter to grease the bottom of a clean bowl. Shape the dough into a ball, place it in the bowl, then lightly brush the top with the remaining butter so a crust doesn't form. Cover with a clean tea towel and leave to rise 30–60 minutes, or until the dough has doubled in size.

Punch down the dough to let the air out, then knead for another 10 minutes. Let the dough rest again for 5 minutes under the tea towel.

Cut the dough in half and form each piece into a ball by pulling the edges toward the center. Let it rest for another 5 minutes.

Meanwhile, preheat the oven to 400°F (200°C). Combine all the egg wash ingredients in a cup or small bowl.

Put a piece of parchment paper on your work surface and, having lightly dusted one ball of dough with flour, roll it out into a thick disc. Now you can use the tip of your finger to make any sort of decoration. I like to make a circle with a grid in the center (see page 35), but you can also make a cross, or any other shape you like. Leave to rest for another 5 minutes.

Leaving the dough on the parchment paper, transfer the dough directly to a baking sheet. Brush the egg wash on top, then sprinkle with seeds of your choice. Bake for 25–35 minutes, or until golden on top and underneath. While it bakes, prepare the second loaf on another piece of parchment paper and leave it under a tea towel, ready for baking when the first loaf is done. (If you have a very large oven, you can bake both loaves together.)

Serve the *sheermal* warm, possibly with butter and jam, or just on its own. It's a bread best consumed on the day of baking (which isn't hard as it's irresistible). If left on the counter, it unfortunately gets stale quickly, so if you do have any leftovers, freeze them. *Sheermal* thaws very well in a hot oven, very lightly splashed with water.

# Shakes & "potions"

Continuing the street foods journey, there must be a stop at an *abmiveh-foroushi*, or juice shop. These shops are tiny, since you're supposed to take your drink to go, and they usually have a counter lined with at least five or six blenders containing bright, thick liquids—strawberry red, black mulberry ruby, mango orange, shades of yellow and beige from bananas and walnuts, and carrot shakes with ice cream (my least favorite; my mom would make me carrot juice with milk as a child, and like a spiteful kitten I'd spill it all on the floor by "mistake"). These are not like the healthy-ish juice bars of recent years—the key here is abundance, and smoothies are served in a tall, big glass topped with dollops of ice cream.

They also sell the "special potion" *ma'joon-e makhsoo*s. The classic juice shop version is a bomb of ingredients—dates and bananas always, to give sweetness and thickness, then any kind of nuts, plus coconut powder and sesame seeds, and so on, all blended with milk, cream, and/or ice cream, then topped with more nuts and honey.

This version of the "potion" is a bit less powerful (read fewer ingredients), but is still a favorite breakfast. Feel free to add or remove ingredients, and to adjust the quantities to your taste. It's your magic cauldron.

*Makes 2 large glasses*

3 dates, pitted
2 cups (500 ml) milk (any kind)
1 banana
2 big dollops of full-fat plain
  Greek-style yogurt
a handful of walnuts
1 tablespoon coconut flour, plus
  extra to garnish
1 tablespoon sesame seeds,
  plus extra to garnish
½ teaspoon ground cinnamon
a pinch of salt
ground pistachios, to garnish
a drizzle of honey, to garnish
  (optional)

Soak the dates in the milk while preparing the other ingredients.

Peel and slice the banana and keep a couple of discs aside for garnishing. Place the rest in a blender with the yogurt, walnuts, coconut powder, sesame seeds, cinnamon, salt, and soaked dates, and blend together until smooth.

Pour into two large glasses and garnish each with some sliced banana, a sprinkling of coconut flour, sesame seeds and ground pistachios, and a drizzle of honey if desired.

Note: The shake also keeps for a day in the fridge, so it's a nice idea to make this the night before for a healthy breakfast on a busy morning.

# A simple porridge with rosewater

*Fereni* | فرنى

*Fereni*, or *firni* (sometimes spelled *phirni*), is one of those foods common across today's Iran, the Levant, and India. You'd know it by the name *kheer* in India—but this is a word you should not really say in front of Iranians, because they'd either laugh at you (and that would be embarrassing), or they'd turn red in the face (as they'd be embarrassed), because it sounds very much like a rude word in Persian for penis.

In the Levant, these "spoon puddings" are made with rice flour or cornstarch (or simply starch), with a base of milk or water, with slightly different flavorings; often orange blossom water is paired with rosewater, and sometimes even a dash of mastic is used. They are similar to the *muhallabia* on page 165, and distantly related to other "cooked milk" puddings such as *latte alla Portoghese*; all of them are distant offsprings of *blancmange* and *isfidhabaj*—ancient "white" dishes that were popular respectively in Europe and in the Middle East even before the Middle Ages. Their velvety consistency and floral aroma, however, persist through different recipes and regions.

This sweet porridge is like a warm hug from someone smelling of roses, and caresses all the way from your mouth to your belly. For me it's a loving memory from those cold Friday mornings as a child when I had a sore throat (or not). It's super easy to prepare, and makes a perfect excuse for a bit of morning mindfulness in the form of stirring.

*Serves 4–6*

½ cup (80 g) rice flour
4¼ cups (1 liter) milk
¼–⅓ cup (55–75 g) sugar,
   or to taste
2 tablespoons rosewater
sliced pistachios and rose petals,
   to garnish (optional)

Mix the rice flour into the cold milk until smooth, then pour into a pot. Cook over medium-low heat, whisking all the time, until the *fereni* starts to thicken; the timing is highly variable, depending on your ingredients, so consistency is the best indicator here.

Stir in the sugar and rosewater and cook for a few more minutes.

You can either serve the porridge hot (the way I prefer it), or let it cool, then refrigerate in individual small bowls and serve cold. Garnish with pistachios and rose petals if you like.

# Date & onion frittata

*Kuku-ye khorma* | کوکوی خرما

I always introduce *kuku* as an Iranian frittata, because it's the most direct way of describing this egg-based dish. The Iranian *kuku* (pronounced *koo-koo*) is usually firmer than the well-known Italian frittata. The main difference is that whereas a frittata is all about the beaten egg to which you add other ingredients, such as vegetables or cheese, *kuku* is all about the ingredients other than egg. The egg is just the glue holding everything together.

I used to think I invented this date *kuku* thanks to my own stroke of culinary genius, but I soon realized (through my mother's ruthless frankness) that it's very similar to a dish called *gheysava* from the Azerbaijan region of Iran.

For a quick lunch or supper, you can make a *kuku* with just about anything—cooked-down vegetables such as fried eggplant or potatoes; meat or fish (such as shredded chicken or lamb, or chopped shrimp); mixed herbs (like the famous *kuku sabzi* with mixed herbs, or just a lot of chives); and even leftover rice, in the same way Italians make *frittata di spaghetti* with leftover pasta.

This *kuku* with dates, eggs, and walnuts, spiced with turmeric, cinnamon, and saffron, makes an extraordinary addition to any brunch (or lunch or dinner) table. You can use any type of dates here.

*Serves 4–6*

1 tablespoon neutral-flavored
    vegetable oil
1 tablespoon golden onion
    (page 16)
14 oz (400 g) dates
    (about 20), pitted and
    chopped into quarters
5 eggs
1½ teaspoons saffron infusion
    (page 18)
¼ teaspoon ground cinnamon
½ teaspoon salt
a pinch of freshly ground
    black pepper
1 teaspoon butter

Heat half the oil in a nonstick frying pan over medium heat. Add the golden onion and dates and keep stirring so the dates don't burn, as their natural sugars can make them caramelize quickly. After 2–5 minutes, when the dates have softened (the timing will depend on the type and freshness of your dates), turn off the heat and transfer the mixture to a plate to cool a little. Wipe or wash the pan clean and set aside.

In a large bowl, beat the eggs together with the saffron infusion, cinnamon, salt, and black pepper. Add the cooled date and onion mixture and combine until well coated with egg.

In the same pan you cooked the dates in, heat the remaining oil over high heat.

Add the *kuku* batter to the hot pan, and flatten any pieces of date sticking out, to give it a smooth and evenly distributed surface. Put the lid on, reduce the heat to low, and cook for 5–7 minutes. Using a spatula, make sure the bottom of the *kuku* is firm enough and not stuck to the pan; if needed, cook for a few minutes longer.

To flip the *kuku*, gently move the *kuku* to the lid with the help of the spatula, add the butter to the pan and let it melt, then put the *kuku* back in the pan, raw side down. Cook, uncovered, over medium heat for another 5 minutes, or until the other side is golden as well.

You can serve this *kuku* at any temperature, but I prefer it warm. If you're serving it for brunch or supper, some tangy cheese, such as feta, or Greek-style yogurt would be nice on the side; some bread would also be good. You can also let the *kuku* cool down, then cut it into small squares and serve it with toothpicks, as a finger food for an informal gathering.

# A light lentil soup

*Adassi* | عدسى

This simple, heartwarming, and delicious lentil soup, together with *haleem*—a wheat and meat porridge also known as *harissa* in the Arab world, and not to be confused with the fiery North African condiment—is a beloved winter breakfast, traditionally cooked in the bazaars of Iran. In the dire cold months when little fresh produce was available, long-storing lentils were cooked together with fried onions (and later potatoes, too) to make a hot, nourishing soup.

Unlike *haleem*, however, *adassi* is very easy and quick to make at home. A good tip is to double the portions and cook this for a warming winter's dinner, then enjoy the rest for breakfast on a cold morning. You can make the soup as thick or as runny you like, but lemon juice is essential.

For a lavish brunch, serve individual small bowls of *adassi* alongside other breakfast dishes such as date *kuku* (page 40), *fereni* (page 38), different types of bread, and cheeses, jams, tahini, and honey.

*Serves 4*

1¼ cups (250 g) brown
    or green lentils
1 tablespoon golden onion
    (page 16)
1 teaspoon salt, or to taste
2¾ cups (650 ml) water
1 potato, about 5½ oz (150 g)
¼ teaspoon ground cinnamon
juice of ½ lemon, plus extra
    lemon wedges to serve
½ teaspoon freshly ground black
    pepper, or to taste
olive oil, for drizzling

Rinse the lentils and place in a large pot with the golden onion and salt. Pour in the water and put the lid on. Cook over medium heat for 30 minutes, checking the lentils regularly: as they cook, they will absorb the water, so you might need to add more, since this is meant to be a rather runny soup.

Meanwhile, peel the potato, cut into large cubes, and keep in a bowl of cold water.

When the lentils have cooked for 30 minutes, add the potato cubes, then cover and cook for another 30 minutes, checking that there's enough water for the potatoes to cook in and for the soup to remain quite liquid.

Stir in the cinnamon and lemon juice, then add salt and black pepper to taste.

Now blend half the soup until quite creamy, but leaving a few small potato chunks; I use a handheld stick blender to partially blend the soup.

Serve in bowls, drizzled with a little olive oil. Serve with lemon wedges on the side, and some bread.

# A sweet saffron omelet

*Gheyghanagh* | قیقناق

Many sweets in Iran, especially the ones from the region of Azerbaijan (where this omelet is from), involve pouring hot syrup over cooked or baked batter—similar to the technique used in making baklava (page 162). This sweet breakfast omelet, from Tabriz in northwest Iran, may be the easiest of them all.

Both my maternal grandparents, born and raised in north Khorasan (in northeast Iran), have always said they're originally from Tabriz. Although the mystery behind their relocation to the other side of our vast country is one I might never be able to solve, the proof of it is shown in my grandparents' food, which not only looks like the food of the Azerbaijan region of Iran, but also the food of Azerbaijan the country. No surprises there, as the nation of Azerbaijan used to be part of what was then Persia, before the Russians conquered all of the Caucasus in the early 1800s—hence the same name for both the Iranian region and the current republic of Azerbaijan, divided by a rather recent border. I was moved to tears, and filled with joy, when I found some of the dishes my grandmother

*Continued* ›

«

used to cook in Olia Hercules's book, *Kaukasis, the Cookbook: A Culinary Journey Through Georgia, Azerbaijan & Beyond*, as I had never come across any written account of those recipes in any Iranian source.

In Tabriz, and in my grandmother's house, *gheyghanagh* is something very sweet, to have only a little taste of after eating *kalleh pache* (aka *khash*, boiled trotters and head), to cut through the heavy, fatty dish. These days, it can also be served like a pancake, with lashings of syrup laced with saffron and rosewater. Since it is so sweet, you only need very small portions of this omelet.

*Serves 2–4*

⅓ cup (80 g) sugar
⅓ cup (80 ml) water
2 tablespoons saffron infusion
    (page 18)
1 tablespoon rosewater, or
    ¼ teaspoon ground cardamom
2 eggs
1 teaspoon all-purpose flour
a pinch of salt
1½ teaspoons butter or ghee

In a small saucepan, heat the sugar with the water to make a smooth and very runny syrup; don't let it thicken. When there are small bubbles and all the sugar has dissolved, add the saffron infusion and rosewater or cardamom. Keep warm on very low heat.

Beat the eggs together with the flour and salt. Melt the butter in a nonstick 8 inch (20 cm) frying pan over medium-high heat, then pour in the egg mixture and let it turn golden, without stirring the egg. After a few minutes, once quite firm underneath, flip the omelet over and cook on the other side for another couple of minutes, until golden.

Very carefully pour in the hot syrup—it will boil ferociously when added to the pan, so be prepared. Cook over low heat for another 5–10 minutes, until the syrup has reduced.

Cut the omelet into wedges in the pan with a wooden or silicone spatula. Leave to rest for 15–30 minutes before serving.

Serve for breakfast or as a snack, perhaps with a cup of black tea or coffee.

# Everyday comfort food
# & small dishes

The recipes in this chapter have a sense of comfort and home. Not all of them may seem easy, but they are nonetheless considered fairly simple and even quick in Iran. Time is one of the most important ingredients in Iranian cuisine, even if we might disagree on how "quick" some of these recipes really are.

These are the dishes you would prepare for your kids when they come back from school, or for a weeknight dinner of *hazeri* (a ready-made meal). Some are indeed technically side dishes that double up as a quick lunch.

Despite their apparent informality, some of these simple recipes are among the staples of Iranian cooking, even if some folks unjustly deem them unsuitable to serve to guests. There's *eshkeneh*, with its hundreds of regional variations, that showcases one of the cores of Iranian cooking: a simple but nourishing soup of onions, herbs, nuts, and dairy, into which a couple of eggs are broken. Equally important is the central role of yogurt to the Iranian table, with the many variations of *borani*.

# A pilaf with green beans & tomato

*Lubia polow* | لوبیا پلو

When it comes to comfort food, the universal palate tends to favor carbs. Bready, noodley, potatoey dishes often top the charts, easily checking the boxes for hearty, warming and, of course, comforting. But I'd like to make a case for tomatoey rice as the ultimate comfort food. Perhaps a little spicy but not too much—just a dash of turmeric, cinnamon, and black pepper. Maybe a bit on the salty side, too, with little fatty bites of meat, and sweet and ever-so-soft chunks of green beans, with the rice keeping the soul of all these ingredients trapped deep within after its long, slow cooking, served with a nonnegotiable bowl of plain yogurt (or a variation with cucumbers, page 68) on one side, and perhaps a bowl of *salad Shirazi* (page 63) on the other. This is *lubia polow*, the smell of home after coming back from school as a kid, and memories of my first-ever attempt at cooking Iranian food as an adult, having lived abroad with fellow Iranians for barely a month, and only beginning to realize just how tough it all was to be an immigrant in another country. Comfort I sought, and *lubia polow* delivered.

As with all *polows*, you can add slices of potato or flatbread for *tahdig*—but I find *lubia polow* makes a great *tahdig* even on its own. This dish owes a great part of its flavor to lamb meat, but if you can't find any, feel free to replace it with another meat, possibly with a good amount of fat. For a vegetarian version, omit the meat altogether and add more green beans.

*Serves 4–6*

For the rice
2 cups (350 g) Iranian or basmati-
   style long-grain rice
¼ cup (70 g) coarse salt
1½ teaspoons vegetable oil
1 tablespoon ghee (or half
   butter, half vegetable oil)

Start by rinsing, then soaking, the rice in water with the salt, following the Iranian rice recipe on page 24, leaving the rice to soak for 2–3 hours, or at least 30 minutes.

To prepare the sauce, fry the green beans in a heavy-based pot with 1 tablespoon of the oil over medium-high heat for about 10 minutes, stirring often. Transfer the beans to a plate.

In the same pot, heat the golden onion together with the remaining oil, then add the meat, and brown for about 5 minutes. When all the surfaces look seared, add the tomato paste and stir for another 5 minutes or so, until the tomato paste brightens a little in color.

Put the beans back into the pot, add 1⅔ cups (400 ml) water, and mix well. Reduce the heat to the lowest setting and cook with the lid on for 40–50 minutes, until the meat is tender. Toward the

For the sauce

1 lb 2 oz (500 g) green beans, trimmed and cut into 1¼ inch (3 cm) lengths

2 tablespoons vegetable oil

2 tablespoons golden onion (page 16)

9 oz (250 g) sheep or lamb meat (shanks or shoulder), cut into ¾ inch (2 cm) cubes

¼ cup (60 g) tomato paste

1 teaspoon salt

½ teaspoon freshly ground black pepper

1 teaspoon ground cinnamon

2 teaspoons saffron infusion (page 18)

end of this time, stir in the salt, pepper, cinnamon, and saffron infusion. Taste and adjust the seasoning if needed.

Meanwhile, parboil and drain the rice according to the Iranian rice recipe on page 22, adding the vegetable oil to the boiling water.

In a large nonstick pot, melt the ghee with a scant 1 cup (220 ml) water. When it comes to a boil, set half of the oily water aside in a cup.

Gently scatter a layer of rice in the bottom of the pot with a skimmer (if you want to make a potato or bread *tahdig*, add that first and then start with the rice), then add a layer of the green bean and meat mixture. Scatter another layer of rice on top, then the sauce mixture, and repeat until you use up all the rice and sauce. Remember to never push the rice down, and to shape the pilaf into a pyramid form in the pot. Pour the reserved oily water on top of the rice.

With the lid on, cook over high heat (preferably on a heat diffuser) for 5–10 minutes, then reduce the heat to the lowest setting. Wrap the lid in a clean cotton tea towel and place it on the pot, making sure the lid seals tightly. Cook over the lowest possible heat for at least 45 minutes, or up to 1½ hours; never remove the lid during this time, or you'll lose all the steam that is cooking the rice.

For serving, very gently move the rice around with the beans and meat so that everything is combined rather evenly, then transfer onto a platter or individual plates using a skimmer, serving spatula, or cake server, trying to scatter the rice evenly without crushing it.

In the right pot, the rice should make a crusty *tahdig* (unless you have used potatoes or bread on the bottom), which you can remove with a wooden or plastic spatula.

*Pictured on pages 50–51*

# Simple egg soup with yogurt

*Eshkene-ye maast* | اشکنه‌ی ماست

What would you do with the seeds of a long, sweet yellow melon after devouring the fruit on a hot, lazy summer afternoon? When my mother was a girl, she and the other kids were given the job of picking out the seeds, removing the fleshy strings, and saving the seeds in a jar—a genius parenting method for bored children in midsummer. Then an adult would wash the seeds, dry them, toast them, then grind them into a powder, and later make a super-simple soup with them, adding the melon powder to sautéed onions and topping them up with water, to make a stock to which eggs were added shortly before serving.

*Eshkeneh* is this simple as a soup. It always starts with onions, and it always finishes with poached eggs. It's one of the flagstones of Iranian cooking, and it has endless variations. Like many other Iranian dishes, *eshkeneh* is more a "mold" that can be filled with just about any ingredients you have at hand, be it herbs, tomatoes, mung beans, potatoes, quince, and even sour cherries—and, of course, powdered toasted melon seeds. The one defining feature, however, is eggs. In Persian, the word *eshkeneh* comes from "breaking," so any soup into which you break an egg would be *eshkeneh*.

This is one of the simplest and most delicious *eshkenehs* ever, using yogurt—another Iranian cooking staple—and walnuts (but not powdered melon seeds). The important thing to remember is to not let the yogurt curdle. Add it last, keep it on low heat, and don't let it come to a boil.

*Serves 2*

3–4 tablespoons neutral-
    flavored vegetable oil
1 onion, finely diced
2–3 garlic cloves, finely chopped
1 teaspoon ground turmeric
½ cup (60 g) chopped walnuts
1 teaspoon salt, or to taste
1 cup (300 g) full-fat plain yogurt,
    preferably Greek-style
2 eggs
freshly ground black pepper

For the mint oil
3 tablespoons oil
1 tablespoon powdered
    dried mint

Start by making the mint oil. In a small saucepan, heat the oil. When it's hot, take the saucepan off the heat and add the mint. Set aside while making the soup.

In a heavy-based saucepan, heat the oil and sauté the onion for 10–15 minutes over low heat, until soft, golden, and translucent. Add the garlic and cook for a minute, then add the turmeric. Mix well for a few seconds, then add the walnuts and salt. Pour in about 1 cup (250 ml) water, put the lid on, and wait for it to come to a boil.

Meanwhile, beat the yogurt with a fork or spoon for a minute so that it becomes homogeneously creamy. Add a few tablespoons of the soup and beat again to thin the yogurt down.

*Continued ›*

«

When the soup comes to a boil, reduce the heat to the lowest setting. Crack in the eggs, then wait for about 30 seconds before stirring in the eggs. Now gently pour in the yogurt mixture and keep stirring. Just before the soup comes back to a boil, take the pan off the heat; the yogurt will curdle if it stays on the heat too long.

Crack in some freshly ground black pepper, then ladle into bowls. Drizzle with the mint oil to make dark-green swirls on the pale yellow soup. Serve immediately, with any kind of bread.

**Note:** Any leftover mint oil will keep in the fridge for a week, and can be used on soups, meats, and vegetables.

# Balls of herbs & flatbread

*Doimaj* | دویماج

Wherever in the world bread is central to a food culture, you will always find recipes to recuperate stale bread—such as *panzanella* salad in Italy (page 191), and *fattah* and *fattoush* bread salads in the Levant (pages 141 and 144). In Iran, we dunk stale bread in our many soups. And then there's *doimaj*, which is a sort of bread salad, turned into little buns.

There are many regional variations, but *doimaj* always involves dry, crunchy flatbread (stale, or heated to dryness), bashed into a coarse powder, then flavored and shaped into little balls to be eaten in a mouthful or two. As one can guess from its name, *doimaj* seems to have Turkic origins, because in Iran, it's most common in Azerbaijan and other regions with Turkic populations. In "deep Turkey" (the Anatolia region) they have a snack very similar to this recipe called *pisik koftesi*, with no cheese, but with the addition of tomatoes, raw onion, and olive oil. Flavor-wise, it reminds me a little of the Tuscan bread soup *pappa al pomodoro*, which also uses stale bread and tomatoes.

Usually, old cheese is used in *doimaj* as well as old bread, killing two birds with one stone, or reviving two stale ingredients within one simple dish. So if you have any odd bits of cheese left in your fridge, or even herbs or onion, feel free to crumble, grate, or chop them and toss into this recipe.

While *doimaj* was developed as a way of using up old flatbreads, a leavened bread without the crust will work just as well.

*Continued ›*

«

*Makes about 10 balls*

5½ oz (150 g) flatbread (about
    2 lavash, or 3 pita breads)
1¾–3½ oz (50–100 g) aromatic
    herbs, such as basil, dill, mint,
    and/or cilantro, trimmed,
    washed, and chopped
3½ oz (100 g) feta, crumbled
¼ cup (30 g) coarsely chopped
    walnuts
3 small scallions, or 2 large ones,
    chopped
1 tablespoon ghee or butter
¼ teaspoon ground turmeric
¼ teaspoon salt
freshly ground black pepper

For this recipe, your bread needs to be completely dry, so it will easily snap and crumble. Preheat your oven to 235°–300°F (120°–150°C), put the bread on a baking pan, and dry it in the oven without burning it. For lavash or pita bread, this shouldn't take more than 10 minutes; just test if it snaps when you bend it.

Break the bread into pieces, gather them in a clean tea towel, tuck in the extremities so they don't escape, then gently bash into crumbs with a rolling pin, jar, or pestle. If some larger pieces remain, that's fine.

In a large bowl, mix the breadcrumbs with the herbs, feta, walnuts, and scallions, preferably with your hands.

Melt the ghee in a small saucepan. Over the lowest heat, add the turmeric and stir for a minute or two, so that the color of the turmeric deepens and the spice cooks. Drizzle this turmeric oil into the bowl of breadcrumbs and mix everything well.

Now, working the "dough" with one hand, pour in about ½ cup (125 ml) water a little at a time, kneading continuously so that everything comes together into a dry-ish dough. The amount of water you need depends on your bread. When you can bring together little balls that don't fall apart, taste one of them, add the salt and black pepper to your liking, and mix again.

Shape the mixture into little balls about the size of a ping pong ball, and set on a plate. Chill in the fridge for at least 10 minutes before enjoying on their own as a snack, or as a light lunch or dinner. They will keep in the fridge for up to 3 days.

# Charred eggplant with egg & tomato

*Mirza ghasemi* | میرزا قاسمی

One hot summer in my earliest years of living in Rome, my friend Amir, a fellow Iranian also recently moved to the Eternal City, was staying at my place for a short period. Neither of us confused twenty-somethings was coping well at the time. It was 2009, and we were still caught up in the psychological and emotional aftermath of the electoral coup that had unraveled in Iran in the previous months. Like most of those in our generation who weren't rallying in the street, or getting beaten up by the forces of the repression, or ending up in jail—or worse, dead—we would spend our days glued to the screen, watching it all happen in detailed graphic videos on Twitter or Facebook.

We would spend our evenings into the early morning hours in Trastevere—back then the only neighborhood in Rome with bars open to host the few people left in the city during August— drowning our trauma and despair in many bottles of beer, followed by many shots of tequila or vodka. For those short hours, we wouldn't gape at people who were laughing and having a good time, wondering how anyone in the world could still be capable of such normalities. Then we would walk the empty and disarmingly beautiful streets of the *centro storico*, before getting on a sketchy night bus that would bring us home, where we would be glued to the screen some more before finally giving in to the elusive luxury of sleep.

In that bloody, sweltering summer, despite shock, trauma, and many hangovers, Amir and I also cooked—seeking a somewhat masochistic relief in sweating next to a boiling hot stove, finding catharsis in charring eggplant into blackness. And this is how I learned this version of *mirza ghasemi*, a dish originally from the north of Iran (where Amir's family is from), but known and loved in all of Iran.

In Amir's version, the eggs are first scrambled with turmeric and blanched garlic, then added to the eggplant and tomato mixture—whereas some people break the eggs directly into the eggplant mixture, which I frankly don't like.

Charring eggplant to the point of burning the skin and then using the smoke-scented pulp is a common practice in the Middle East, and is also used in the much loved *baba ghanoush*, sometimes known as *moutabal* (page 130).

The best way of charring eggplant is of course over an open fire, but a gas burner works just as well. I have seen people alarmed by the idea of placing an eggplant directly on a gas flame until it burns— but it's all right, folks! Several generations of Middle Eastern people guarantee it. If you don't have a gas burner or can't brave the mess or the risk, blacken the eggplant on a pan in a hot oven, right under the broiler; you won't get that smoky flavor if you just bake it in the oven.

*Continued* ›

«

While the heavenly pairing of eggplant and tomato is widely celebrated all over the Mediterranean, what makes this dish distinctly *shomali* (from the north of Iran) is the abundance of garlic, so don't be parsimonious with it.

The "green line" of northern Iran, where the climate is most like Europe thanks to being sandwiched between the Caspian Sea and the high Alborz Mountains, is so in love with garlic that even rental beach houses have a faint whiff of garlic about them.

I have used a moderate amount of garlic for this recipe. You can add an extra clove, or remove one, but I beg you to keep this delicious dish as garlicky as it deserves to be. If you like, you can blanch the garlic (see Note) to soften its flavor.

*Serves 4*

3 large eggplant, or 4 small ones
   (about 3 lb 5 oz/1.5 kg)
¼–⅓ cup (60–80 ml)
   vegetable oil
1 lb 2 oz (500 g) tomatoes, diced,
   or a 14 oz (400 g) can of diced
   or whole peeled tomatoes
1 teaspoon salt
4–6 garlic cloves, chopped
1 teaspoon ground turmeric
3 eggs
½ teaspoon freshly ground
   black pepper

Wash and dry the eggplant, leaving the skin on.

If you don't have a gas burner, preheat your oven to 425°F (220°C). Line a baking sheet with parchment paper, put the eggplant on top, and place the tray right under the broiler. Bake the eggplant for 40–60 minutes, until the skin is completely darkened and the flesh is tender and cooked; you may need to turn them over halfway through baking to char the skin uniformly. Leave to cool for 5–10 minutes.

If you do have a gas burner (or even better, a charcoal fire!), put each eggplant over a medium-sized burner and turn the flame up to maximum. Let the skin completely char and burn, carefully rotating the eggplant with the help of two wooden spoons, so they char evenly all over. Once blackened and collapsed, which should take about 30 minutes, depending on their size, transfer the eggplant to a tray and leave until cool enough to handle.

Scoop the flesh of the cooled eggplant directly into a large pot, removing any big chunks of charred skin; it's okay if a few tiny pieces remain. Drizzle with half of the oil and place over medium heat, breaking the eggplant flesh apart with a wooden spoon. Add the tomatoes, breaking them up if whole, then sprinkle with half the salt. Put the lid on, turn the heat down to medium-low and cook for 20–30 minutes.

Meanwhile, add the garlic to a frying pan with the remaining oil over medium heat. Add the turmeric and stir around a bit. Beat the eggs in a bowl with the remaining salt. When the garlic is

just golden, add the beaten egg. Let it firm up, then casually stir, as if to scramble the egg. At this point, we want to cook the egg completely; this will take about 5 minutes.

Now add the garlicky-turmeric egg mixture to the pot with the eggplant mixture. (You can also add the egg mixture at the end, but I like to add it sooner so that all the flavors are well combined.) Break everything up with a wooden spoon and sprinkle with the pepper. The dish is ready when the mixture has thickened and any excess water has evaporated. Serve hot or at room temperature, with bread or plain rice.

**Note:** If you'd like a milder garlic flavor, blanch the garlic cloves before frying them with the oil and turmeric. To do this, peel the whole garlic cloves and place in a small saucepan. Cover barely with water, bring to a boil, then discard the water. Repeat this process 7–10 times; the garlic cloves will become soft in texture and smell. You can now chop them and proceed with the recipe.

# The unthinkable Iranian "*makaroni*"

ماکارونی

Some time in recent history, the modern form of Italian-ish pasta found its way into Iran. However, it's a mistake to think that Iranians have been strangers to noodles and pasta in general. In fact, one of the oldest written records of noodles is *lakhsha*, known in eastern parts of Iran and Afghanistan as *lakhshak,* supposedly "invented" by the Sasanian King Khosrow. The same word traveled to Central Asia and Eastern Europe, becoming *lapsha* in Russia and *laska* in Hungary, both meaning "noodles." Perhaps the most famous noodle in Iran today is *reshteh* (literally meaning "string"), which stars in the hearty bean, herb, and noodle dish *ash reshteh,* and *reshteh polow* (pilaf with noodles). *Khingal*, a popular dish in Azerbaijan (and one I grew up eating at my grandmother's house), is made of wide noodles, not unlike lasagne, that are boiled, then dressed with ground lamb and onion, a lot of yogurt, and minty oil—a condiment also used for many noodle dishes in Turkey, such as *manti* (mini dumplings).

In Iran, any pasta in general is now called *makaroni* in domestic use (if we don't count the trends of recent years, where you can find penne and fusilli on restaurant menus, complete with amusing Iranian pronunciations). The typical *makaroni* sauce is definitely inspired by a classic bolognese, but somewhere along the way it's been tamed and domesticated to fit the Iranian palate, with so much golden onion, a touch of turmeric, cinnamon, and saffron, and only just a hint of tomato paste. Remarkably, the method for cooking Iranian *makaroni* is precisely the same as for Iranian rice (page 22)—parboiled, drained, and then steamed under a tea towel–clad lid for too long a time for pasta, which as a reward results in an awesome *makaroni tahdig*, soaked in the oils and flavors of the Iranian sauce.

This was a kids' favorite when I was in school, and—brace yourself—we ate it with huge spurts of ketchup. However, I have cooked spaghetti (and better yet, its thicker cousin spaghettoni) this way for my Italian friends, and they have approved, as the flavor very much resembles that of *pasta al forno*, a classic pasta bake. The trick is to undercook the pasta in the first step (the parboiling), so that it won't be overcooked after the long second stage (the steaming).

Expect a final dish a lot less saucy than your average Italian pasta. In fact, I won't judge you if you put a bottle of ketchup on the table when serving. It's an Iranian *makaroni,* after all.

*Continued ›*

«

*Serves 4*

### For the sauce
3 tablespoons vegetable oil
1 tablespoon golden onion
   (page 16)
10½ oz (300 g) ground meat
¼ teaspoon ground turmeric
¼ teaspoon ground cinnamon
¼ cup (60 g) tomato paste
scant 1 cup (200 ml) hot water
1 teaspoon saffron infusion
   (page 18)
½ teaspoon salt, or to taste
¼ teaspoon freshly ground
   black pepper, or to taste

### For the pasta
12 oz (350 g) spaghetti
   or spaghettoni
1 tablespoon ghee (or half butter,
   half vegetable oil)
1 potato, peeled and sliced
   crossways into ¼ inch (5 mm)
   discs, kept in a bowl of water
   to avoid oxidation

Begin with the sauce. Heat the oil in a large heavy-based pot with the golden onion. Next, brown the meat over medium-high heat for about 5 minutes, until no pink parts are left. Add the turmeric and cinnamon and cook for another few minutes, then stir in the tomato paste and cook for about 5 minutes, or until the tomato paste brightens in color. Pour in the hot water, reduce the heat to low, and cook with the lid on for 15 minutes.

Stir in the saffron infusion salt, and pepper, then adjust the seasoning to taste. This sauce will have very little liquid, and should not be as saucy as an Italian *ragù*. Set aside.

Meanwhile, bring a large heavy-based nonstick pot of water to a boil and season with salt. Add the pasta and cook for about half the time indicated on the package.

From here on, the steaming steps are very similar to those for making Iranian rice (page 22) and *lubia polow* (page 48). Drain the pasta and, in the same pot, bring the ghee and a scant 1 cup (200 ml) water to a boil. Set half of this oily water aside in a cup.

Cover the bottom of the pot with the potato discs, to make *tahdig*. Then add one layer of spaghetti on the potato slices, then top with one layer of the meat sauce. Repeat until you run out of both, then pour the rest of the oily water over the top.

Put the lid on and cook over high heat for 7–10 minutes. Now reduce the heat to the lowest setting (on a heat diffuser, if you have one), wrap the lid in a clean cotton tea towel, place it snugly on the pan, and cook for 30 minutes to 1 hour.

Mix the pasta gently with the meat mixture and serve immediately, scraping the *tahdig* off the bottom of the pot with a wooden spatula.

# A simple Iranian salad for summer & winter

*Salad Shirazi* | سالاد شیرازی

This humble salad, together with a bowl of plain yogurt, is an essential part of an Iranian table, the way I have known it to be. It's usually the last thing to be prepared before sitting down to eat. By this time the rice is ending its "brewing" time, or maybe the *kuku* (page 40) is fried on both sides and somebody is already setting the table. The younger people of the house make the salad, in order to help.

In essence it's just cucumber, tomato, onion, salt, and some acid—preferably verjuice, which we love in Iran. This combination, sometimes with a few more ingredients, appears as a salad in many parts of the Levant as well as Turkey and Greece, and it also reminds us of the vegetable base of the Tuscan bread salad, *panzanella* (page 191). The fresh juice of Shirazi limes (which are small, a bit bitter, and slightly yellow) or even bitter oranges is just as suitable, although fresh lemon or lime juice will also do. A touch of mint, dried or fresh, is much appreciated, too. This is a simple salad, and it's best to not mess with it. Just use the best ingredients possible, and don't make it more than

*Continued ›*

«

15 minutes before serving, or it will become soggy. There is no oil in *salad Shirazi*—but if you'd like to add a splash of good olive oil, no one should protest.

In winter, the classic *salad Shirazi* tastes horrible—because out-of-season tomatoes and cucumbers taste horrible. However, I just can't fathom a proper Iranian table without this salad on it, so, for my cooking classes in Rome, which I usually hold before Christmas, I came up with this winter version, which is inauthentic but utterly delectable. The ruby red pomegranate seeds make up for the acidity of bright red tomatoes, and the texture and anise-like aroma of fennel stand in beautifully for the aromatic crunch of cucumbers.

Both salads will make one medium bowl. Simply mix all the ingredients in a bowl and serve.

## Classic summer version

2 cucumbers, or 4 Persian/Lebanese cucumbers,
    about 9 oz (250 g), peeled and diced
2 small tomatoes, diced
½ large red onion, or 1 small one, diced
1 heaped tablespoon dried mint, or a handful
    of fresh mint leaves, finely chopped
2 tablespoons lime or lemon juice
½ teaspoon salt, or to taste
a sprinkling of freshly ground black pepper

## Unorthodox winter version

1 fennel bulb, trimmed and diced into
    ½ inch (1 cm) pieces
1 small red onion, diced
seeds of ½ pomegranate
1½ teaspoons dried mint, or a handful
    of fresh mint leaves, finely chopped
2 tablespoons lemon or lime juice
1 teaspoon salt

*Pictured opposite*

# Many Iranian ways with yogurt

The Iranian adoration of yogurt is a love story going back to ancient times, with yogurt appearing as "Persian milk" in Al-Baghdadi's celebrated thirteenth-century cookbook, *Kitab al-tabikh* ("The Book of Dishes"). Yogurt is ever-present on the Iranian table, mostly just in plain form as something to spoon alongside literally everything, but especially rice, and in particular mixed *polows* such as *lubia polow* (page 48).

Vegetables—even raw, but often cooked—when drowned in yogurt are called *borani* in Iran. Indeed, in *A Safavid Period Cookbook*, documenting the food of the Persian court in the 1600s, it says "all types of *qalie* (stews/*khoresh*) to which yogurt and garlic are added are *borani*." This could indicate that *boranis* used to have meat in them, too—or that multiple varieties of meat were added to the kings' *borani* merely to please the royal palate.

I have been told that in Isfahan, the historical and cultural heart of Iran—sometimes known as the "Florence of the Orient," and incidentally also the capital of the Safavid dynasty—the ultimate show-off move at a wedding would be to serve the yogurt stew *khoresh-e māst*. Served cold or at room temperature, *khoresh-e māst* is a stretchy "cream" made of shredded and pounded lamb, mixed with thick strained yogurt, sugar, and enough saffron to make the plate shine like a glorious sunset on the table. Garnished with almond slivers and barberries, this dish could well be a souvenir of the meaty *boranis* of the Safavid Empire.

However, the late scholar and literary translator Najaf Daryabandari writes in *The Rt. Honorable Cookbook: From Soup to Nuts* that *borani* is in fact a form of salad, where instead of "drizzling" the dressing over the ingredients, we submerge them in the sauce (yogurt).

In *Sofre-ye Atma'eh*, a cookbook from the 1800s Iranian court, the king's cook mentions seven types of *borani*, none of which has meat in them: spinach (and other greens such as chard), marrow, beet, eggplant, green bean, cardoon, and mushroom. Basically any vegetable, fried, grilled, or charred (like the eggplant in *mirza ghasemi*, page 57), drowned in yogurt, perhaps with grated garlic, would make a delicious *borani*.

Iranian yogurt is usually thick. In mid-spring, amazing sheep yogurt appears, but yogurt is mostly just made from cow's milk these days. For most dips, it's advisable to use strained yogurt—*mast chekideh* in Persian and *labneh* in Arabic (see recipe on page 170; omit the jam). I also find that a good full-fat yogurt works well—and that organic yogurts do taste better.

*Continued ›*

《

# The one with cucumber

*Mast-o khiar* | ماست و خیار

Please don't confuse this with *tzatziki*, the famous Turkish/Greek yogurt and cucumber dip. Although it is undoubtedly very similar, the Iranian version is softer in flavor, mainly due to the lack of garlic. The simplest Iranian *mast-o khiar* contains only finely diced cucumber and a pinch of salt, and perhaps a garnish of dried mint. This is a slightly fancier one with walnuts and raisins, which I adore, but feel free to omit these. Serve as a fabulous side dish for grilled meats; I also enjoy it for lunch on a hot summer day.

*Makes about 3 cups (675 g)*

2 cucumbers, or 4 Persian/
    Lebanese cucumbers,
    about 9 oz (250 g)
3 tablespoons coarsely
    chopped walnuts
3 tablespoons raisins
1½ teaspoons dried mint,
    or a handful of fresh mint
    leaves, finely chopped
½ teaspoon salt
1⅓ cups (400 g) plain
    Greek-style yogurt
Damascus rose petals,
    to garnish

Peel the cucumbers and dice into ¼ inch (5 mm) pieces. Combine in a bowl with the walnuts, raisins, mint, and salt.

Fold the yogurt through and mix well. Serve cold, with rose petals scattered on top.

*Pictured on page 67, center*

# The one with spinach

*Borani-e esfenaj | بورانی اسفناج*

In this classic *borani*, you can replace the spinach with any leafy greens, such as chicory, chard, kale, and wild leeks. Saffron and golden onion are crucial to a *borani* made with greens, whereas in *boranis* made with vegetables like eggplant, green beans or summer squash, I'd replace these with grated raw garlic.

*Makes about 3 cups (475 g)*

5½ oz (150 g) cooked spinach
  (see Note)
1⅓ cups (400 g) plain
  Greek-style yogurt
1½ teaspoons golden onion
  (page 16)
¼ teaspoon salt
¼ teaspoon freshly ground
  black pepper
½ teaspoon saffron infusion
  (page 18), to garnish (optional)

Combine the spinach very well with the yogurt, trying to break the spinach apart with a spoon. Mix with the onion, salt, and pepper. Serve in a bowl, drizzled with the saffron infusion if desired.

**Note:** To yield this amount of cooked spinach, start with about 9 oz (250 g) frozen spinach, or 1 lb 2 oz (500 g) fresh spinach.

*Pictured on page 67, bottom*

# The one with beets

*Borani-e laboo | بورانی لبو*

Another classic *borani*, but with a wonderfully different flavor palette. I like this one on the sweet side (hence the sugar), but not everyone does. If your beets have the stems and leaves intact, you can cook these, chop them up, and mix them through the dip as well. I like to keep in some chunky bits of beet, as it gives the dish a better mouthfeel. Throw in a handful of coarsely chopped walnuts as well if you feel fancy.

*Makes about 3 cups (550 g)*

10½ oz (300 g) beets, cooked
  and peeled
1⅓ cups (400 g) plain Greek-style
  yogurt, strained
½ teaspoon salt
1 tablespoon sugar, or to taste

Dice the beets, some finely, some coarsely, and combine in a bowl with the yogurt, salt, and sugar. Rest for at least 10 minutes in the fridge before serving.

*Pictured on page 67, top*

# The anatomy of an Iranian feast

This chapter contains recipes for dishes that are mostly served at house parties or celebrations. When I was a child, the women in my family each had their own cooking repertoire, which meant you could expect certain dishes at each household. As a guest in an Iranian household you should expect legendary hospitality, much *taarof* (compliments), and almost always too much food.

My mother would start her parties with a barley and chicken soup, and would then serve a simple Iranian rice (page 22), at least one type of elegant mixed pilaf such as jeweled rice (page 78) or sour cherry pilaf (page 79), or a fava bean and dill pilaf, and at least one type of *khoresh* (stew). Then there would be the cold dishes such as *salad olivier* (Russian salad) and sometimes *dolmeh* (stuffed vegetables). Next to these would be little bowls of pickles, yogurt, and platters of fresh herbs with a slab of feta.

These dishes need a bit of time and attention, in both cooking and serving.

# Upside-down saffron rice cake, two ways

*Tahchin* | تهچین

For a lavish, fragrant, and highly celebratory dish that is usually prepared for gatherings or ordered in restaurants, *tahchin* is relatively easy to make. The rice is parboiled as in the master Iranian rice recipe on page 22, but is kept a little more al dente, because its second cooking (steaming or "brewing") will be in a batter of yogurt and eggs spiked with saffron and freshly ground black pepper.

*Tahchin* gets its name from laying pieces of either lamb, chicken, or condiments at the bottom of a cooking pot. But don't confuse it with *tahdig*, which is literally the crust at the bottom of a pot of rice, and can be made with anything from plain rice to slices of potato, flatbread, or winter squash, and even lettuce (not a favorite of mine). *Tahchin* is always a rice cake that, when unmolded, keeps the shape of its container, thanks to the batter of yogurt and eggs. And there's always a stuffing of meat, poultry, or vegetables. Amazingly, it looks a lot like another lavish rice cake from Naples, called *sartù di riso* (page 237), which hails from a time when cooks of the court were challenged to come up with a rice dish delicious enough to satisfy the *maccheroni*-loving Neapolitan royals—a dish in which the rice is also held together with a batter of eggs and parmesan, encasing a filling of *ragù* and fried meatballs, and sometimes eggplant or other ingredients.

One of the finest *tahchins* in Iran uses large pieces of delicate, fatty lamb neck or shoulder, marinated overnight in yogurt and saffron, as a filling. But I find *tahchin* is a wonderful way to turn leftover meat—particularly from roasts—into another marvelous dish; think of the salvation it can be after Thanksgiving or Christmas, or how it can give another life to the meat from that chicken you've boiled for several hours simply to make a broth or stock.

Vegetarian *tahchins*, although not an innovation, are more uncommon. The one opposite with fried eggplant is an absolute delight, but you can easily use pumpkin or squash instead. The point is, just about any ingredient, if properly flavored, can make an excellent filling for a *tahchin*.

One last tip: the barberry garnish may seem fussy or unnecessary, but those tiny pockets of pure acidity work wonders in your mouth against the rich, eggy, and fatty rice. Don't skip them. While I have been known to voice strong feelings against topping random dishes with pomegranate seeds in the name of making them "Persian," for this particular recipe, if you can't find barberries, a fistful of raw pomegranate seeds added right before serving will do the job, and look quite festive too.

# The one with fried eggplant

*Tahchin-e badenjan* | تهچین بادنجان

*Serves 4–6*

**For the rice**
2 cups (350 g) Iranian or basmati-
  style long-grain rice
¼ cup (70 g) coarse salt
1½ teaspoons vegetable oil

**For the *tahchin***
2 lb 4 oz (1 kg) eggplant, peeled
  and sliced ½ inch (1 cm) thick
½ teaspoon salt, plus extra for
  salting the eggplant
vegetable oil, for shallow-frying
¼ teaspoon ground turmeric
⅔ cup (200 g) plain Greek-style
  yogurt (or strained yogurt)
3 eggs
3 tablespoons saffron infusion
  (page 18)
¼ teaspoon freshly ground
  black pepper
3½ tablespoons ghee (or half
  butter, half vegetable oil)
½ teaspoon ground cinnamon
2 tablespoons golden onion
  (page 16)

**For garnishing**
¼ cup (35 g) dried barberries
1 teaspoon butter
½ teaspoon sugar

Start by rinsing and soaking the rice in water with the salt, following the Iranian rice recipe on page 22, leaving the rice to soak for 2–3 hours, or at least 30 minutes.

Meanwhile, rub the eggplant slices with salt and leave in a colander in the sink for at least 30 minutes to drain off any bitter juices. Rinse with water, then pat dry with paper towels.

Heat a few tablespoons of frying oil in a frying pan (the quantity you'll need depends on the size of your pan). In batches, fry the eggplant slices over high heat for a few minutes on each side until golden; it doesn't matter if the center seems uncooked, as the eggplant will cook through in the rice later. Lay the fried eggplant in a dish lined with paper towels to absorb the excess oil, and sprinkle the turmeric on top.

In a large bowl, mix the yogurt with the eggs, saffron infusion, salt, and pepper. If the yogurt is too thick, add a splash of water.

Discard the water from the soaking rice, then parboil the rice according to the recipe on page 24, adding the vegetable oil to the parboiling water, and cooking the rice for a shorter time so that it is a little more al dente than usual. For some types of basmati rice, this will take only a couple of minutes; others can take up to 10 minutes. Drain and rinse the rice as directed on page 24, then gently fold into the bowl of saffron yogurt.

In a 9–11 inch (23–28 cm) heavy-based nonstick pot, heat the ghee over high heat. When it's really hot, add half the rice and yogurt mixture and gently push down with the back of a spoon. Cover with half the eggplant slices, sprinkle with the cinnamon and golden onion, then cover with the remaining eggplant. Finally, add the remaining rice mixture and push it down.

Wrap the lid with a clean tea towel and place it on the pot, ensuring it seals well. After 5–10 minutes over high heat, reduce the heat to the lowest setting; ideally, use a heat diffuser here. Cook—without ever lifting the lid—for 80–90 minutes. Turn the heat off and let the *tahchin* rest for 5 minutes.

*Continued ›*

«

While the *tahchin* is resting, rinse the barberries and place in a small saucepan. Cook them with the butter over medium-low heat for a minute or two. Add the sugar, stir them around a bit, then immediately turn off the heat so the sugar doesn't burn.

### TURNING OUT THE TAHCHIN

Now let's flip the *tahchin* onto a large serving plate. This part is a bit tricky, and everything is very hot, so be careful. Remove the lid and place your serving plate (which should be flat, and a bit larger than the pot) upside down over the pot. Using oven mitts or pot holders, hold the pot handles and the dish together, then flip the pot over in one movement and put them on the counter or a table. Gently remove the pot. Your *tahchin* should be inverted onto the serving plate like a nice saffron cake.

Pile the barberries (or raw pomegranate seeds) in the center of the *tahchin*. Cut into slices to serve, possibly with *salad Shirazi* (page 63) or yogurt, although these aren't strictly necessary.

**Note:** You can also bake *tahchin* in the oven, either in a tall baking dish, or preferably in a cast-iron pot—although, being heavy, it'll make the *tahchin* harder to flip. The important thing is to have the oven preheated to 350°F (180°C), and have both the baking dish and the oil very hot before starting to layer in the rice and filling. Seal tightly with a lid or foil and bake for 80–90 minutes.

*Pictured on pages 76–77*

# The one with saffron chicken

*Tahchin-e morgh* | تهچین مرغ

This dish is perfect for using up any leftover saffron roast chicken from page 83—or any kind of leftover meat, for that matter. If you're using chicken meat left over from making a stock or broth, make sure you season it well. If you're cooking chicken from scratch, simply braise the chicken pieces in a tiny amount of water, maybe with a small onion, adding some of the saffron infusion at the end of the cooking process. Leave to cool, then shred the meat and proceed with the recipe.

*Serves 4–6*

**For the rice**
2 cups (350 g) Iranian or basmati-
    style long-grain rice
¼ cup (70 g) coarse salt
1½ teaspoons vegetable oil

**For the *tahchin***
2 tablespoons oil
14 oz–1 lb 5 oz (400–600 g)
    shredded saffron roast chicken
    (page 83), or any kind of
    cooked meat
1 cup (250 ml) chicken broth
    (or the juices of roast chicken
    diluted with water)
½ teaspoon salt, plus extra to
    taste
¼ cup (60 ml) saffron infusion
    (page 18)
⅔ cup (200 g) plain
    Greek-style yogurt
3 eggs
½ teaspoon freshly ground
    black pepper
3½ tablespoons ghee (or half
    butter, half vegetablel oil)

Start by rinsing and soaking the rice in water with the salt, following the Iranian rice recipe on page 22, leaving the rice to soak for 2–3 hours, or at least 30 minutes.

Heat the oil in a frying pan, add the shredded meat, and fry for about 5 minutes, until partly golden. Add half the broth and 1 tablespoon of the saffron infusion, then add some salt to taste.

In a large bowl, dilute the yogurt with the remaining broth. Beat the eggs in with the ½ teaspoon salt, pepper, and remaining saffron infusion.

Parboil and drain the rice according to the Iranian rice recipe on page 24, adding the vegetable oil to the parboiling water. Gently fold the rice through the saffron yogurt mixture.

In a 9–11 inch (23–28 cm) nonstick, heavy-based pot, heat the ghee over high heat. When it's really hot, add half the rice and yogurt mixture and gently push down with the back of a spoon. Top with the shredded meat, making sure to pour in all the juices, too. Cover with the remaining rice, pushing it down.

Wrap the lid with a clean tea towel and place on the pot, ensuring it seals well. After 5–10 minutes more over high heat, reduce the heat to the lowest setting; ideally, use a heat diffuser here, if you have one. Cook—without lifting the lid—for 80–90 minutes. Turn the heat off and let the *tahchin* rest for 5 minutes.

Carefully flip the *tahchin* onto a large serving plate, following the instructions for the eggplant *tahchin* (see opposite page), and cut into slices to serve.

# Iranian jeweled rice

*Morasa' polow* | مرصع پلو

It's not hard to imagine where this dish gets its name from, with the rice covered in generous quantities of brightly colored barberries, candied orange peel, pistachios, almonds, and saffron rice. These are pricey ingredients, so the name "jeweled rice" isn't a reference to its appearance alone. That's also why I remember *morasa' polow* mostly from weddings, or rare formal family gatherings where somebody felt the need to make a bold statement.

This contemporary version is not nearly as "jeweled" as those from the Safavid era. As well as almonds, pistachios, and barberries, the recipe in *A Safavid Period Cookbook* from the 1600s also lists fried noodles, dates, dried figs, golden raisins, chestnuts, boiled chickpeas, lentils, and small meatballs. Large pieces of braised lamb were hidden within the mound of rice, and a syrup was drizzled over it all before serving, as many pilafs of that time were served sweet.

Although the ingredients for jeweled rice have diminished over time, the obsession to serve it in a painterly fashion persists to this day. "You may cook [*morasa' polow*] poorly, but you should not serve it inadequately," advises *A Safavid Period Cookbook*. This is a dish with a mission: to impress with its accessories. Just like a woman who walks into a party wearing shiny diamonds and rubies and emeralds, jeweled rice must turn heads when brought to the table.

You can serve the jeweled rice with any poultry dish (such as the ones on pages 83 and 86), tiny meatballs, or roast pumpkin or winter squash.

*Serves 4–6*

For the rice
2 cups (350 g) Iranian or basmati-
   style long-grain rice
¼ cup (70 g) coarse salt
1½ teaspoons vegetable oil
1 tablespoon ghee (or half butter,
   half vegetable oil)

Start by rinsing and soaking the rice in water with the salt, following the Iranian rice recipe on page 22, leaving the rice to soak for 2–3 hours, or at least 30 minutes.

Meanwhile, if you're using barberries for the "jewels," rinse them and cook them in a pan with half the butter, adding the sugar just when they become bright. After a minute, turn the heat off and set aside. If you're using pomegranate seeds, skip this step.

Parboil and drain the rice according to the Iranian rice recipe on page 24, adding the vegetable oil to the parboiling water.

In a large nonstick pot, bring 1 cup (250 ml) water to a boil, together with the ghee. Set half of this oily water aside in a cup.

For the "jewels"

½ cup (50 g) dried barberries,
   or the seeds of ½ pomegranate

2 teaspoons butter

1½ teaspoons sugar

scant 1 cup (100 g) blanched
   slivered almonds

¾ cup (100 g) pistachios, cut
   into slivers

½ cup (100 g) candied orange
   peel, thinly sliced

2 tablespoons saffron infusion
   (page 18)

1 tablespoon rosewater
   (optional)

Scatter the rice ever so gently in the pot, without pressing down, to form a cone. With the end of a wooden spoon, poke a few holes into the rice to let the steam rise. Pour the reserved oily water over the rice. Gently spoon the almonds, pistachios, and candied orange peel on top, keeping them all separate.

Put the lid on and cook over high heat for 5–10 minutes, until the rice "sweats" and condensation forms under the lid. Now wrap the lid in a clean folded tea towel, then place the lid on the pot, making sure it seals tightly. Cook the rice over the lowest possible heat for 45 minutes to 1¼ hours; a heat diffuser is best here, especially if cooking on a gas burner.

To assemble the jeweled rice, first gently scoop the pistachios, almonds, and candied orange peel into separate bowls. In another bowl, gently mix about 2 cups of the rice with the remaining teaspoon of butter, the saffron infusion and rosewater, if using. Use a skimmer or slotted spoon to gently fluff and spoon out the rice onto a platter in a scattering movement, then "jewel" it with separate stripes of almonds, pistachios, orange peel, saffron rice, and barberries or pomegranate seeds. For the best visual effect, try to put contrasting colors next to each other.

To serve, put a little of the "jewels" onto plates, then reach for the rice hidden beneath. It would be impolite for the first person to take all the jewels and leave only rice for everyone else. This dish can be served on its own, or with roast chicken or lamb, grilled meat, or even little meatballs.

# Sour cherry pilaf

*Albaloo polow* | آلبالو پلو

While most children feast on candies and other sweets as snacks in Iran, what drives kids crazy with an almost manic delight is the sourest treat you can find. Think very tart fruit leathers made mostly of plums but also barberries, pomegranates, or tamarind. Or dried and salted sour cherries, crisp and sour greengage plums in spring (sometimes sprinkled with salt), and *qareh qurut* or black

*Continued ›*

«

*kashk*, a byproduct of yogurt (usually a hard paste with the most exquisitely sour flavor you can imagine). At the very north of Tehran, where the capital merges into the foothills of Mount Damavand, there are country-style restaurants and many snack stalls selling all these treats and more, some going the extra mile in feeding this hysterical appreciation for sourness by actually adding citric acid and food colorings, giving a slightly psychedelic look to the bright fuchsia mounds of prunes and many assorted folded fruit leathers. In Iran we're trained to love sourness, and a sour condiment is almost ever-present in recipes, be it lemon juice, Seville orange juice, verjuice (the juice of unripe grapes), vinegar, or the molasses of sour fruits such as pomegranates or plums.

In *A Safavid Period Cookbook*, Nour-allah, the chef of Shah Abbas the Great (1571–1629), dedicates an entire chapter to sour *polows*, in which he describes different pilaf recipes using lemons, quinces, Seville oranges, sumac berries, pomegranates, vinegar, unripe grapes, black mulberries, cornelian cherries, tamarind, barberries, and sour cherries as the main flavor, enhanced with many other ingredients. Barberries and sour cherries are the stars of two favorite Iranian dishes to this day: *zereshk polow*—pilaf with barberries, often served with saffron chicken—and *albaloo polow*, pilaf with sour cherries, often served with chicken kebabs or tiny meatballs. While the former is very common, the latter is a bit less so, due to the seasonality of sour cherries. This delicate balance between sweet and sour can be found also in the cuisine of Aleppo, in Syria. When eating the Iranian sour cherry pilaf with meatballs, ever so lightly sprinkled with pistachios, you can't help being reminded of *kebab karaz*—Aleppian meatballs stewed with sour cherries and topped with toasted pine nuts (page 161).

*Serves 4–6*

For the rice
2 cups (350 g) Iranian or basmati-
    style long-grain rice
¼ cup (70 g) coarse salt
1½ teaspoons vegetable oil
1 tablespoon ghee (or half butter,
    half vegetable oil)
1½ teaspoons butter
1 tablespoon saffron infusion
    (page 18)

For the sour cherries
1 lb 2 oz (500 g) pitted sour
    cherries, either fresh or frozen
    (see Note), or 12 oz (350 g)
    dried, pitted sour cherries
½–¾ cup (100–150 g) sugar

Start by rinsing and soaking the rice in water with the salt, following the Iranian rice recipe on page 22, leaving the rice to soak for 2–3 hours, or at least 30 minutes.

Meanwhile, if you're using fresh or frozen cherries, let them macerate with the sugar for at least 30 minutes. If using dried cherries, soak them in 1 cup (250 ml) hot water until rehydrated.

Put the cherries in a saucepan, either with the released juices if using fresh or frozen ones, or with the sugar to taste if using dried cherries. (This is a sweet and savory dish, so some sugar is needed.) Cook with a lid on for 8–15 minutes, until the cherries are soft but nowhere near falling apart. Remove them from the syrup. Keep about ½ cup (125 ml) of the juices for the rice, and store the remaining syrup to make *sharbat* (page 117).

Parboil and drain the rice according to the Iranian rice recipe on page 24, adding the vegetable oil to the parboiling water.

*Continued ›*

«

Melt the ghee with ½ cup (125 ml) water in a heavy-based nonstick pot over medium-high heat. With the pot still on the heat, gently scatter in a layer of rice with a slotted spoon, then add a layer of sour cherries. Repeat this layering (never pushing down on the rice), to create a little mountain of rice and sour cherries. Now, using the other end of the slotted spoon, dig some holes in the mound of rice and sour cherries to let the steam rise from the bottom to the top.

In a small saucepan, heat the reserved cherry syrup with the butter, then drizzle it all over the mound of rice. Wrap the lid in a clean folded tea towel, then place the lid on the pot, making sure it seals tightly. Leave for 5 minutes over medium heat, then turn the heat down to the lowest setting possible; a heat diffuser is best here, especially if cooking on a gas burner.

Since you can't really make *tahdig* with this pilaf (the sugar in the cherry juices burns quickly), reduce the cooking time to 35–50 minutes. Never remove the lid during this time.

Have your saffron infusion ready in a bowl. Add some spoonfuls of the rice from the top of the pilaf (without any sour cherries) and mix gently but thoroughly to color the rice a bright saffron yellow.

Serve your *albaloo polow* on a platter, with the saffron rice scattered on top. You can serve it as a vegetarian main dish, or with chicken (such as the saffron chicken opposite) or meatballs. At feasts and weddings, slivers of almonds and pistachios are sometimes added to the saffron rice.

**Note:** Instead of fresh or frozen sour cherries, you can also use canned ones, which are already half-cooked. Taste them and check the ingredients list. If they're not sweet, heat the sour cherries in a saucepan with the juices from the can, adding sugar to your taste; you may not even need to add any sugar. As soon as the sugar has dissolved, turn off the heat, so as not to overcook the cherries. Remove the cherries, reserve about ½ cup (125 ml) of the syrup for the rice, and store the remaining juices to make *sharbat* (page 117).

# Saffron roast chicken stuffed with dried fruit

*Morgh-e shekam por* | مرغ شکم پر

In all cultures, sitting down to feast on a whole roast chicken, stuffed or otherwise, brings about feelings of comfort and abundance. Until not so long ago, beheading one of the family's precious chickens for lunch was a luxury only few could afford, and for festive occasions alone. While a roast chicken has nowadays become an easy casual dinner—something you'd happily eat with your hands, then lick those juices off your fingers and lips—a properly stuffed saffron roast chicken on an Iranian table still holds some prestige and elegance, albeit with the same joyful finger licking.The roast chicken would be like the golden centerpiece of a lavish spread for a gathering, next to trays of rice—of at least two kinds, one simple (page 22), perhaps another with fava beans and dill—and possibly lamb stew with zucchini (page 91) or eggplant.

I am very fond of this filling for roast chicken, not only because of the richness of sweet and sour flavors from the dried fruit, but because it reminds me of the *mehmooni* (family gatherings) of my aunt, who's been living in Germany with her family for about 20 years now. She snatched the Azeri-inspired recipe from my grandmother, of course, and, being more daring than my mom in all matters in life, ended up being the only sister who could pull off two stuffed roast chickens to serve to her guests. My mom stuck to her fail-safe *khoresh*—stews—which gained her the reputation of an excellent cook among family and friends.

You can also stuff this saffron chicken with the *lavangi* filling from the stuffed trout on page 88.

For the chicken
1 whole chicken, gutted,
    about 4 lb (1.8 kg)
1½ tablespoons salt
1 lemon, halved

For the stuffing
1 cup (200 g) prunes, pitted
½ cup (100 g) dried apricots,
    halved
scant 1 cup (100 g) dried
    barberries or cranberries
2 tablespoons butter
⅔ cup (80 g) walnuts,
    coarsely chopped
⅓ cup (50 g) golden raisins
    (optional)

Several hours before cooking, or even the night before, pat the chicken dry with paper towel. Rub the salt on the chicken skin and in the cavity. Squeeze the lemon juice into the cavity of the chicken and leave the squeezed lemon inside the cavity. Leave to rest in the fridge, preferably uncovered.

About 2 hours before cooking, bring the chicken out of the fridge and let it reach room temperature. Discard the lemon.

For the stuffing, soak the prunes, apricots, and cranberries (if using) in water in separate little bowls for 15–30 minutes. If using barberries, simply rinse them with water.

Melt most of the butter in a pan. Drain the prunes, apricots, and cranberries, then add to the pan with the walnuts and raisins

*Continued ›*

«

1 teaspoon sugar
   (if using barberries)
2 tablespoons golden onion
   (page 16)
2 tablespoons saffron infusion
   (page 18)
½ teaspoon salt
¼ teaspoon freshly ground
   black pepper

For the saffron butter
7 tablespoons (100 g) butter
3 tablespoons saffron infusion
   (page 18)
1½ teaspoons salt

(if using). Cook over gentle heat for a few minutes. If you're using barberries, melt the remaining butter in a small pan, add the barberries, and cook for a minute or two over low heat; add the sugar and keep stirring until it dissolves, then mix with the rest of the fruit. Add the golden onion, saffron infusion, salt, and pepper. Give it a stir for 2 minutes, then take off the heat.

Preheat the oven to 425°F (220°C).

For the saffron butter, melt the butter and mix well with the saffron infusion and salt.

To prepare the chicken for the saffron butter rub, first put it on one side, then use a sharp knife to score three deep incisions on one leg. Turn the chicken around and repeat with the other leg. This will allow the legs and breast to cook at the same time.

With the chicken legs facing you, gently pull the skin at the end of the breast toward you with one hand, then insert two fingers of the other hand between the breast and skin. Repeat this carefully and gently, as much as you can, to separate the skin from the meat without tearing it.

Fill the cavity with about half the stuffing, reserving the rest for serving. Tie the chicken legs together with butchers' twine and place the chicken in a baking dish. Using a pastry brush, rub as much of the saffron butter as you can on all sides of the chicken, and under the skin.

Roast the chicken for about 1 hour 20 minutes, brushing it with more saffron butter every 30 minutes. Once the chicken is cooked through, remove from the oven and leave to rest for at least 30 minutes.

To serve, strain the juices at the bottom of the baking dish, and use about ¼ cup (60 ml) to heat the remaining stuffing to use as a garnish. Pour the remaining juices into a gravy boat to serve alongside the chicken.

Serve with jeweled rice (page 78) or sour cherry pilaf (page 79), although since the chicken is stuffed with dried fruit, I prefer plain rice (page 22). You could also serve it with roast potatoes. Any leftovers can be used in the *tahchin* rice cake on page 75.

# Chicken braised with pomegranate

*Khoresh-e nārdoon* | خورش ناردون

Please don't confuse this with *fesenjan* or *fesenjoon*, the famous Iranian chicken with pomegranate molasses and a hefty amount of ground walnuts that has been celebrated a lot recently in Western media. You see, *fesenjan*, like so many other Iranian stew (*khoresh*) recipes, is a "mold" that you can fill with almost any ingredient. In *fesenjan*, just like Circassian chicken (page 152), the defining characteristic is the abundant use of ground walnuts—or sometimes even ground almonds, hazelnuts, or pistachios—slowly cooked for several hours, until the oil of the nuts appears on top of the stew. The classic walnut leaves a more "spiky" taste in the mouth, whereas the other nuts have a more rounded flavor. However, not all *fesenjans* use pomegranate molasses—and sometimes slices of pumpkin, fried eggplant, prunes, spinach, large amounts of herbs, and even yogurt (replacing the molasses) are added to the stew.

Having said that, the name of this dish—*nārdoon*, or *nārdaneh*—is another word for *anār*, or pomegranate, in Persian. Before the arrival of tomatoes from the "New World" and their integration into the cuisines of the Old World in the eighteenth and nineteenth centuries, acidic flavorings for meats were achieved by the use of vinegar, wine, or fruit molasses. A good example is *peposo all'imprunetina*, a Tuscan stew from the fifteenth century in which beef or veal is cooked in abundant amounts of red wine (Chianti, from vineyards close to the town of Impruneta, near Florence). In different regions of Iran (and other parts of the Middle East and Central Asia), the molasses of prunes, apricots, and pomegranates has been used for the same purpose, giving meat that delectable and satisfying sour flavor. Indeed, *Scents and Flavors*, a cookbook from thirteenth-century Syria, has a whole chapter on sour chicken recipes cooked with pomegranates, barberries, rhubarb, tamarind, and bitter oranges. Unfortunately, a lot of this culinary nuance is disappearing through the overuse of tomato sauces and pastes.

This is a simple recipe for cooking chicken or duck in pomegranate molasses and juice. Other game birds also benefit from this approach, with *faraona alla melagrana* (guinea hen with pomegranate, page 240), from central Italy, being another example. In fact, the uncanny resemblance between these two dishes from two apparently distant cultures helped inspire the research that led to this book you're now holding in your hands.

In this recipe you can adjust the sweetness to your taste. If the pomegranate juice is sweet, you may not need any sugar.

*Serves 4–6*

⅓ cup (80 ml) vegetable oil
2 lb 10 oz (1.2 kg) chicken (legs,
 or thighs and drumsticks)
2 tablespoons golden onion
 (page 16)
3–4 garlic cloves, finely chopped
⅓ cup (80 ml) pomegranate
 molasses
1¼–1⅔ cups (300–400 ml)
 pomegranate juice
1 teaspoon salt
1–1½ tablespoons saffron
 infusion (page 18)
freshly ground black pepper
1 tablespoon sugar (optional)
seeds of 2 small pomegranates
 or 1 large one

In a tall pot large enough to fit all the chicken pieces, heat half the oil and brown the chicken pieces on all sides over medium-high heat for about 10 minutes, or until golden brown. Remove the chicken to a dish using tongs (never a fork, as it'll puncture the meat and the precious juices will come out).

Add the remaining oil to the same pot, reduce the heat to medium, and stir the golden onion and garlic around for a minute or two, until the garlic is fragrant. Pour in the pomegranate molasses and stir for another minute or so, taking care not to burn the mixture.

Pour in the pomegranate juice and mix well, then put the lid on and bring to a boil. Now add the salt to the sauce and put the chicken pieces back in. Reduce the heat to low, then cover and cook for 20–30 minutes.

Add the saffron infusion and season with black pepper. Cook, uncovered, for another 15–20 minutes to let the sauce thicken. Taste the sauce to adjust the seasoning. If the sauce is too sour for you (it depends on the variety of pomegranate juice and molasses), add the sugar.

Check that the chicken is cooked (the juices should run clear when the flesh is pierced with a knife, and the meat should have separated from the bone). If not, cook a little more until it is.

Just before serving, mix half the pomegranate seeds through the sauce, then sprinkle the rest on top when serving. Serve with Iranian rice (page 22) or bread.

# Trout stuffed with herbs, barberries & walnuts

*Mahi-e shekam por* | ماهی شکم پر

Among the more than 80 recipes in this cookbook, those containing seafood can be counted on the fingers of one hand. I believe geography is the reason for this. Growing up in Iran, a vast country of mostly desert, and with the sea only in the north—the Caspian, beyond the high Alborz Mountains—and in the far south, I was little exposed to fish. I am willing to argue that those of us living in any part of Iran except the sea regions can't really cook fish well. I grew up absolutely hating fish. This changed when I moved to Italy, a thin, long peninsula surrounded by the Mediterranean that knows its way around seafood so well it converted even a non-fish-believer like me.

There's a very important reason why this specific recipe couldn't be missing from this chapter. As un-expert as most Iranians (in my opinion) might be with seafood, at least once a year all the nation tries its best to cook a herby pilaf with fish—*sabzi polow ba mahi*—for one of the most important Iranian meals: Norouz, the Persian New Year celebration on March 20, which marks the beginning of spring. While the herby pilaf (*sabzi polow*)—which includes large quantities of finely chopped parsley, dill, and cilantro, a touch of fenugreek, and fresh garlic—is more or less the same all around the country, the type of fish varies from family to family. After years of insisting, it wasn't until my mother adopted this *lavangi*-style trout recipe that I started eating fish with my *sabzi polow* for Norouz. (Before that, I would just have some tantrums, and then a fried egg, hastily cooked by my frustrated and resigned mom.)

*Lavangi* refers to the style of stuffing—aromatic herbs in abundance, finely chopped, then sautéed and cooked in pomegranate molasses mixed with barberries, walnuts and, of course, a healthy dose of garlic. The influences are from the region of Gilan in northern Iran, along the Caspian Sea, and it stretches into the Iranian region of Azerbaijan and beyond. You will also find variations of *lavangi* stuffing in the south of Azerbaijan the country, around the Lankaran area. You can use this filling for roast chicken too, such as the golden saffron one on page 83.

In Italy, I have often made this dish with trout, sea bass, or other whole fish for Christmas Eve, when it's customary to eat seafood.

*Continued ›*

«

*Serves 4–6*

### For the *lavangi* stuffing

3 tablespoons vegetable or
  olive oil
5–6 garlic cloves, finely chopped
14 oz–1 lb 2 oz (400–500 g)
  fresh herbs—at least three of
  the following: chives, cilantro,
  dill, parsley, basil, and/or
  scallions—washed, trimmed,
  and finely chopped
½ teaspoon salt
¼ cup (60 ml) pomegranate
  molasses
juice of 1 lemon
½ cup (60 g) walnuts,
  coarsely chopped
⅓–½ cup (25–30 g) dried
  barberries
½ teaspoon butter
½ teaspoon sugar
freshly ground black pepper

### For the fish

2 tablespoons butter
2 tablespoons saffron infusion
  (page 18)
zest of 1 lemon
½ teaspoon salt
2 whole trout, about 3 lb 12 oz
  (1.7 kg) in total, gutted and
  cleaned (ask your fishmonger
  to do this for you)

To prepare the stuffing, heat the oil in a large pot with the garlic over medium heat. After a minute, or as soon as you can smell the garlic, stir in the herbs and salt. Turn the heat down to low and keep stirring for about 10 minutes, until the herbs wilt down and release their juices. Now add the pomegranate molasses, lemon juice, and walnuts and cook for about another 10 minutes, to absorb all the liquid.

Meanwhile, rinse the barberries. Melt the butter in a small pan and cook the barberries over gentle heat for a moment or two, then add the sugar and stir.

Add the barberries to the herb mixture with some black pepper and mix well. Now let everything cook together for about another 10 minutes, or until all the juices are absorbed. Set the stuffing aside.

Preheat the oven to 350°F (180°C).

To prepare the fish, melt the butter, then stir in the saffron infusion, lemon zest, and salt. Place the fish on a lined baking sheet large enough to fit them both. Brush the butter mixture into the cavity of each fish, then fill each fish with half the stuffing. Tie each fish with three pieces of butchers' twine to enclose the filling. Brush more of the butter mixture all over each fish—top, bottom, head, and tail.

Roast the fish for 30 minutes. Brush the tops with the remaining butter mixture and roast for another 30 minutes, or until the skin has separated from the flesh; the cooking time may vary, depending on the size of your fish.

Serve with plain rice, herbed rice, roast potatoes, or a winter version of *salad Shirazi* (page 63).

# Mutton braise with zucchini & tomato

*Mossama-ye kadoo* | مسمای کدو

The world of *khoresh*—the Iranian stews and braises often served with plain Iranian rice (page 22) and sometimes bread—is so vast and varied that entire cookbooks could be written about them alone. *Mossama* (or *mossaman*) is a type of *khoresh* that is more of a braise than a stew, with largeish pieces of fried vegetables added to the meat. These vegetables can be just about anything, but the most popular is eggplant, which is the star of several popular kinds of *khoresh*. Summer squash and zucchini, pumpkins and winter squashes, okra, and even celery (together with a large amount of parsley and mint) are also commonly used. Indeed, many households fry eggplant and summer squash when they're at their prime in summer, then freeze them to use in a wintertime *khoresh*. Even now that these vegetables are available year-round, sticking to the season is the key to a delicious *khoresh*—or in fact any other dish.

Time is the secret ingredient in Iranian cooking—and a *khoresh* is the very embodiment of this principle. Some women even cook their *khoresh* the day before, letting it simmer ever so gently for many hours. Naturally, the fried vegetables can't cook in the stew for too long, or they'll disintegrate, so these are added toward the end. The presentation of this dish matters a lot. The fried vegetables should be in the spotlight, so they're first removed from the pot while we serve the meat in the main serving dish, and they are then placed neatly next to or on top of the meat—all very gently so they don't break apart.

Mutton (but not a young lamb, which doesn't have enough meat or flavor) is the ideal meat for *khoresh*, although veal can work, too. It is also best if the meat is still on the bone and not too lean, as the bone gives an unbeatable depth of flavor during the long cooking of this dish. Remember that a *khoresh* is meant to be a little brothy, and you are supposed to bathe your rice or bread in that delicious juice while enjoying the vegetables and meat.

*Continued ›*

«

*Serves 4–6*

¼ cup (60 ml) oil, plus extra
    for frying the zucchini
1 tablespoon golden onion
    (page 16)
1 lb 5 oz–1 lb 12 oz (600–800 g)
    mutton, in large chunks
2 cups (500 ml) hot water
8–9 small zucchini, or
    6 large ones, about
    2 lb 12 oz (1.25 kg); I love
    Roman zucchini in summer
1 teaspoon salt, plus extra for
    salting the zucchini
¼ teaspoon freshly ground
    black pepper
¼ teaspoon ground cinnamon
¼ cup (60 ml) lemon juice,
    approximately
3 tomatoes, cut in half

Heat the oil in a heavy-based pot and add the golden onion. Sear the mutton pieces for about 5 minutes over medium-high heat. Pour in the hot water, bring to a gentle simmer, reduce the heat to low, then cover and cook slowly for 1 hour.

Meanwhile, peel the zucchini (unless they're really young and tender) and rub generously with salt. If they're large, cut them in half lengthways; if small, keep them whole. Make a long lengthways slit along the middle of each one, then let them sit in a colander in the sink for an hour to lose their "bitter" water. Rinse the zucchini well with water, then dry them.

After the meat has been cooking for 1 hour, stir in the salt, pepper, cinnamon, and lemon juice. Put the lid back on and cook for another hour.

Meanwhile, heat enough oil in a large frying pan for frying the zucchini. Working in batches if needed, shallow-fry each zucchini over high heat for 5–10 minutes, until golden on all sides; at this stage, we only want to brown the zucchini, not cook them entirely. Leave to drain on a plate lined with paper towel. In the same oil, fry the tomato halves on both sides for just 2–3 minutes, then set aside.

When the meat has cooked for about 2 hours, gently transfer it to a dish. Cover to retain some of its heat, then set aside.

Using tongs, very carefully place the fried zucchini in the pot, in the meat juices, and place the tomatoes on top. Put the lid back on and cook for 20–30 minutes over very low heat until the zucchini are very soft but not falling apart.

Using tongs, neatly place the zucchini in a deep serving dish, parallel along one side, and place the tomatoes in the middle of the dish. Heat the meat pieces briefly in the juices, then arrange neatly on the other side of the serving dish. Pour all the juices over the meat and the vegetables.

Serve with Iranian rice (page 22) or bread.

# Savory stuffed apples

*Dolme-ye sib* | دلمه‌ی سیب

In a parallel world, instead of calling this book *Pomegranates & Artichokes*, I would've named it *Oh, the Glorious World of Stuffed Vegetables*, as nothing showcases culinary affinities all the way from Central Asia to the heart of the Mediterranean quite like stuffed vegetables. Known as *dolmeh* in Iran, *dolma* in Turkey, *gemista* in Greece, and *mehshi* in Arab-speaking countries, they are scattered throughout this book—stuffed bell peppers on page 145, *Imam bayildi* (Turkish stuffed eggplant) on page 149, stuffed tomatoes on page 249, and stuffed artichokes on page 228— with each recipe diving a little into their cultural history. Across these regions, there are as many varieties of stuffing for these vegetables as there are families.

As well as vegetables, fruit such as apples and quince are occasionally also stuffed with a savory filling. In her *New Book of Middle Eastern Cooking,* food legend Claudia Roden describes these as Iranian dishes, even using their Persian names, *dolmeh sib* (stuffed apples) and *dolmeh beh* (stuffed quince).

My mother had never tried savory stuffed apples, and neither had I. The version in Najaf Daryabandari's cookbook, *The Rt. Honorable Cookbook: From Soup to Nuts,* uses many varieties of dried fruits in the filling, with optional ground meat and no rice. I wanted this recipe to be vegetarian (or vegan, if you omit the butter), but you could add some ground meat right after the onion if you wanted to.

I also wanted this recipe to have the flavor of certain Iranian *dolmeh*. One of the practices specific to Iranian cooking is the use of a vinegar syrup in savory dishes—which in medieval Arab cookery texts is referred to as *sikbaj*, the Arabized word for *sik-bā*, which in turn is Middle Persian for "vinegar stew," and which later gives birth to many other dishes in the Mediterranean, such as *escabeche* in Spain and *scapece* in Italy (fried zucchini marinated in vinegar), and other seemingly unrelated recipes.

The *agrodolce* ("sour-sweet") flavor of vinegar syrup (often with a touch of saffron) is still present in many Iranian savory dishes, in particular some stuffed vegetables, but it varies greatly from region to region and from family to family. For example, my mother would make stuffed cabbage leaves and stuffed zucchini with vinegar syrup, but would not touch stuffed vine leaves if flavored this way. Instead, she uses a thick yogurt in her vine-leaf filling, a nod toward Central Asia and the Balkans.

The filling for these stuffed apples is similar enough to other Iranian *dolmeh*, with rice and a few split peas, except that there's no meat. It also contains raisins and walnuts—which, apart from being a heavenly match with apples, also reminds me of how some Iranian Jewish families use dried fruits in their *dolmeh*, in common with Jewish families in Aleppo, Syria; stuffed vegetables are a

*Continued ›*

«

favorite among Jewish communities everywhere because they can be made in advance and served at room temperature. Just as the tomato and herby rice filling makes the stuffed bell peppers on page 145 typically Turkish and Eastern Mediterranean, and the breadcrumbs and anchovies make the stuffed artichokes (page 228) very southern Italian, the vinegar syrup with saffron also makes these *dolmeh* very Iranian. So, although I hadn't actually tasted this recipe before, and have developed it based on research, I feel confident enough to call it "authentic." Do use Red Delicious or similar apples, as they need to hold up to baking. They are also best cooked in a lidded glass baking dish, so you can see what's going on.

*Serves 4–6 as a side or appetizer, 2–3 as a main*

### For the filling
3½ tablespoons basmati rice
2 tablespoons yellow split peas
2 tablespoons vegetable oil
1 tablespoon golden onion (page 16)
3 tablespoons coarsely chopped walnuts
2 tablespoons raisins
2 tablespoons saffron infusion (page 18)
1 teaspoon salt
½ teaspoon ground cinnamon
freshly ground black pepper

### For the syrup
⅓ cup (70 g) sugar
2 tablespoons white wine vinegar

### For assembling
6 Red Delicious apples
juice of ½ lemon
½ teaspoon salt
1 tablespoon saffron infusion (page 18)
1½–2 tablespoons butter, melted

To make the filling, start by soaking the rice in some water for 20–30 minutes. Meanwhile, in a small saucepan, boil the split peas for 20–30 minutes, or until soft but still al dente. Drain.

Heat the oil in a pan with the golden onion. Drain the rice, then add to the pan with ⅔ cup (160 ml) water. Cook for 5–10 minutes, so that the rice is not completely raw and a lot of liquid is still left. Take off the heat and add the split peas, walnuts, raisins, saffron infusion, salt, cinnamon, and some black pepper. Set aside.

To make the vinegar syrup, bring the sugar, vinegar, and ⅔ cup (160 ml) water to a boil in a small saucepan. Reduce the heat and simmer for 2–5 minutes, then remove from the heat. It's likely that you won't need all of this syrup; any leftovers will keep indefinitely in a sealed jar in the fridge, and can become the base of *sharbat sekanjebin* (page 120) if you cook some mint in it.

Preheat the oven to 400°F (200°C).

Cut the tops off the apples to keep as "lids." Using a teaspoon, carefully scoop the flesh out of the apples, leaving a ¼ inch (5 mm) shell. Reserve the scooped-out apple flesh, but discard the cores. Rub the inside of the apple shells and the bottom of the "lids" with lemon juice so they don't discolor.

In a roasting pan large enough to fit all the apples, place the reserved apple flesh, salt, saffron infusion, half the melted butter, and ¼ cup (60 ml) of the vinegar syrup and mix well.

Arrange the apples on top, then stuff each with the filling, leaving a little space for it to swell. Pour 1 tablespoon of the vinegar syrup into each of the apples. Put the "lids" back on, then drizzle the remaining melted butter over the apples.

Cover with foil (or a lid, if your pan has one). Bake for 45–55 minutes, until the apples are a little shriveled. Remove from the oven, then let the apples cool, uncovered, for at least 15 minutes, before transferring them very gently to a platter.

Transfer all the juice and pulp at the bottom of the roasting pan to a blender. Blend into a thick sauce, spoon it around the apples on the platter, and serve.

# By—or instead of—the tea

One of the rudest things one can do in Iran is to not offer tea to someone who enters your home—although on very hot days in summer, you're allowed to swap the tea for a *sharbat* (cordial), or sometimes ice cream. But even then the kettle is always on, and tea is served all day long, before meals, after meals, and between them.

It's common for the tea to be accompanied by something sweet—sweets that, apart from being snacks, often signify "good news." In case of any happy occasion—be it a promotion, an engagement, or a resolved conflict—you're expected to "give its sweets," which means "bring a box of pastries."

You'll notice the recurrent theme of Norouz in this chapter, as the arrival of spring and the beginning of the new year is the ultimate good news, for which sweets are required. Norouz baking is very diverse and regional in Iran, Afghanistan, Tajikistan, and among Kurds—although many buy their Norouz sweets these days rather than baking them.

There are sweets for religious ceremonies and funerals as well. Iranians celebrate, and commiserate, with sugar.

# Iranian raisin cookies

*Naan-e keshmeshi* | نان کشمشی

These are very simple cookies. Wonderfully so, with no fuss, and only very basic ingredients—velvety and comforting butter in abundance, plus a hint of cardamom, which can be replaced with vanilla. Unlike many other Iranian cookies and candies that are supposed be tiny, delicate, and meticulous, as if they have been cut out of a page of an illustrated manuscript of Persian poetry, these raisin cookies have a more informal and inelegant way about them, making them easy to both make and eat—often in quick succession.

*Makes 20–30 cookies*

4 cardamom pods (or
  ¼ teaspoon ground
  cardamom)
¾ cup (170 g) butter, diced
  and at room temperature
⅔ cup (140 g) sugar
3 eggs
1½ cups (190 g) all-purpose flour
⅔ cup (100 g) raisins

If you're using cardamom pods, bash the pods in a small mortar to break them open and release the seeds. Discard the pods (or save them to infuse into a tea), then grind the seeds with ½ teaspoon of the sugar until you have a powder.

Preheat the oven to 475°F (240°C). Line two or three baking sheets with parchment paper.

Cream the butter with the sugar and cardamom, either by hand or using an electric mixer. When the mixture is fluffy and white, add the eggs one at a time, mixing well but without over-beating. Sift the flour and gently fold it through the batter, then mix in the raisins.

Using two tablespoons, put walnut-sized dollops of batter on the baking sheets. Make sure the dollops are very well distanced, as they will expand to twice their width or more in the oven.

Bake for 8–10 minutes, until the edges turn golden brown; don't overbake the cookies. Leave to cool on the baking sheets for 5–10 minutes to firm up before transferring them to a rack to cool for another 30 minutes.

These cookies are best eaten the same day or within a few days of baking; store in an airtight container in the pantry.

# Saffron rice pudding with almonds

*Sholeh zard* | شله زرد

My grandmother's mother had her only child when she was just 14, nearly a century ago. Which means she was only 34 when she first became a grandmother, when my oldest uncle was born. She was so thrilled with her first-born grandson that she made a *nazr*, a vow, to cook this saffron rice pudding with rosewater and almonds every year on a holy day for the health and well-being of this child.

After her death, when my uncle was a young twenty-something, my grandmother took over her mother's vow, and she cooked the very same sweet rice pudding ever since to be distributed among family, friends, and passers-by on a holy day. My mom recalls when they would cook and stir the pudding in a huge cauldron in their backyard. For quite some years, however, the quantity of this *sholeh zard* was reduced to only a hundred small bowls for passers-by, and their tradition was only ever stopped due to the 2020 coronavirus pandemic. Sadly, my grandmother passed away in 2022.

A *nazr* is an homage paid to a saint, either for a prayer come true, the health of an ill beloved, the serenity of the soul of a deceased parent, or even purchasing a house. The debt of gratitude is usually paid by a sort of charity, such as "sacrificing" (butchering) a sheep and distributing the meat among the poor, making a monetary donation, or feeding a crowd, whether with a meal, a small banquet, or just something sweet, like a tray of dates. The oblation can be offered once, for a special occasion, or annually, like my grandmother's *sholeh zard*, which year after year contributed to building a family tradition.

Nowadays, fewer and fewer people prepare large amounts of food as *nazri* for family, friends, and total strangers—partly because it's so much work, requiring considerable time and many helping hands, both harder to come by in this era of digital connection. Also, the religious fabric of Iranian society has been severely torn during the past four decades of the Islamic Republic (oh, the irony!), and with that, many traditional rituals have perished as well. Most sadly, those who do feel like making a donation—to honor a deceased person, or for the health of a beloved—often feel it's a waste to feed those who probably don't need a square meal, when there are so many who actually do. Instead, those who can afford it make donations to one of the many nongovernmental organizations that try to help the ever-growing number of families in difficulty. Decades of economic sanctions, mismanagement, and corruption have taken more than just bread from the Iranian table—and those who are lucky are left with only the hunger for the human interactions that not so long ago were provided through dance and music parties with family and friends, and in rituals of feeding a large crowd in the name of a saint, even if just once a year.

*Continued ›*

«

Rice puddings, especially those cooked in milk, are one of those universal comfort foods with a fascinating interconnecting history going back centuries (see the *muhallabia*—milk pudding—recipe on page 165). Middle Eastern ones often contain rosewater, orange blossom water, or cardamom. The ones with orange zest and warm spices have traveled west, too, such as the rice cake from southern Italy on page 264. *Sholeh zard*, which is very similar to the Turkish *zerde*, has no milk, taking its name from the generous amount of saffron used (*zard* means "yellow").

The cooking time will depend on the quality of your rice and how much water it absorbs. When done, it shouldn't feel like a risotto; it should be rather watery yet well mixed when you add the sugar.

*Makes 6–8 small bowls*

1½ cups (300 g) high-quality
   long-grain white rice,
   such as basmati
1 teaspoon salt
2 tablespoons saffron infusion
   (page 18)
1½ cups (300 g) sugar
3½ tablespoons butter
3½ tablespoons rosewater
½ cup (50 g) blanched
   slivered almonds
ground cinnamon, to garnish
ground or slivered pistachios
   and/or almonds, to garnish
   (optional)

Put the rice in a bowl, fill with water, rinse gently, then discard almost all of the water. Repeat two or three times.

Put the rice in a saucepan together with the salt, half the saffron infusion, and 4¼ cups (1 liter) water. Stirring often, cook over low heat for about 30 minutes, or until the rice is well cooked but the mixture is not too thick.

Now add the sugar and keep stirring while cooking for another 10 minutes. If the mixture feels too thick, add some extra water. To check if the pudding is cooked, pour a spoonful onto a dish; if it doesn't flow, it's ready.

Stir in the butter, rosewater, almonds, and the remaining saffron infusion. Wrap the lid in a clean tea towel and place it on the pan, ensuring it seals snugly, then cook over the lowest heat possible for another 10 minutes.

Ladle the pudding into bowls. Sprinkle the cinnamon over, in decorative lines or shapes. Garnish with pistachios and/or almonds if desired.

Leave to cool, then refrigerate until chilled; the puddings will keep in the fridge for up to 5 days. Serve cold.

**Note:** You can reduce the amount of sugar by ¼–½ cup (50–100 g), but be aware this may make the pudding too bland.

# An imitation of traditional Iranian ice cream

*Bastani sonnati* | بستنی سنتی

I love cooking, but I'm also a great champion of laziness in the kitchen, whenever possible. Sometimes I'll go through a labor of love to create something as time consuming and detailed as *sartù* (page 237), but other times I just want something that quenches a craving without going through the trouble of a long preparation.

In Iran, we don't just enjoy our traditional ice cream, *bastani sonnati*. Indeed, I was once obsessed with an American ice cream, Baskin-Robbins, that mysteriously appeared in Iran, despite decade-long trade sanctions. (Equally mysterious is how we get the latest iPhones before they make it to Europe, when part of those economic sanctions means we're not able to use any credit cards in Iran.)

Traditional *bastani sonnati*, though, is a delight. Its texture is different from regular ice cream, as there are no eggs, and the main ingredient is *sahlep*, a flour made from orchid roots! This is what gives *bastani sonnati* its stretchy quality, and *sahlep* is also present (together with mastic, a tree resin) in *bakdash booza*, the famous ice cream from Damascus—which, apart from being stretchy, is also chewy. *Bastani sonnati* is often served between two paper-thin wafers, like a sandwich, and it has chunky pieces of frozen clotted cream in it, too.

The recipe below is an ode to laziness and a bit of cunning in the kitchen. It's not the traditional recipe: it's how to take a tub of plain ice cream and make it as similar to *bastani sonnati* as possible. No orchid roots, no tree resin, and no vigorous mixing. Unsurprisingly, as with many other Iranian sweets, the "secret" is in the use of rosewater, saffron, and pistachios. Easy, floral, and impressive.

*Serves 4–6*

1 lb 2 oz (500 g) milk-flavored
   or vanilla ice cream
12 cardamom pods (or 1 teaspoon
   ground cardamom)
a tiny pinch of sugar (if using
   cardamom pods)
3 tablespoons saffron infusion
   (page 18)
2 tablespoons rosewater
a large handful of pistachios,
   bashed into a coarse powder
Damascus rose petals,
   to garnish (optional)

Leave the ice cream at room temperature to soften for about 10 minutes.

In a small mortar, bash the cardamom pods to break them open and release the seeds (save the pods to infuse into a tea). Add the sugar, then crush the cardamom seeds into a fine powder. (Skip this step if you're using ground cardamom, obviously—but apart from giving you a more fragrant cardamom powder, this step would also give you the sense of actually having done something to make this sumptuous dessert.)

Prepare the saffron infusion based on the recipe on page 18, but use one-third of the indicated water and dilute it with the rosewater. Mix in the cardamom powder.

*Continued ›*

« Transfer your ice cream to a large bowl, reserving the container, then soften the ice cream with the back of a rubber spatula. Spread a thin layer of ice cream at the bottom of the container; this layer doesn't have to be perfect. Using a teaspoon, splash around large drops of the saffron mixture, then sprinkle with some of the pistachios. Repeat with more layers, until the container is full again with your Iranian ice cream.

Cover and place it back in the freezer to set for 4–5 hours.

For maximum effect, serve in colorful glass cups, sprinkled with torn dried rose petals.

# A simple cake with date frosting, inspired by the South

One of the best chocolate cakes in the world, in my opinion, comes from a famous pastry shop in Tehran called Bibi. Most of the shop's popularity is due to their moist, luscious, and yet light chocolate cake, which is somehow, always perfectly, only *just* sweet but never too much. It's nothing like the sticky and thick Sacher torte, for example—which I happen to not like.

Cakes and tarts from confectionery shops have been part of Iranian afternoon teas, gatherings, and *mehmooni* for many decades now, but if we go back barely a century, next to those teas there would've been small or large traditional cookies, baklavas, sweet or salty nuts, or maybe some sweet breads—but no cakes. Cake is a relatively new Western addition to the sweet-loving Iranian palate. My mom never remembers her mother baking a cake at home, although she does remember her mother deep-frying leftover dough or even stale flatbread and then sprinkling it with sugar and cinnamon to serve as a sweet afternoon snack.

No one could describe my mother as an adventurous woman, but she did start baking cakes, so my own childhood memories are filled with freshly baked homemade cakes and small sweets. She started with recipes from *Honar-e Ashpazi* (*The Art of Cooking*) by Rosa Montazami, a cookbook considered so fundamental by Iranian families that generations of new brides received it as a gift, and even during the eight years of war with Iraq in the 1980s, there was a coupon for this cookbook for every household in the rations booklet for essential goods. Later, my mom continued to collect recipes from friends and family, magazines, and television cooking shows.

I loved watching her bake. I learned at the age of ten that your whisk and bowl need to be very clean if you want perfectly stiff beaten egg whites; that you need to fold flour gently into a batter in large circular movements; and to never open the oven door when a cake is baking, otherwise it will not rise much. Whatever my mom was baking, I lived for those moments when I could lick the batter off the bowl and spatula.

So, homemade cakes were at our house when people came for tea, in our freezer for future guests, and in my schoolbag as snacks.

In homage to those days, here is a simple yogurt cake that my mom made most often from Rosa's cookbook. The date frosting, however, is inspired by the warm and earthy sweets of southern Iran—in particular a simple halva from Bushehr called *ranginak*, in which dates are stuffed with walnuts, drizzled with a loose batter of flour cooked in butter, and everything is sprinkled with cinnamon. You can use the date frosting for other purposes, too: spread it on your pancakes, swirl it through your yogurt—or simply eat it by the spoonful.

*Continued* ›

«

*Makes an 8 inch
(20 cm) cake*

4 eggs
⅔ cup (120 g) sugar
1 cup (250 g) full-fat yogurt
scant ½ cup (100 ml) sunflower
    oil or melted butter
zest of ½ orange
1 teaspoon baking powder
½ teaspoon baking soda
a pinch of salt
1 teaspoon ground cinnamon
scant 1 cup (100 g) whole wheat
    flour
1¼ cups (150 g) all-purpose flour

## For the date frosting
10½ oz (300 g) dates, pitted
1 cup (250 ml) hot water
½ teaspoon ground cinnamon
¼ teaspoon salt
2 tablespoons butter
¼–⅓ cup (30–40 g) walnuts,
    coarsely chopped

Preheat the oven to 325°F (170°C).

Line an 8 inch (20 cm) round cake pan with parchment paper. In a large bowl, whisk the eggs vigorously with the sugar using an electric mixer, until the eggs double in size and become a light, foamy cream. Whisking a little more slowly, gradually incorporate the yogurt, then the oil, with the orange zest.

In another bowl, mix the baking powder, baking soda, salt, and cinnamon with the flours. Gently add the dry ingredients to the egg mixture, folding slowly and in a large circular motion.

Pour the batter into the cake pan and bake for 40 minutes, or until the top is golden and a toothpick comes out clean from the middle of the cake. Remove from the oven and leave to cool in the pan for about 15 minutes. Transfer to a wire rack and leave to cool completely, so the frosting will glide on more easily.

To prepare the frosting, soak the dates in the hot water to soften them for 10–20 minutes, depending on how hard the dates are. Drain the dates, reserving the soaking water. In a food processor, blend the dates with the cinnamon, salt, and half the soaking water, until you get a very smooth paste (or you can sieve this later, but I never do). If needed, add more of the soaking water 1 tablespoon at a time.

Transfer the smooth date cream to a small saucepan. Add the butter and keep mixing with a rubber spatula over very low heat while the butter melts, making sure the cream is not sticking to the pan. When the mixture is smooth and homogenous, transfer to a bowl, leave to cool completely, then chill it in the fridge.

When the cake has cooled down, use a rubber spatula to spread a thick layer of the frosting on top of the cake; it doesn't need to look neat or a certain shape. Sprinkle the walnuts on top. Consume within a couple of days.

**Note:** Instead of combining whole wheat and all-purpose flour, you could use 2 cups (250 g) all-purpose flour.

# Saffron & lemon toasted almonds & pistachios

During the two weeks of Norouz holidays and the beginning of the Iranian new year with the spring equinox, it's customary to leave on tables plates of sweets (such as the tiny cookies on pages 113–114) and a big bowl of *ajil*—salted pistachios, almonds, cashews, chickpeas, pumpkin seeds, and hazelnuts—for friends and family who call on you for new year greetings.

It often happens, however, that stretched on a sofa, watching too much holiday TV, you'd find yourself in front of that big bowl of *ajil*, munching the hours away on salty, sour, scrumptious, and irresistible pistachios, almonds, and cashews—leaving the bowl half full only with the dried chickpeas and pumpkin seeds.

Since this was too familiar a scenario at our home, my mom would implement a strategy to save both my waistline and her wallet: she'd store all the sweets and *ajil* in plastic boxes and hide them in the most unlikely places. This meant that when she'd go out during the Norouz holidays—often to some great-aunt's house—I'd start my treasure hunt. Never in the pantry or kitchen cabinets, because that would've been too obvious, but more likely among my mom's shoeboxes, on top of her wardrobes behind heavy sweaters, deep in her chest of drawers concealed by hair sprays and jewelry boxes, or between stacks of sheets and duvets. And once I did find them, it was hard to not keep raiding them whenever I had the chance—so my mom would find her strategically hidden boxes of *ajil* half empty nonetheless. She would say "we have a little mouse in the house" when her exasperation eventually waned.

What makes these nuts irresistible is the sourness of lemon and a scent of saffron, in addition to the salt. They're very easy to prepare, and they make a perfect match for *aperitivo* drinks, such as a spritz (page 203) or negroni (page 204).

## Salted saffron-toasted almonds *Badam shoor* | بادام شور

*Makes about 1½ cups (200 g)*

1 tablespoon saffron infusion
   (page 18)
1 tablespoon hot water
1 teaspoon salt
¼ cup (60 ml) fresh lemon juice
1½ cups (200 g) whole almonds

Place a nonstick frying pan over medium-high heat. While the pan is heating, mix the saffron infusion, hot water, salt, and lemon juice in a bowl until the salt has dissolved.

When you can feel the heat of the pan with your palm held 4 inches (10 cm) above it, reduce the heat to medium and toast the almonds, constantly turning and flipping them so they don't burn. After about 10 minutes, or when they smell toasty and nutty and they have darkened slightly, quickly add them to the

*Continued ›*

«

saffron mixture and mix well, making sure all the almonds are equally absorbing the liquid. Leave to soak for 10–15 minutes.

Wipe out the pan, so that any small crumbs don't burn, and keep it warm over low heat.

Once the almonds have rested, turn the heat back up to medium and return the soaked almonds to the hot pan, with all the juices left in the bottom of the bowl. Keep moving and flipping the almonds with a wooden spoon so that they don't burn. After another 10–15 minutes, the almonds should be perfectly dry. Remove from the heat and let them cool for 20–30 minutes before eating, as they may be very hot inside.

If you somehow manage not to eat all these toasted almonds at once, it's crucial to let them dry completely—either in the open air, spread out in a single layer for 24 hours, or in a 200°F (100°C) oven for about 2 hours—before storing them in an airtight container at room temperature. If you don't do this, any humidity left inside the almonds will make them moldy, and that would be a great pity.

## Salted saffron-toasted pistachios *Pesteh-ye shoor* | پسته شور

*Makes about 9 oz (250 g)*

2 tablespoons saffron infusion (page 18)
¼ cup (60 ml) fresh lemon juice
2 tablespoons hot water
1 teaspoon salt
9 oz (250 g) unshelled pistachios

Place a nonstick frying pan over medium-high heat. While the pan is heating, mix the saffron infusion, lemon juice, hot water, and salt in a bowl until the salt has dissolved.

Now toast the pistachios in exactly the same way as the almonds above, adding 5–10 minutes more to each stage of the toasting described above, as pistachios need a little more time to get properly toasted because of their shells.

Before storing, let them dry completely—either in the open air, spread out in a single layer for 24 hours, or in a 200°F (100°C) oven for about 2 hours. They will then keep in an airtight container at room temperature for 2–3 weeks.

# Two types of tiny cookies

On the large platters to celebrate Norouz, you'll find many little cookies and sweets. My mom is an expert at baking these for the holidays, instead of buying them from confectionery shops as most families do. The fabulous thing about these two cookies is that one uses egg yolks, and the other uses egg whites, which means you can make two types of cookies with the same amount of eggs, with some other simple pantry ingredients. The ridiculous easiness of the walnut cookies makes up for the somewhat effortful stirring required for the coconut ones. Both are feather light and melt-in-the-mouth sweet, and are supposed to be tiny, pale, and delicate, so don't overbake them.

## Tiny coconut cookies *Shirni nargili* | شیرینی نارگیلی

*Makes about 40 tiny cookies*

2 egg whites
½ cup (100 g) sugar
½ cup (60 g) coconut flour
   (see note, next page)
2 tablespoons oil
1 tablespoon fresh lemon juice
a pinch of ground pistachios,
   to garnish

Preheat the oven to 350°F (180°C). Line your largest baking sheet with parchment paper, and prepare a piping bag (or make your own by snipping off the corner of a clean ziplock plastic bag to create a ¼ inch/5 mm opening).

In a saucepan, whisk the egg whites and sugar together with a fork. This is not a meringue, so we're not looking for a thick, firm cream; we just want to dissolve the sugar in the egg white. Now add the coconut flour and oil and combine well.

Put the saucepan over medium-low heat and stir continuously with a rubber spatula, making sure the batter is not browning or sticking to the pan. (A better baker than me would tell you to do this step using a double-boiler or bain-marie, but I honestly can never be bothered.)

After about 15 minutes, or when the batter is too hot for you to touch with your fingers (this is how you test it), and when the mixture has somehow thickened and become a lot whiter than the initial translucent gray, take the saucepan off the heat and immediately add the lemon juice. Mix well and set aside to cool off a bit.

Transfer the batter to your piping bag. Pipe the batter onto the baking sheet, to make cookies a bit larger than a hazelnut, spacing them about 1¼ inches (3 cm) apart. Sprinkle each cookie

*Continued ›*

«

with a tiny bit of ground pistachios. (You may need to bake these cookies in two batches, depending on the size of the pan.)

Bake for 10–15 minutes, or until only the bottom edge of the cookies darkens a bit but the top is still pale; I suggest you keep watching them closely, as they're very sensitive, so you don't want to overcook them—and it's a good meditation.

Take the cookies out of the oven and let them cool on the pan before removing; they should come off easily, but if they don't, give them a nudge with a spatula. The cookies will keep in an airtight container in the pantry for up to 2 weeks.

**Note:** You can substitute coconut flour with almond flour.

*Pictured opposite, left*

## Tiny walnut cookies *Shirni gerdooyi |* شیرینی گردویی

*Makes 40–50 tiny cookies*

2 egg yolks
2 tablespoons sugar
a few drops of natural
    vanilla extract
⅔ cup (80 g) very coarsely
    chopped walnuts
finely ground pistachios,
    to garnish

Preheat the oven to 315°F (160°C). Line a baking sheet with parchment paper.

Using an electric hand mixer or stand mixer, beat the egg yolks with the sugar and vanilla until the mixture is white and fluffy, doubled in size, and no grain of sugar can be felt if you rub some between your thumb and index finger. Fold the walnuts through in circular motions.

With the help of two teaspoons, put little mounds of the batter, the size of a large hazelnut, on the baking sheet, leaving about 2 inches (5 cm) of space in between. Sprinkle each cookie with a little bit of ground pistachios. (You may need to bake the cookies in two batches, depending on the size of the pan.) Bake for about 10 minutes, or until the edges of the cookies are golden; don't let them brown.

Remove from the oven and let them cool for 15 minutes on the pan before gently removing with a spatula. Once cooled, the cookies will keep in an airtight container in the pantry for a couple of weeks, if you can resist eating them all in one sitting.

*Pictured opposite, right*

# Sharbat, many refreshing drinks for hot days

Tea is ever-present for Iranians, night and day—to wake you up, to drink when you're tired or thirsty, or when you're in company. But sometimes in the summer when it's too hot for tea, you offer your guests *sharbat*, a sweet cold drink not unlike diluted syrups.

The basic *sharbat* is made using water, rosewater, and sugar, and is usually kept ready in the fridge, or served with ice cubes. You can add many different seeds and spices to your *sharbat*, depending on how much time you have and how dear to you your guest is. The best *sharbats*, in my opinion, are made when the best jams are made; the excess syrup of the jam is kept in a bottle, then served at the bottom of each glass, which is then filled with ice and topped with water. These fruity *sharbats* also make excellent edible gifts.

## Saffron & rosewater sharbat
*Sharbat-e golab-o za'feran* | شربت گلاب و زعفران

This simple recipe is a great way to use any leftover saffron infusion. You can adjust the sweetness to your taste; Iranians often drink their *sharbat* very sweet. The amount of rosewater you need will also depend on its quality and how fragrant it is, so adjust the quantity to suit.

*Serves 3–4*

4¼ cups (1 liter) water
3 tablespoons sugar
2 tablespoons rosewater,
   or to taste
2 tablespoons saffron infusion
   (page 18)
ice cubes for each glass
dried rose petals, to garnish
   (optional)

In a jug, mix together the water, sugar, rosewater, and saffron infusion, stirring until the sugar has completely dissolved.

Pour into three or four glasses, add ice cubes, sprinkle with rose petals if desired, then serve.

*Pictured on page 118, right*

# Sharbat with sour cherry syrup *Sharbat-e albaloo* | شربت آلبالو

Fruit *sharbats* are a byproduct of jam making. Usually, once the jam is done, the extra syrup is separated and stored in bottles, to be served in a glass of iced water on a hot day, just like any other *sharbat*. What follows is a recipe to make sour cherry *sharbat* without making the jam; this recipe can be applied to strawberries, too. The syrup will keep in the fridge for months. About two tablespoons of syrup is enough for each individual drink, which is then topped with water and ice.

*Makes about
4 cups (950 ml)*

5 cups (1 kg) sugar
1 lb 2 oz (500 g) sour cherries—
    fresh ones are best, but frozen
    ones are also fine
ice cubes for each glass
water, for topping each glass

In a large bowl, combine half the sugar with the sour cherries. Mix well, cover with a tea towel, and let macerate overnight.

The next day, bring 4¼ cups (1 liter) water to a boil and pour it over the sour cherries. Leave to soak for another 4–5 hours.

Line a colander with cheesecloth and place it over a bowl. Gently tip the cherries into the colander to filter the syrup, enclosing the cherries in the cheesecloth and squeezing them to release more juices. At this point the syrup will have lots of residue from the cherries so let it sit again for at least 1 hour, so the sediments settle to the bottom of the bowl.

Carefully pour the syrup into a saucepan, leaving the residue in the bowl. Add the remaining sugar and let it simmer until the syrup thickens a little, and a mark remains if you pass a finger on the back of a spoon dipped into the syrup. The syrup will always be thicker when cold, so be careful that the syrup doesn't end up too thick. Leave to cool.

To serve, pour 2–3 tablespoons or ½ inch (1 cm) of syrup into each glass. Fill each glass with ice cubes and pour water over. If you like, you can serve with a long, slender spoon, so each person gets to mix their own *sharbat*.

**Note:** You can also make the *sharbat* using leftover sour cherry syrup, such as the one from the sour cherry pilaf on page 79, or the juices from canned sour cherries. Put a scant 1 cup (220 ml) light sour cherry syrup in a saucepan with ¾–1 cup (150–200 g) sugar, depending on how sweet the syrup is; if it isn't sweetened at all, use 1 cup (200 g) sugar. Gently simmer until the syrup thickens a little and serve as directed above.

*Pictured on page 118, left*

# Sharbat with vinegar & mint syrup, cucumber (& gin)

*Sekanjebin khiar* | سکنجبین خیار

*Sekanjebin*, a combination of the words *serkeh* (vinegar) and *angebin* (syrup), is a very old Iranian recipe. It used to be served as a medicinal recipe in ancient Perso-Arab medicine by Avicenna, who believed *sekanjebin* could cure different malaises based on changing the ratio of vinegar and sugar.

These days, *sekanjebin* is a synonym for summer afternoons. The simplest summer snack would be a head of romaine lettuce next to a bowl of this syrup. You'd simply peel off each leaf, fold it, dip it in the syrup, and eat it.

Another summer favorite is this *sharbat* with cucumber, which I love from the depths of my heart, partly because the match of mint with cucumber is made in heaven. They say this is a very good way to quench a summer thirst. I have also discovered that gin works great in this recipe, and now this is my favorite summer cocktail.

*Serves 4–6*

For the vinegar
 & mint syrup
½ cup (125 ml) water
generous 1 cup (220 g) sugar
¼ cup (60 ml) white wine vinegar
1 small bunch of mint,
 washed

For serving
1–1¾ fl oz (30–50 ml) gin
1 cucumber, or 2 Persian
 cucumbers, washed
 and grated
ice cubes for each glass
sparkling water, for topping
 each glass
fresh mint leaves, to garnish

To make the syrup, bring the water to a boil in a small saucepan and add the sugar. When the sugar has dissolved, add the vinegar and the bunch of mint and gently simmer for 5–10 minutes, or until the syrup thickens a little. Remember that syrup thickens on cooling, so don't overcook it. Set aside to cool down completely, then remove the mint bunch.

To serve, pour 2–3 tablespoons of the syrup into each glass, then the gin. To each glass add a teaspoon or two of grated cucumber. Fill with ice cubes, top up with sparkling water, garnish with mint leaves, and serve with a long, slender spoon for each person to stir their own drink.

*Pictured on page 118, center*

In
between

As the empire selectively swings its drawbridge open for some, others must climb in uninvited. Over barbed fences and across miles of sand. Over bureaucratic red tape and across seas of hypocrisy.

Walé Oyéjidé, "After Migration: The Once and Future Kings," *The Good Immigrant USA*

"*Bir tane çai lütfen.*" I ask for tea at Istanbul airport almost like a local, thanks to years of hearing Azerbaijani Turkish at my grandparents' house. This is something to be savored, this airport tea, poured from a proper large teapot into a proper glass cup, with a proper sticky baklava next to it. It's the last good tea before going back to Italy—where coffee is great but tea is dreadful. It's also a much appreciated refresher after the overwhelming security check and passport control at the border, which will soon be partly repeated before boarding the plane.

The usual warmth and hospitality of the Turks can't be expected of their flight crew. They have a huge responsibility; as the guardians of our "fence," it's their job to protect the other side from our "invasion."

Our fence is drawn here, next to the Mediterranean Sea. In the midst of these beautiful lands, of old, old civilizations, old religions, old cultures, fragmented by new borders. This is the closest that people from my side of the world can get to the other side without undergoing racial profiling, or spending a lot of money and time to go through the humiliating process of getting a visa.

Sipping my tea, I look around. These strangers look familiar to me, with their big gorgeous eyes, dark hair, thick eyelashes and eyebrows, light skins, dark skins, green eyes, brown eyes. People I don't know but whose stories I can partly guess, because like me, they're waiting to be dispersed somewhere on the other side; to Rome, London, Hamburg, Amsterdam, Paris. A bit further into the airport others are headed to Sydney, New York, Los Angeles, Toronto.

Although Istanbul, like Dubai or Beirut, is the end of our fenced free range, migration has always been central to the history of the Mediterranean. The reasons were the same—escaping persecutions, or seeking social prospects in a land that offered more opportunities. The difference was in the direction of migrations: roughly from the sixteenth century to the early twentieth century, many from Europe moved to the Middle East and North Africa in search of a better life.

Now those of us here, about to board a plane, are the lucky ones. We have obtained permissions, visas, and sometimes are fortunate enough to have a second "good" passport. We've worked hard for our luck, or maybe our parents have before us. We're the lucky ones because the most we have to endure are rude flight crews at departure and perhaps a little interrogation on arrival, especially if we have a beard or are wearing a hijab.

We're the lucky ones, because in order to get to the other side of the fence we don't have to look death in the eye: by sailing on rickety little boats, or crossing the harsh mountains with our life savings in the hands of a trafficker, or by hiding underneath cargo trailers.

We, in the airport, are lucky because we won't be detained in some infamous camp in Lesbos, or Lampedusa. We get to be on the plane to fly over the fence, not desperately hang off its wheels while it takes off.

We're lucky. We're not fleeing bombs and war and occupation. We're lucky because we know that had that been the case, we'd have been rated second-class refugees, "fake" refugees, because we don't look or pray like those on the other side of the fence. Because it would not have been "unimaginable" to see our houses bombed—by bombs that had been funded by creators of the fence.

The cities of "in between," some on one side of the fence, some on the other, look familiar to me, as if in a déjà vu. They remind me of Italy, and they remind me of Iran. I know these ancient Roman columns, the colorful mosaics. I know the olive trees on the horizon, the citrus ones adorning the streets, from Shiraz to Beirut to Palermo, and their flowery scent upon the air in spring. I know the dark eyes and dark hair of passers-by, and the words in the mouths of strangers whose language I don't speak but a part of me understands nonetheless.

Despite the differences in religion and culture, so much is the same here: the bells of the churches, the song of the moazin calling to prayer, the shouts of street vendors, and the horns of cars, the melody of oud, the beat of the tanbur, and the desire to dance. I know the inebriating smell of kebabs, of the fat dripping on charcoal, the bright flavor of sumac and the pepperiness of olive oil, the zing of lemons. I know those breads with toppings: pide, pita, pizza. The anise-like heat of arak, raki, ouzo in my mouth, the stickiness of baklava, and the teas and coffees. The freshly juiced pomegranates, and fast peeling of artichokes, the prayers on Fridays and Mass on Sundays.

I know that common ache, too. The nostalgia on both sides of the fence. We mourn our glorious past days, the missed opportunities, and our current shortcomings, our rich cultures, that are often undermined, inside and outside.

And Istanbul reminds you of Tehran, which reminds you of Rome, which reminds you of Athens. I know this land, like a place I have inhabited in a dream, or the home that I could one day have. My soul recognizes its flavors, its lights and sounds, that essence that cannot be fenced. The part that welcomes me as if I were returning to a waiting mother's arms.

Here, against all odds, I am home.

# THE "IN BETWEEN" PANTRY

There's a good chance you'll find everything you need for Eastern Mediterranean and Levantine cooking in a Middle Eastern grocery store. I buy mastic powder and dehydrated sour cherries online.

**Tahini:** The sesame paste that breathes soul into many beloved dips and dressings, and could totally replace peanut butter in any pantry. Go for a quality one, and shake and mix before using. I like Palestinian and Lebanese ones best.

**Lemons:** We know we are in the Mediterranean by the bright presence of citrus. Together with tahini and garlic, lemons are more prominent in Lebanese and Greek dishes; Syrian and Levantine dishes are more sweet and sour.

**Pita bread:** Not only an accompaniment but also the backbone of many dishes, holding stews and meatballs and grills for serving and, when toasted, adding crunchiness to salads. I like the ones you can easily split into two discs.

**Spices:** Cumin, paprika (sweet and smoked), cinnamon, Aleppo pepper, black pepper, sumac, and baharat (the Lebanese seven-spice mix) are most commonly used.

**Nuts:** Using pistachios, almonds, walnuts, and pine nuts, both savory and sweet dishes from this area are rich with nuts.

**Filo pastry:** Many of the sweet and savory pastries from this region use filo pastry, a relic of the Ottoman Empire, when many large households even had their own filo pastry master in the kitchen.

**Flower petals and essences:** In a region where roses and citrus grow abundantly, both rosewater and orange blossom water—together with mastic—contribute the iconic flavors of local desserts and sweets. Dried rose petals and orange blossoms are also used aesthetically and for flavor.

**Yogurt, kaymak, and feta:** A thick, full-fat yogurt, often strained (and what you may know as "Greek-style" yogurt), may appear at any meal of the day, in both sweet and savory dishes. *Kaymak* is mostly paired with honey for breakfast, or used to top sweets like *knafeh*, whereas the uses of feta-like cheese are almost unlimited.

**Pomegranate molasses:** Of Perso-Aleppian heritage, the tangy sourness of pomegranate molasses appears in some sweet dishes (mostly only as a topping) as well as many savory ones.

**Herbs:** Much attention is given to parsley here, which is often abundant, followed very closely by dill. Oregano is also much loved and comes in different varieties, although it's almost always dried.

**Olives and olive oil:** These have been ever-present on the tables of the Eastern Mediterranean and the Levant for thousands of years, as well as in literature and art.

**Other frequently used ingredients** include garlic, honey, tomato and its derivatives, and various forms of bell pepper.

# Recipes from the Levant
# & Eastern Mediterranean

The fact that the recipes in this chapter are from countries such as Turkey, Lebanon, Syria, Greece, and so on does not mean the cuisine of the Middle East and Eastern Mediterranean is a monolith. In fact, the cuisine of each of these nations is regionally specific, influenced by, and in turn influencing, the food of its neighbors. The dishes in this chapter merely connect the dots between the previous chapter and the following one.

# Creamy eggplant & tahini dip

*Baba ghanoush / moutabal el-batinjan | بابا غنوج / متبل الباذنجان*

In the last few centuries, eggplant have been at the heart of Levantine cuisine, just as they are in Italian cuisine today. Long before that, however, its dark color and bitter taste gave the eggplant a reputation for being toxic. Amusingly, the same mistrust that met the humble eggplant in Italy when it was first brought there by the Arabs—gaining the name "unhealthy apple," *la mela insana*—had also greeted this tasty vegetable back in the ninth century when it entered Arab cuisine. In a passage from an eleventh-century text, when asked whether he likes eggplant, a Bedouin responds: "Even if Maryam the mother of Jesus split it, and Sarah the wife of Abraham cooked it, and Fatima the daughter of the Prophet served it, I would have no taste for it."

Charring eggplant over an open fire must be my favorite method of cooking them. We do this for *mirza ghasemi* (page 57) in Iran, and all over the Levant, people do it for *baba ghanoush* and other eggplant dishes.

There's a bit of confusion about the name of this dish, as it is called *baba ghanoush* (or *ghanouj*) in some parts and *moutabal* in others, in particular Lebanon. *Moutabal* in Arabic means "spiced" or "flavored," coming from the verb *tabbala*: to dress with lemon and garlic. In *moutabal* the texture of the pulp is still present, whereas in *baba ghanoush* the texture is more uniform. There's also a smoked eggplant purée flavored with only lemon juice and garlic. I have spoken to people from Syria, Lebanon, Palestine, Egypt, Israel, Jordan, and Kuwait about *baba ghanoush*, trying to find what changes. Not much, apparently, since the borders between these countries are much more recent than the existence of this dish. It turns out there's no perfect recipe. Just add tahini, lemon juice, garlic, and maybe a bit of cumin to your taste.

One thing that struck me hard when speaking to Rania Hammad, a Palestinian friend based in Rome, is that she has noticed that *baba ghanoush* has a different flavor in Palestine. Like many Palestinians, she has relatives all around the region (and the world) who have been displaced from their land by the Israeli occupation. Rania says everything—in particular, vegetables—tastes a bit better in Lebanon and Syria, in her opinion. People in Palestine didn't have access to enough fresh eggplant, so they made up for it with extra tahini. Sadly, a 2019 United Nations report on the occupied Palestinian territories describes how barrier walls separate Palestinian farmers from their fields and how the water flow is restricted. The little that they can grow in these conditions is at risk of spoilage due to frequent power cuts in the West Bank and Gaza. Farmers have been losing their livelihoods as agriculture becomes more and more difficult. No wonder *baba ghanoush* tastes different in Palestine.

*Continued ›*

«

*Makes 2–3 cups*

4 eggplant, about 2 lb 12 oz
   (1.25 kg) in total
¼ cup (65 g) tahini
juice of 1–2 lemons, to taste
1 garlic clove, peeled
1 teaspoon salt
a pinch of ground cumin
   (optional)
olive oil, for drizzling
pomegranate seeds or
   pomegranate molasses,
   to garnish (optional)
chopped parsley, to garnish
   (optional)

Preheat the oven to 400°F (200°C). Arrange the eggplant on a baking pan lined with parchment paper and bake for 1½ hours. Then either put the eggplant under the broiler for 10–15 minutes to char the skin, or char them over a gas flame for a few minutes, if you have a gas burner. (Alternatively, rather than baking them in the oven first, you can cook the eggplant solely by charring them on a gas burner, as described in the recipe for *mirza ghasemi* on page 57; for a delicious *baba ghanoush*, you must get that smoky flavor going, one way or another.)

When the eggplant are cool enough to handle, scoop out the flesh with a spoon, discarding any excess water with the charred skins.

Place the eggplant flesh in a blender. Add the tahini, lemon juice, garlic, salt, and cumin, if using. Blend in several pulses; ideally, the *baba ghanoush* must maintain some texture, rather than being blended into a smooth cream. Taste and adjust the seasoning.

Serve on a large plate, smoothed over with the back of a spoon, leaving some swirls to hold the olive oil.

Drizzle with olive oil, sprinkle with pomegranate seeds or molasses and parsley if desired, and serve with flatbread.

*Pictured on page 131, bottom*

# Scarlet spread of bell peppers, pomegranate molasses & walnuts

*Muhammara* | محمرة

I first tried this surprisingly sweet, sour, hot, and smoky dip at Hummustown, an organization founded by Shaza Saker, a Syrian-Italian woman who, in her own words, sick of feeling sad, frustrated, and helpless watching the civil war in Syria blundering on year after year, decided to be the change she wanted to see in the world. She created Hummustown as a way of giving independence to Syrian refugees in Rome, helping them integrate by doing what they do best: offering their excellent home cuisine to Romans, such as *kibbe* and meat kebabs, fragrant pilafs, colorful dips and *mezze*, bright, citrusy, and fresh salads, and decadent, syrupy, aromatic sweets.

Thankfully, the ingredients and flavors of Syrian cuisine are Mediterranean enough for Romans—who often regard almost any dishes from elsewhere as "ethnic food"—not to wrinkle their noses at it. Here, as in most of the West, it is the food of the immigrants that is called "ethnic"—which, in the words of Krishnendu Ray, a New York University professor of food studies, is a descriptor for "What we don't know much about, don't understand much about, and yet find it valid to express opinions about." I know this only too well from my own experience with Iranian food here in Rome, which makes me want to rejoice in Hummustown thriving.

*Muhammara* is a testament to how an ancient cuisine has interacted with the food of the "New World." When bell peppers were being made into *peperonata* (page 193) or roasted with chickens in Italy, Syrians added their own signature flavor of pomegranate molasses to them and made *muhammara*.

The amount of spices is totally down to your taste. We're looking for deep flavors, but if you're missing a type of paprika, fear not. If you can't find Aleppo pepper (also known as *pul biber*), simply use some chile powder.

*Makes 1–2 cups*

3 red bell peppers, about
    2 lb (900 g) in total
¼ cup (30 g) dried breadcrumbs
Generous 1 cup (150 g) walnuts,
    roughly chopped
3 tablespoons pomegranate
    molasses, plus extra
    for drizzling
juice of 1 lemon, or more to taste
1 teaspoon salt
1 teaspoon smoked paprika
½ teaspoon sweet paprika
½ teaspoon Aleppo pepper
    or chile powder
1 tablespoon olive oil,
    for drizzling

Char the bell peppers on a gas burner (see page 57) until the skin is burned and the flesh is soft. Alternatively, roast the bell peppers in a 400°F (200°C) oven for 40 minutes to 1 hour, until the skin is dark and almost burned.

Put the charred or roasted peppers in a large bowl, cover with a plate, and leave to "sweat" for 10–20 minutes, to make them easy to peel. Discard the skins, seeds, membranes, and excess water.

Toast the breadcrumbs in a dry frying pan over medium heat for a few minutes, tossing regularly, until lightly toasted.

Put the bell pepper flesh, breadcrumbs, walnuts, pomegranate molasses, lemon juice, salt, and spices in a food processor and pulse until well combined but not puréed; you want to keep some of its texture.

Spread the *muhammara* on a plate, leaving swirls to hold drizzles of olive oil and extra pomegranate molasses. As ever, flatbread should be served on the side.

**Note:** A smoky touch enhances the flavor of this dip, which is why I like charring the bell peppers over a gas burner, open fire, or on the grill.

*Pictured on page 131, top*

# Filo triangles stuffed with feta

*Tyropitákia* | Τυροπιτάκια

*Tyropitákia*, which means "small cheese pie" in Greek, is the best airport food you will ever find if you're flying out of Greece or Turkey—which is probably a sad enough event for you to need an extra-tasty snack.

Whether it is indeed from Greece is more debatable. It all started with an ancient Greek cheesecake called *placenta*—and no, it did not contain any human body parts (thank heavens). But even Cato, the ancient Roman historian, had a recipe for it, before it appeared with a similar Latin name in the Byzantine Empire centuries later.

There's also the undeniable legacy of Anatolian cooking, with its many varieties of dough and its love of filo pastry. Just think of *börek*, so versatile and popular that it traveled with the Ottoman Empire much farther than the current borders of Turkey and the Levant, into the Balkans and beyond. Even the famous Russian *pirog* or *pirozhki* could be a love child of the *börek* family.

The technique of layering many thin sheets of dough goes back to the Turkic peoples of Central Asia, who are also believed to be the original creators of baklava (page 162). Until the early twentieth century, many wealthy families in Turkey would have a baker at home just to make the filo dough for all their *böreks* and baklavas.

Then there's the word *pita*, meaning "pie" in Greek but "flatbread" in many parts of the Levant. Apparently this is the origin of *pita*, which later gave birth to *pizza* in southern Italy and to *pide* in Turkey.

This, however, is not a quest to find who did what first. It's simply a joyful reflection on the thousands of years of history of a simple cheese pie, which can now be made very easily at home using store-bought filo pastry. As a romantic and a lover of ancient stories, a part of me does want this cheese pie to be from ancient Greece, to go on a journey eastward through other empires and then come back home and be called *tyropitákia* again. Ulysses, coming back to Ithaca.

Folding these triangles may look complicated, but in fact it's very easy. Just look for the right angle and keep folding the triangle in upon itself.

These pies are a great way to use up any odd bits of cheese left in the fridge, so just use whatever you have—including small portions of cooked vegetables or roast meat.

Remember to drip melted butter in between the pastry layers for extra-crispy results. I do like to drizzle honey on the regular cheese ones.

*Continued ›*

«

*Makes 9–10 little pies*

5½ oz (150 g) feta cheese,
    finely crumbled
5½ oz (150 g) semi-hard cheese,
    such as gruyère, gouda,
    emmental, or fontina, grated
1 egg
2 tablespoons milk
1 tablespoon dried oregano,
    and/or a small bunch of dill,
    finely chopped
5½ tablespoons (80 g) butter
9–10 filo pastry sheets; mine
    measured 10 inches x
    14½ inches (25 cm x 37 cm)
2 tablespoons honey,
    or to taste
black and white sesame seeds,
    for sprinkling (optional)

Preheat the oven to 350°F (180°C).

Mix the cheeses, egg, milk, and herbs together. Melt the butter and set aside.

Have a damp, clean tea towel ready before you open the package of filo pastry, and work with one filo pastry sheet at a time, keeping the rest very well covered with the damp cloth so they don't dry out. I also like to cover my work surface with parchment paper when making this recipe, so the dough doesn't stick to the surface, and to catch any drips from the melted butter.

Place one sheet of filo pastry on your work surface, with the short side facing you. Drizzle a little melted butter over it (drizzling supposedly gives a flakier pastry than brushing it with butter). Fold the sheet in half lengthways, so that you have a long, narrow rectangle, with the short side facing you. Drizzle again with melted butter.

Put a spoonful or two of the cheese mixture near the bottom edge of the filo. Take the bottom left corner of the pastry and fold it over to the right, at a right angle, so that the filling is covered with a triangle of pastry. Now fold this triangle onto itself and away from you so you're left with a rectangle again. Keep folding like this until you end up with a final triangle. Once you start folding, you'll get the hang of it, I promise.

Place the *tyropitákia* on a baking sheet and make the others in the same way. If any melted butter is left over, drizzle it over all of the little pies before baking.

Bake for 20–25 minutes, or until golden and crisp.

To serve, arrange on a platter, drizzle lightly with honey, and sprinkle with sesame seeds, if desired. Serve warm, for breakfast, a snack, or a light lunch with a bit of salad.

# Zucchini patties with feta & dill

*Kolokythokeftedes* | Κολοκυθοκεφτέδες

On the drive from the airport to where I was staying with friends, Athens felt a lot like Mashhad in Iran, the city of my mother where I went to school. In the markets of Athens, however, I felt I was back in Tehran, in the Tajrish bazaar, going back home after a long day. The cafés reminded me of Istanbul, and the majestic ancient ruins—Western civilization's foundation stones—of Rome.

More than anywhere else perhaps, Athens felt like home. The concept of a fluid and multiple home washed over me, and I felt I truly belonged to Tehran, Mashhad, Rome and the Italian south, and all the land in between. Greece, however, is on the other side of the fence, inaccessible for those of us without permission to enter the West, and therefore a destination with heavily guarded borders for migrants on small boats. And yet, for a country on the other side, it is remarkable how Middle Eastern its capital feels, especially in its hospitality. On my first night there, our hosts took us to a humble but absolutely delightful barbecue eatery—something similar to a *kababi* in Iran or a *trattoria* in Rome, for lack of a better description.

*Continued ›*

《

The place is famous for serving all your grilled meats and fries on paper—a lot less hassle and cleaning. But before they brought us our mountain of every kind of grilled meat, we were served velvety fava dips, bright tomato salads with feta and rusks called *dakos* that undoubtedly would remind you of the Tuscan *panzanella* (page 191), filo triangles with cheese and honey (page 134), and these incredible zucchini patties, which have a Turkish cousin called *mücver*. While cute cats roamed the halls unbothered, too irresistible and mewing at our feet for a share of grilled meat, we feasted in a haze of joy and culinary ecstasy.

People used to make these patties only in summer, the season of zucchini abundance, when they hollowed out zucchini to make *dolmas/dolmades*; their name, *kolokythokeftedes*, literally means "kofta of zucchini."

If you can resist eating all of them while making them, you could prepare the patties a day or two in advance to take on a summer picnic or barbecue.

*Makes about 12 patties*

1 lb 2 oz (500 g) zucchini
2–3 teaspoons salt, for salting
    the zucchini
7 oz (200 g) feta cheese,
    crumbled
a handful of chopped dill
1 scallion, thinly sliced
2 eggs
freshly ground black pepper
⅔ cup (75 g) all-purpose flour,
    approximately
¼ cup (60 ml) oil, for pan-frying,
    approximately

Coarsely grate the zucchini into a bowl. Rub and squeeze the zucchini with the salt, to help release its water, and leave for 15–30 minutes. Drain off the excess water, then squeeze the zucchini pulp to make sure it's all quite dry, as this is the secret to delicious *kolokythokeftedes*.

In a clean dry bowl, mix the zucchini pulp with the feta, dill, scallion, eggs, and a sprinkling of black pepper. Sprinkle the flour over and gently mix through until just combined; it's very important to not overwork the batter.

Heat 2–3 tablespoons of the oil in a frying pan. When sizzling hot, dollop in about 2 tablespoons of the batter and flatten it with the back of a spoon. Fry a few patties at a time over medium-high heat, flipping them midway to make sure both sides are golden; it only takes a few minutes for each batch to cook. Repeat with the remaining batter, adding more oil to the pan as needed.

Serve, possibly with some bubbly (Greek) wine and perhaps some *tzatziki*.

# Two bread salads from the Levant

A few years ago for Norouz, the Persian New Year, I decided to invite people over for dinner. All over the world, the Iranian diaspora holds tighter to the community during these first days of spring, as it can feel lonely to celebrate without the flowers and goldfish tanks and mirrors and candles and sweet wheat puddings and colorful eggs that flood every city and town in Iran.

The dinner I was planning was a quiet one, though. I invited a couple of friends, and one of them brought along her Kurdish Syrian friend, Hellen, as Kurds also celebrate Norouz.

Hellen is from Aleppo, a city she had to flee with her family when the war broke out. She has now joined her family in Turkey—along with 3.6 million other registered Syrian refugees—where she is deputy director of an NGO working to build understanding, peace, and prosperity between local and immigrant communities, mostly Syrians and Turks.

Hellen made us an Aleppian specialty, something Kurds enjoy on Friday mornings and other special occasions such as Norouz. I watched as she brushed triangles of pita bread with olive oil and toasted them in the oven, toasted pine nuts in butter, then layered the bread with a garlicky yogurt sauce with tahini and chickpeas. This was a chickpea *fattah*, Hellen told me—one of the many variations of this bread dish in Levantine cooking.

The bread salads of the Levant, like those of other places where bread is an important staple, were born out of the necessity of reusing stale bread. *Fattah* has many varieties, some with meat and/or eggplant, but I love the chickpea and yogurt version here, especially as a substantial addition to a *mezze* table.

The second salad, *fattoush*, a Syrian peasant dish, is strikingly similar to the Tuscan *panzanella* (page 191), apart from the dressing, where the typically Syrian pomegranate molasses and sumac are used. There is no real "recipe" for these salads; just taste as you go.

Before leaving Italy shortly after that dinner, Hellen applied for many academic positions in Europe, but being a Syrian passport holder made it almost impossible for her to get a visa. While she could have applied for political asylum, as she cannot return to Syria, she didn't want to be a refugee— even though it cost her professional opportunities and it would cost a whopping $4,000 to renew her passport in Turkey, where she now resides. I was shocked to learn that there are no Syrian embassies in Europe. "We can't go back home, and with no embassies to go to either, it feels like we have no home anywhere," she said. "It's a terrible feeling of unconnectedness and unsafeness."

For those of us who count merely as escapees of some "undesirable" country to the "gate-keepers" (visa grantors), freedom of movement is never taken for granted. Not for those like Hellen, who couldn't get a visa for a postdoctorate degree in Europe despite her PhD in ancient archaeology from Rome. We know the true value of being allowed on the other side of the fence, and we know no one would put their children and themselves on a small wobbly boat crossing the sea, or clinging to the outside of a plane in takeoff, to get to the other side, if there were a legal, safer, and more compassionate way.

## Fattah
فتّة

*Serves 4*

2 pita breads, or 4¼ oz (120 g) flatbread
2–3 tablespoons olive oil
14 oz (400 g) can chickpeas, drained (about 8 oz/230 g) (see Note)
¼ cup (40 g) pine nuts
1½ tablespoons butter
mint leaves, to garnish

For the yogurt sauce
2 cups (500 g) full-fat plain Greek-style yogurt
2 tablespoons lemon juice
2 garlic cloves, grated or finely chopped
3 tablespoons tahini
¼ teaspoon ground cumin
1 teaspoon salt
freshly ground black pepper

Cut the bread into triangles and drizzle with the olive oil, then toast for a few minutes in a hot oven until crispy and golden.

Meanwhile, rinse the chickpeas, then heat them briefly in a pan with a splash of water so that they're lukewarm. Set aside.

In a small pan, toast the pine nuts in the butter until golden.

In a small bowl, mix together all the yogurt sauce ingredients until well combined.

To assemble, arrange the toasted pita triangles on a platter, top with a layer of warm chickpeas, then add dollops of the yogurt sauce. Repeat the layers until the ingredients run out. Top with the pine nuts and the melted butter, garnish with mint leaves, and serve immediately.

In Syria *fattah* is enjoyed as a weekend breakfast, but I like it as a weeknight meal in summer, or as part of a *mezze* feast.

**Note:** Instead of canned chickpeas, you could use ⅓ cup (80 g) dried chickpeas. Soak them overnight, then cook them in plenty of water seasoned with salt until tender. Drain, then use while still warm.

*Pictured on page 142, left*

*Continued ›*

«

# Fattoush
فتـوش

*Serves 4*

## For the salad

2 cucumbers, or 4 Persian/
    Lebanese cucumbers
2 large tomatoes, or 5 small ones
1 small onion
½ head of romaine or
    butter lettuce
4–5 radishes
a handful of mint
a handful of parsley
1 pita bread
2 tablespoons olive oil
ground sumac, for sprinkling

## For the dressing

2 tablespoons olive oil
1 tablespoon pomegranate
    molasses
1 tablespoon white wine vinegar
zest and juice of 1 lemon
1 garlic clove, grated
2 tablespoons ground sumac
½ teaspoon salt, or to taste

Peel the cucumbers (if preferred), cut in half lengthways, and remove the seeds, then slice as thinly or thickly as you like. Cut the tomatoes into fairly large cubes, catching all the lovely juices, and thinly slice the onion. All goes in a large bowl. Wash and dry the lettuce head, then tear the leaves into the bowl. Thinly slice the radishes, coarsely chop the mint and parsley, and toss them into the bowl.

Carefully separate the pita bread into two thin discs, then toast them in a hot oven for a few minutes. Break them into chunks and drizzle with the olive oil so they keep their crunch.

Combine all the dressing ingredients in a cup, small bowl, or a little jam jar, mixing well.

Toss the salad with the dressing, then arrange on a large platter—not in a bowl—with the toasted pita chunks in the middle. Sprinkle with sumac and serve immediately, so the salad doesn't get soggy. Enjoy as a meal on its own, or as a side to just about any dish.

*Pictured on page 143, top*

# Two ways with stuffed bell peppers

*Dolma / Mehshi / Gemistés | Dolmeh /* محشی */ Γεμιστές*

The wonderful, varied, and delicious world of stuffed vegetables expands all the way from Iran to the Levant and the Middle East, to Turkey and the Balkans, and to Italy. In Turkish, *dolma* literally means "stuffed"; so does *mehshi* in Arabic and *gemista* in Greek. In Iran, we use the Turkish word with a slightly different pronunciation, *dolmeh*. Although stuffed vegetables have been around for millennia, there is no doubt that *dolma* traveled as far as the Balkans and all of the Levant because of the Ottoman Empire.

In Turkish, stuffed vine leaves and cabbage leaves are not called *dolma* but *sarma*. Amusingly enough, it is the rolled things in Greek that are called *dolma (dolmadakia)*, as opposed to *gemista*, which are hollowed-out vegetables such as bell peppers. In Iran, we call them all *dolmeh*. In Arabic, *mehshi* is used for most hollowed-out vegetables, while the literal name is used for stuffed vine leaves, *warak el enab*—just as stuffed cabbage in Italy is most commonly called by its literal description, *involtini di verza*.

The filling recipes are highly variable. Rice is often used, but meat is also very important. So important that in Turkish, a *dolma* with no meat is called *yalanci*—a fake, a lie. Mostly ground meat is used together with rice, although our family recipe in Iran uses finely diced meat.

Herbs are also often used in the filling; some Greek versions have a lot of parsley and dill. There are no herbs in our family recipe, but it turns out this is a rarity in Iran. My family, with roots in the Azerbaijan region of Iran, uses yogurt in the rice filling for vine leaves. An Iranian Jewish friend told me they use nuts and dried fruit in their *dolmeh*, and apparently the Jewish tradition in Syria is the same. Since *dolma* of all kinds are often consumed at room temperature, they're perfect for Shabbat, as they can be prepared in advance.

In Italy, breadcrumbs are often used to stuff zucchini, bell peppers, and even artichokes (page 228), whereas in the Balkans, other grains are also used for stuffing vegetables.

You can use the following two fillings for tomatoes and eggplant, too. Stuffed eggplant is in a world of its own; see the *Imam bayildi* recipe on page 149, a very different recipe from a *dolma*. No matter what vegetables you're stuffing, make sure they're roughly the same size and perfectly ripe, or they won't cook through evenly. Adding spices such as cinnamon to the vegetable cavity is a Middle Eastern trick that is also used for the Italian stuffed tomatoes on page 249. Many people (including a young version of myself) don't eat the vegetable shell, just the filling—and that's okay. I prefer cooking these bell peppers on the stove. Keep an eye on the liquid at the bottom of the pot—there shouldn't be too much, but the pot shouldn't be dry, either. Let the *dolmeh* rest without the lid on for some time before serving. As mentioned earlier, they taste amazingly good the next day.

*Continued ›*

<<

*Makes 4 large stuffed bell peppers or 6 smaller ones*

filling of choice (see below and next page)
4 large red, yellow, or orange bell peppers, or 6 smaller ones, about 3 lb 5 oz (1.5 kg) in total
½ cup (125 ml) hot water
2 tablespoons olive oil
1 tablespoon tomato paste
1 teaspoon salt, plus extra for sprinkling inside the bell peppers
freshly ground black pepper
1–2 potatoes, peeled (optional)

Ready the filling of your choice.

Cut the top off each bell pepper, to use as a "lid." Remove the seeds and white membranes from inside each bell pepper.

Pour the hot water into a small bowl, add the remaining ingredients, and mix well.

Sprinkle the cavity of each bell pepper with some extra salt, then fill each pepper with your chosen filling, leaving some space for the rice to swell. Put the "lids" back on and secure them with a toothpick.

Arrange the bell peppers snugly in a pot. If there's too much space left, fill it with a peeled potato or two, so that the peppers stay upright.

Gently pour in the tomato paste mixture, at the side of the pot. Cover and cook over medium-low heat for about 1 hour, or until the bell peppers are soft on the top, and the skin is wrinkled. Add a little more water if needed.

Remove the lid and let the bell peppers rest a bit before serving.

## Greek-inspired meatless filling

1 cup (200 g) short-grain white rice
4 tomatoes (7 oz/200 g), chopped
1 onion, or 2–3 scallions, chopped
1 big bunch of parsley, chopped
1 big bunch of dill, chopped
1 cup (250 ml) hot water
2 tablespoons olive oil
1½ teaspoons tomato paste
1 tablespoon sugar
2 teaspoons salt
½ teaspoon freshly ground black pepper
1 teaspoon ground cinnamon
1 teaspoon smoked, hot, or sweet paprika

Mix the rice with the tomatoes, onion, and herbs.

Pour the hot water into a small bowl, add the remaining ingredients, and mix well. Pour over the rice mixture, stirring until well combined.

When using this filling, make sure you only stuff the bell peppers two-thirds full, as the rice will swell during baking. Also, make sure you add enough of the liquid into each bell pepper so the filling doesn't dry out, and to ensure the rice is fully cooked. Feel free to add a splash more water if needed.

Cook the bell peppers as directed in the main recipe above.

*Pictured opposite*

## Iranian-inspired filling with meat

2 tablespoons yellow split peas
¾ cup (150 g) basmati rice
2 tablespoons oil
1 onion, diced
½ teaspoon ground turmeric
5½ oz (150 g) diced or
    ground lamb
1½ teaspoons tomato paste
2 tablespoons saffron infusion
    (page 18)
2 teaspoons salt
½ teaspoon freshly ground
    black pepper
1 teaspoon ground cinnamon

Cook the split peas in a small saucepan of boiling water for about 20 minutes. Meanwhile, soak the rice in a bowl of water.

Heat the oil in a large frying pan, then sauté the onion over medium heat for about 5 minutes. Add the turmeric, then sear the lamb in this mixture for 3–5 minutes. Stir in the tomato paste and cook for a few minutes, until its color brightens slightly.

Drain the split peas and rice, then add them to the pan. Add 1 cup (250 ml) water and cook for 10 minutes. Turn the heat off and stir in the saffron infusion, salt, pepper, and cinnamon.

When using this filling, make sure you only stuff the bell peppers two-thirds full, as the rice will swell during cooking. Also, make sure you add enough of the liquid into each bell pepper so the filling doesn't dry out, and to ensure the rice is fully cooked. If you need a bit more liquid, pour an extra ½ cup (125 ml) water into the pan you cooked the filling in (to take up any spices left behind, to add extra flavor to the filling), then add some to each bell pepper.

Cook the bell peppers as directed in the main recipe at the top of the previous page.

# Turkish eggplant in tomato sauce

*Imam bayildi | İmambayıldı*

This classic Turkish dish has its roots in legend. Quite a few theories circulate around its name, which literally translates to "Imam fainted." Some say the fried eggplant with the tomato sauce and onion filling was so ridiculously good that the Imam fainted. A counter argument to this theory is that the Ottoman cuisine of the time was so lavish with meat, eggs, dairy, animal fats, nuts, and dried fruit, that this relatively simple dish could hardly qualify to make an Imam—who would be used to it all—faint. Another version of the story is that upon hearing how much precious olive oil was used to make the dish properly, the Imam fainted. I like to think the final version has the most truth to it, because to fry the eggplant the way you must for this dish, you really need a whopping amount of oil.

Smaller, long eggplant are best, as *Imam bayildi* is an elegant dish. Although it is meat-free, it reminds me of the Arabic Levantine *sheikh el mahshi* ("lord of the stuffed vegetable"), and the Iranian *shekam pareh* (meaning "split belly," referring to the eggplant being split in the middle)— which is the same as the Turkish *karnıyarık*, which translates exactly the same. I found a recipe for "A Jewish Dish of Eggplants Stuffed with Lamb" in a book about the cooking of Andalusia and Maghreb from the thirteenth to fifteenth century that sounds a lot like those two meat-stuffed eggplant dishes. It seems eggplant were an ingredient of choice for the Jewish community in these lands, who were quick to embrace this underappreciated vegetable when it was first introduced into southern Europe with the Arab conquest.

As with eggplant parmigiana (page 243) and *mirza ghasemi* (page 57), using ripe and in-season produce will make a significant difference. Don't be too sparing with your best olive oil, either. We wouldn't want to prevent the Imam from fainting.

*Serves 4–6*

6 thin eggplant,
   or 3 large round ones
salt, for salting the eggplant
⅓ cup (80 ml) olive oil,
   for pan-frying, plus
   extra if needed
chopped parsley, to garnish
   (optional)

Peel some stripes off each eggplant, leaving the rest of the skin on for a decorative effect; alternatively, you can leave the eggplant unpeeled. If you're using large round eggplant, cut them in half lengthways.

Cut a long slit lengthways along the middle of each eggplant but not all the way through, to serve as a pocket. Rub all parts of the eggplant generously with salt. Leave in a colander for 30 minutes to 1 hour for them to release any bitter juices.

*Continued ›*

《

### For the filling
¼ cup (60 ml) olive oil
3 onions, sliced
3 garlic cloves, finely chopped
1½ teaspoons tomato paste
4–5 tomatoes, about
   14 oz (400 g), diced
2 teaspoons salt
1½ teaspoons sugar
1 teaspoon sweet paprika
a pinch of freshly ground
   black pepper

### For the sauce
1½ teaspoons tomato paste
½ cup (125 ml) hot water
1 teaspoon salt

Meanwhile, make the filling. Heat the olive oil in a large pot and sauté the onion over high heat for 5–7 minutes. Add the garlic and cook for 2–3 minutes, until fragrant. Stir in the tomato paste and diced tomatoes. Cook for a minute or two, then season with the salt, sugar, paprika, and black pepper. Stir in ½ cup (125 ml) water and simmer gently over low heat for 15 minutes.

Wash and dry the eggplant. Heat the olive oil in a large frying pan and lightly pan-fry the eggplant on all sides over medium-high heat. We don't want to cook them thoroughly at this stage, just soften them and add a bit of flavor. If frying the eggplant in batches, you may need to use some more oil.

Arrange the eggplant in a large saucepan. Open the slits down the middle and stuff each one with 2–3 tablespoons of the filling, drizzling in any remaining liquid as well.

Mix the sauce ingredients together until well combined, then pour into the pot from the side. Cover and cook over medium heat for about 30 minutes, then remove the lid and cook for another 15–25 minutes, until the liquid has reduced and the eggplant are completely soft. You may need to add a bit more water if they take longer to cook. (Instead of cooking them on the stove during this final stage, you can also bake the eggplant in an oven preheated to 350°F/180°C for about 1 hour—but I personally prefer the stovetop method.)

Serve at room temperature, garnished with parsley if desired, with flatbread or Iranian rice (page 22) on the side.

# Circassian chicken with walnuts

This chicken dish has been perhaps the most surprising recipe that I tested for this book. What first drew my attention to this dish was certainly not its appearance, as it's a grayish-beige blob, sometimes garnished with a sprinkling of paprika or walnuts. What it lacks in looks, though, it mightily compensates for in flavor.

What intrigued me was the main ingredients: shredded chicken with heaps of ground walnuts. As an Iranian, the first thing this combination brings to mind is the famous *fesenjan* stew, with chicken (or other poultry, sometimes even little meatballs), ground walnuts and, most characteristically, plenty of pomegranate molasses. The similarity is noteworthy enough to have been mentioned also by Claudia Roden in her legendary *New Book of Middle Eastern Food*.

As its name implies, this chicken recipe belongs to the Circass people from around the Black Sea and above Georgia; it is also common in Turkey. Geographically speaking, the Iranian province of Gilan is not that far from the Circass, and according to the thirteenth-century Syrian cookbook *Scents and Flavors*, similar recipes were also enjoyed in what is now modern Syria.

For me, the surprise of this recipe is its mind-blowing delicious flavor despite the absence of any acidic ingredient. But there is a trick: you must use the best chicken you can afford. The broth is an essential part of this dish, and so the better the chicken, the more rewarding the final result. It does take a little time to make the broth from scratch and strain it, but the dish keeps very well for a couple of days in the fridge, making it great for last-minute gatherings and a worthy dish for picnics, too.

*Serves 6–8 as an appetizer, 2–4 as a main*

2 lb 4 oz (1 kg) chicken (a mixture of different pieces with the bones in, or an entire chicken)
1 large onion, quartered
1 bay leaf
3½ oz (100 g) stale bread (about 3 slices, no crust)
2⅓ cups (300 g) walnuts
2 garlic cloves, peeled
1 teaspoon salt
½ teaspoon freshly ground black pepper
2 tablespoons olive oil or walnut oil, for drizzling
1 teaspoon sweet paprika

Put the chicken in a pot with the onion and bay leaf. Fill with just enough cold water to cover the chicken. Bring to a boil, then reduce the heat, cover, and simmer for 1–1½ hours, or until the chicken is tender and falls from the bone.

Remove the chicken from the pot. Discard the bay leaf and onion. Skim off any scum, then strain the broth through a fine-meshed sieve into a large bowl.

As soon as the chicken is cool enough to handle, pull the meat off the bones and shred it into small pieces with your fingers, placing it in a large bowl. Discard the skin and bones.

Put the bread in a small bowl. Add some of the chicken broth, to soften the bread and absorb the flavor.

Reserving a few walnuts for garnishing, grind the rest into a fine powder in a blender or a food processor, loosening it with a little of the chicken broth as you go. Add the soaked bread and its broth, the garlic cloves, salt, pepper, and enough of the broth to reach the consistency of a thick soup, not a purée. Taste and adjust the seasoning if necessary.

Set aside about one-third of the walnut sauce. Pour the rest over the shredded chicken and mix very well.

Spread the chicken on a large platter, then cover it completely with the reserved walnut sauce. Drizzle with the oil, sprinkle with the paprika, and garnish with the reserved chopped walnuts. Serve cold or at room temperature with toasted flatbread.

# Lamb kebabs with tomato sauce & yogurt

*Giaourtlou*

All the senses are engaged when visiting the cities of the Levant and the Eastern Mediterranean, with the stunning natural scenery and historical landmarks, the sound of church bells, the call to prayer from the mosques, the shouts of street vendors, the horns of cars, and the melodies of the lute-like oud. Before we get to taste the remarkably delicious food, there comes the smell—and the smell of this land for me is that of fatty meat grilling on charcoals: the smell of kebabs.

I'm not a phenomenal griller myself at all, but here's a recipe for simple tiny kebab skewers that can be made at home on a grill pan, or on a barbecue if you're lucky enough to have access to one.

Instead of ground lamb (which is my preference here), you can use any ground red meat, as long as there's a good percentage of fat. Indeed, in Istanbul and western Turkey, where lamb is expensive and harder to find than in eastern Turkey, many kebab places use mostly beef with only some lamb tail fat to add that gamey, greasy flavor. I don't recommend this.

*Kebab giaourtlou* is a common dish in Greece, although it's originally from Turkey, where it's called *yoğurtlu kebap*. It means "kebab with yogurt"—not to be confused with *iskandar kebab*, which is similar but has yogurt on the side, with the meat served on a bed of chunky bread pieces dressed in butter and a pool of tomato sauce. These little skewers are served on a whole pita bread (and topped with another one, to keep them warm), and the tomato sauce and yogurt are served on top, or on the side as a dressing to add to each mouthful of meat wrapped in bread.

As with all kebabs and meatballs that use ground meat, remember that you need to knead the meat with the spices and let it rest, so that it won't fall off your skewers.

If you have wooden skewers, make sure you soak them in water for at least an hour before using them, so they don't burn.

*Continued* ›

«

*Serves 4–6*

For the kebabs

1 lb 2 oz (500 g) ground lamb
1 small onion, or ½ large one,
    grated
1 handful of chopped parsley
1 garlic clove, grated
1 tablespoon olive oil
1 tablespoon dried breadcrumbs
1½ teaspoons tomato paste
1½ teaspoons salt
½ teaspoon freshly ground
    black pepper
1 teaspoon sweet paprika
1 teaspoon ground cinnamon
½ teaspoon ground cumin
½ teaspoon dried oregano

For the tomato sauce

2 tablespoons olive oil
1 small onion, or ½ large
    one, diced
14 oz (400 g) can diced
    tomatoes, or 3–4 fresh
    large tomatoes, diced
1 teaspoon sugar
½ teaspoon salt
½ teaspoon smoked, hot,
    or sweet paprika

For serving

2 tablespoons olive oil,
    for grilling
3–4 large flatbreads
1 cup (300 g) plain Greek-style
    yogurt, whipped
chopped parsley, to garnish
paprika and/or ground sumac,
    for sprinkling
onion slices, to garnish (optional)

If you're using bamboo skewers for your kebabs, soak 8–12 of them in water for at least an hour so they don't burn on the grill.

Combine all the kebab ingredients in a large bowl. Knead well for 5–10 minutes, until the color has slightly changed. Chill in the fridge for at least 30 minutes, or even overnight.

To make the tomato sauce, heat the olive oil in a pot and sauté the onion over medium heat for about 5 minutes, or until translucent and quite soft. Add the tomatoes, with a splash of water if needed. Stir in the sugar, salt, and paprika and simmer on low heat for 20–30 minutes, stirring occasionally.

Meanwhile, heat a grill pan or barbecue grill plate to high and drizzle with olive oil.

Take 2–3 tablespoons of the kebab mixture at a time and work it in the palm of your hand into a sausage shape. Place a skewer right in the middle and squeeze your hand around it several times to shape the kebab around the skewer. Make sure the top and bottom are secured tightly around the skewer.

Grill each kebab for a couple of minutes on each side until brown and sizzling; meanwhile, warm the flatbreads for serving.

Place the flatbreads on a serving platter/s and lay several skewers on each. Add dollops of yogurt on the kebabs, then spoon the tomato sauce on top. Scatter with parsley, paprika and/or sumac, and onion slices, if desired, and serve immediately. As with most kebabs and street foods, this is a hands-on dish—tear off a piece of bread and, holding the kebab in it, remove the skewer before eating.

Alternatively, you could simply keep all the kebabs warm under one flatbread, then cut the rest into large wedges and serve on a platter, with separate bowls of yogurt, tomato sauce, parsley, and onion, so that each person can assemble their own.

**Note:** You can prepare the kebabs a few hours before grilling and keep them in the fridge on a plate, separating them with parchment paper if necessary to ensure they're not sticking to each other. Give them an extra squeeze just before grilling to make sure the meat is sticking to the skewers.

# The Palestinian upside-down triumph of rice

*Maqluba* | مقلوبه

There are many rice and pilaf recipes in the Levant, most with a selection of warm spices, often with a range of fried vegetables, and almost always with a kind of meat—with chicken or lamb being the most frequent choices.

*Maqluba*, which literally translates as "upside down," is a Palestinian specialty, loved and cooked all over the Arab world. Of the three rice molds in this book—the other two being the Iranian *tahchin* on page 72, and the Neapolitan *sartù* on page 237—*maqluba* is perhaps the easiest to make. Cauliflowers are often used in winter, and eggplant in summer, usually together with tomatoes, both having been fried first. If you're Italian and you see an eggplant *maqluba*, which often looks like a cake with eggplant slices perched on top like the petals of a flower, you will be reminded of *timballo di melanzane*, the Sicilian dish made in the same way but with pasta instead of rice. As explained in the *sartù* recipe, the word "timballo" comes from the Arabic *tabl*, or drum.

While this *maqluba* is eggplant-free, given that the Iranian *tahchin* has an eggplant variation (page 73), you can use eggplant here if you want to. In an attempt to eat more plant-based dishes, I have also omitted the meat but incorporated chestnuts, which are an unusual choice alongside the more typical pine nuts or toasted almonds. Do add baharat (Lebanese seven-spice) if you have any; otherwise the cinnamon, pepper, and nutmeg should suffice.

The recipe might seem daunting at first glance, but you only need one pot for this dish, and it works great for weeknight dinners.

*Serves 6–8*

2½ cups (500 g) basmati rice
4 teaspoons salt
½ cup (125 ml) olive oil
2 onions, sliced
1 lb 2 oz (500 g) carrots, cut into thick matchsticks
1 small cauliflower (1 lb 5 oz– 1 lb 12 oz/600–800 g), split into florets
¼ cup (50 g) raisins
3½ oz (100 g) peeled and boiled (or roasted) chestnuts

Wash the rice gently with cold water and rinse at least three times, discarding the water. Add 1 teaspoon of the salt, gently mix, and set aside.

In a tall nonstick lidded pot (which we'll use as the "mold" for this rice dish), heat about 3 tablespoons of the olive oil. Sweat the onion over medium heat with ½ teaspoon of the salt for about 15 minutes, until soft and translucent. Remove and set aside.

In the same pot, heat another 2 tablespoons olive oil. Gently cook the carrot over medium heat with another ½ teaspoon salt for about 15 minutes, until soft with a few brown edges. Remove and set aside.

2 tablespoons tomato paste

1 tablespoon ground cinnamon
or Lebanese seven-spice
(baharat)

1 teaspoon freshly ground
black pepper

½ teaspoon ground cumin

½ of a whole nutmeg, grated

Heat another 2 tablespoons olive oil in the pan. Add the cauliflower and 1 teaspoon salt. Cover and cook over low heat for 15–20 minutes, then add the raisins and chestnuts. In a kettle, bring 2½–3 cups (600–700 ml) water to a boil (the exact amount you'll need will depend on the size of your pot). Pour into a bowl, stir in the tomato paste, all the spices, and the remaining salt and olive oil and mix well. (Instead of water, you can also use stock of your choice—watch the salt, though.)

Shape the cauliflower mixture in the pot into a low cone. Layer the sautéed onion on top, making sure it's an even layer, and top it with the sautéed carrot. Discard the soaking water from the rice, cover the vegetable mixture with the rice, then gently pour in the spice liquid; the total amount of liquid must be about ½–¾ inch (1–2 cm) above the rice.

Place a heatproof plate (smaller than the circumference of your pot) upside down on top of the rice, so everything remains in place. Cook over medium heat for about 10 minutes, until there are bubbles in the surface of the rice and no liquid is visible on top.

Very carefully remove the plate. Taste the rice and cook with a lid on for another 5–15 minutes over medium heat, until the rice has no "bite"; the time will vary depending on your rice.

Turn off the heat, wrap the lid with a tea towel, and place it snugly over the pot. Let the rice rest for about 15 minutes.

Choose a tray or serving dish quite a bit larger than the pot's circumference. Place it upside down on the pot, then carefully flip the pot onto the tray. Very gently remove the pot and unmold the *maqluba*. Some parts of the rice might crumble, but that's okay—you can put them back into the "cake" with a spoon and no one will know.

Serve hot, perhaps with some yogurt on the side. You can also serve this dish with meat of your choice, or maybe a fresh salad such as *salad Shirazi* (page 63).

# Meatballs with sour cherries from Aleppo

*Kebab el-karaz* | كباب الكرز

Although the cuisines of different Levantine countries share many similarities, there are some important distinctions as well. For example, whereas Lebanese food is more citrusy, bright, and Mediterranean, Syrian food—especially that of Aleppo—is known for its use of *agrodolce* ("sweet-sour"), particularly in savory dishes. In this, Aleppo cuisine reminds us a lot of Iranian cuisine.

I am particularly fond of a thirteenth-century Syrian cookbook, translated into English as *Scents and Flavors*. In it, as well as the Persian-Arab heritage of Baghdad cuisine of the previous centuries, new Turkish influences are detectable, especially in baking recipes. Among the recipes are many with chicken using different fruit (mostly sour)—tamarind, rhubarb, barberries, quince, sour cherries—and some sugar. Some of these recipes are cooked in almost exactly the same way in Iran today.

Perhaps the best example of these sweet-and-sour meat recipes with fruit is the legendary *kebab karaz* (sour cherry meatballs), which uses both sour cherries and pomegranate molasses—another ingredient that is distinctive to Aleppo and nearby Anatolia and Iran—together with warm spices. It's so delicate yet rich in flavor, that it's no wonder Aleppo was once known as the capital of Middle Eastern food.

This dish is traditionally served on Arab pita bread—but if you serve it on white basmati rice, it would be almost indistinguishable from *albaloo polow*, the Iranian sour cherry pilaf on page 79.

If you can't find fresh sour cherries, use frozen ones or dehydrated ones. Remember to keep the water you use for reviving dried sour cherries, to use in the sauce.

*Serves 4–6*

For the meatballs
1 lb 2 oz (500 g) ground lamb
1 small onion, or ½ large onion, grated and squeezed dry
½ teaspoon salt
½ teaspoon freshly ground black pepper
1 teaspoon ground cinnamon
¼ nutmeg, grated
2 tablespoons olive oil

Start with the meatballs. In a large bowl, mix together the lamb, onion, salt, pepper, and spices. Knead well for about 10 minutes, until all the ingredients are thoroughly combined and the color has changed slightly. Cover and chill in the fridge for at least 1 hour, or even overnight.

Near serving time, combine all the sauce ingredients in a large pot. Bring to a gentle boil, then cover and simmer for 15–20 minutes over low heat.

Meanwhile, shape the meat into small balls about ¾ inch (2 cm) in diameter, using about ½ tablespoon of meat for each meatball.

*Continued ›*

«

For the sour cherry sauce
2 lb 4 oz (1 kg) fresh or frozen
    sour cherries, pitted (see Note)
3 tablespoons sugar
2 tablespoons pomegranate
    molasses
½ teaspoon salt
1 clove

For serving
2–3 pita breads
2–3 teaspoons butter or ghee,
    melted
¼ cup (40 g) pine nuts, toasted
a handful of chopped parsley

Heat the olive oil in a frying pan over medium-high heat and brown the meatballs all over, in batches if necessary; they do not need to be fully cooked at this point.

Add the meatballs to the sour cherry sauce and simmer for another 10–15 minutes to cook through. Remove the clove.

To serve, warm the pita breads, cut neatly into wedges, and arrange on a large platter. Drizzle with the melted butter. Spoon the meatballs and sauce on top of the bread. Scatter with the pine nuts and parsley and serve immediately.

**Note:** Instead of fresh or frozen sour cherries, you could use 12 oz–1 lb 2 oz (350–500 g) dehydrated pitted sour cherries. Soak them in 2 cups (500 ml) hot water for at least 30 minutes to revive them. Add them to the sauce ingredients with the soaking liquid and simmer as directed.

# Baklava beyond borders

باقلوا

Baklava, with its many buttered layers of filo pastry, stuffed with chopped nuts—usually pistachios but also walnuts and almonds—then baked and drenched in syrup, is a sweet that connects the Levant to North Africa, to Central Asia, and even to India. There are regional variations in the syrup, such as the addition of honey in Greece and some Balkan countries, which makes their baklava much sweeter and stickier, and the addition of rosewater and orange blossom water in the Levant, and cinnamon or lemon juice in other places, but no aromatics in the Turkish version.

The technique of layering many sheets of flatbread and then pouring syrup over them apparently comes from the Turkic people who resided in the current Azerbaijan, and it was later adapted by the Seljuks and perfected in the kitchens of Istanbul's Topkapi Palace during the Ottoman Empire. The syrup-drenching method is still used a lot in Azerbaijan, and by the Turkic Azeris of Iran.

Making baklava is quite easy with store-bought filo pastry. For a perfect result, don't overcook the syrup. After thoroughly drenching with the syrup, let the baklava rest completely overnight. Surprisingly, it gets less sweet if left to rest for longer.

*Continued ›*

«

*Makes a 7 x 9½ x 2¾ inch
(18 x 24 x 7 cm) panful*

¾ cup (180 g) butter, melted
30 filo pastry sheets, measuring
about 7 inches x 9½ inches
(18 x 24 cm)—or 15 filo pastry
sheets, measuring 9½ inches
x 14¼ inches (24 x 36 cm),
cut in half
3½ cups (300 g) ground
pistachios

For the syrup
1 cup (250 ml) water
2 cups (400 g) sugar
2 tablespoons rosewater
2 tablespoons orange
blossom water

To make the syrup, heat the water in a small saucepan with the sugar. When the sugar has dissolved, add the rosewater and orange blossom water and bring to a gentle boil. Simmer for 5 minutes, then remove from the heat and leave to cool completely. You can make the syrup a few hours ahead, or even the night before.

Preheat the oven to 350°F (180°C). Generously brush the bottom and the sides of a 7 x 9½ x 2¾ inch (18 x 24 x 7 cm) brownie pan or baking dish with some of the melted butter. Have a damp, clean tea towel ready before working with the filo pastry, as it tends to dry out very quickly.

Place a sheet of filo pastry at the bottom of the pan or dish (keep the rest well protected under the damp cloth) and brush it lightly with melted butter. Layer another 14 pastry sheets on top, brushing each sheet with melted butter. Spread half the ground nuts on top, then gently push down on them with your hands to make a compact layer.

Layer 5 more pastry sheets on top, brushing butter over each of them. Spread the remaining nuts on top, again pushing down lightly. Top with the remaining pastry sheets, brushing butter between each layer and drizzling the remaining butter on top.

Using a very sharp knife, very carefully score a series of straight lines across the baklava, 1¼ inches (3 cm) apart, then score another series of lines diagonally across, to make diamond shapes. Now cut deeply all the way down through each scored incision, taking care that the top layers of pastry don't move too much.

Bake for 30–35 minutes, until the top is golden. As soon as you take your baklava out of the oven, immediately drizzle it with the cold syrup. Before cutting into it again, let the baklava sit at room temperature for 7–8 hours, or overnight. The resting time is essential to the flavor, as it takes away the extreme sweetness of the syrup and allows the pastry and nuts to suck in all the flavors.

Once the baklava has rested, cut it into diamond-shaped pieces and serve with (or without) tea. It will keep in an airtight container at room temperature for a few days, unless it's very hot out, in which case it will keep in the fridge for a week or more.

# Milky, silky tricolor pudding

*Muhallabia* | محلبية

*Muhallabia* is a white pudding that shares its intriguing thousand-year-old roots with the French *blancmange*, Italian *panna cotta*, and other similar white puddings everywhere.

It starts with *isfidhabaj* ("white stew"), which in medieval texts on Arab cooking is often mentioned as a Persian dish. The name is in fact Arabized from the Persian *sepidba*, with *sepid* meaning "white" and *ba* "soup." The Iranian lexicographer Dehkhoda defines *sepidba* as "a soup without yellow spices (turmeric, saffron, cinnamon), something to be given to the frail or sick." Sometimes it had chickpeas and sometimes almonds (which later appeared in the medieval European *blancmange* as a precious ingredient that came from the East).

In other recipes, these "white stews" were based on ground rice—and they often had meat in them too, which was probably used as a thickener and was later replaced with gelatin; like many other medieval savory recipes, they also contained sugar. (To this day, the Iranian *halim*, a wheat porridge made with pounded meat, is served with sugar and cinnamon. In Turkey there are still white puddings that use chicken breast: *kazan dibi* and *tavuk göğsü*. The chicken breast is very overcooked, so you don't taste it at all; you just see the fibers stretching off your spoon.)

Then there is *harire badam*, which I was literally brought up on. In the Arab world, *harire* is a type of soup, but in Iran it is a porridge made of almonds, with or without rice flour. My mother tells me this is how she started weaning me at the tender age of two months, as it was traditional to give *harire badam* to babies and the frail, a nod to its ancestor *isfidhabaj* that was used for the same purpose. Similarly, in Italy, *mangiare in bianco* or "eating white food" (without tomato sauce and condiments) is still recommended for the frail and sick, reminding us of *isfidhabaj* once again.

*Isfidhabaj* and *blancmange* are ancestors to rice puddings everywhere: from *kheer* or *fereni* (page 38) to *sholeh zard* (page 101) and its Turkish cousin *zerde*, to the rice puddings that later became cakes, such as the orange rice cake on page 264 and, of course, our *muhallabia*. Medieval *blancmange* is also the distant parent of other white puddings thickened with eggs, such as *latte alla Portoghese* and *crème caramel*.

Today, white puddings are flavored with the aromatics of each region—rosewater in India and Iran, and mastic in the Levant, as well as orange blossom water. Mastic is a tree resin that gives a stretchy quality and satisfyingly bitter aftertaste to desserts across Turkey, Greece, Lebanon, and Syria. For this *muhallabia* I used a mastic powder that I bought online. The saffron and cocoa tricolor effect is something my mother used to do and that I've noticed in some Levantine recipes as well.

So embrace those humble milk puddings. They are truly an international dish, connecting all people since ancient times with their white velvety sweetness.

*Continued ›*

«

*Serves 3–5*

⅓ cup (50 g) rice flour (see Note)
¼ cup (30 g) cornstarch
4¼ cups (1 liter) whole milk
1 tablespoon unsweetened
  cocoa powder
3 tablespoons saffron infusion
  (page 18)
½ cup (100 g) sugar
1 tablespoon rosewater
1 tablespoon orange
  blossom water
¼ teaspoon mastic powder
  (optional)
chopped pistachios and/or
  almonds, to garnish

In a small bowl, mix the rice flour and cornstarch with a scant ½ cup (100 ml) of the milk until smooth, making sure no lumps are left. In a largish bowl, dissolve the cocoa powder in a few tablespoons of the milk. Pour the saffron infusion into another bowl that is about the same size.

Bring the remaining milk to a boil in a pot with the sugar over low heat, stirring occasionally so that the bottom doesn't stick and a skin doesn't form on top. Add the rice flour mixture and start stirring; the milk should thicken in next to no time. When it does, stir in the rosewater, orange blossom water, and mastic, if using, and cook for another few minutes.

Pour about one-third of the warm milk mixture into the bowl with the cocoa powder, mixing well. Another one-third goes into the bowl with the saffron infusion; the third color (the white milk mixture) remains in the pot.

To assemble the puddings, hold a bowl at a bit of an angle in your hands and pour in a large spoonful or two of one of the pudding mixtures. Keep holding the bowl at an angle for a few seconds, to give the pudding time to firm up a bit, then rotate the bowl and add a second colored pudding mixture to another corner. Wait again, then add the third color. Repeat with more bowls.

Garnish with chopped pistachios and/or almonds. Chill and serve cold as a sweet treat or dessert.

**Note:** Instead of using a mix of rice flour and cornstarch, you could use either ½ cup (80 g) rice flour or ⅔ cup (80 g) cornstarch.

# Syrupy baked quince, spicy & drunken

Years ago, I bought a small copper pot from Tehran's Tajrish Bazaar and brought it back with me to Rome. Besides enhancing the aesthetics of my kitchen, dangling from a bar above the stove, it was the pot I wanted to cook quince in, once a year.

In Iran you are taught to make quince jam—or anything with quince—in a copper pot, to bring out the very deepest red color. We believe this is why the color of quince jam from Iran is so different from the Italian one (and also *cotognata*, a thick quince jam or paste that in southern Italy is served around Christmas).

Quince has a special place in the cuisine of this whole area, often appearing in savory dishes—in Iran in stews, or stuffed the same as apples (page 95); in Syria in another stew, the famous *kibbeh safarjaliyeh*. Even in Italy, quince sits next to pork beautifully (similar to the recipe on page 247, although I use pears there). In the Levant, quinces have been poached in syrup since medieval times—often scented with "rosewater, musk, raw ambergris," according to some accounts. These days, warm spices such as cinnamon and star anise are also popular, as (thankfully) we don't normally use ambergris or musk in cooking anymore.

In Muslim countries, the story ends here, but in Greece—similar to how pears are poached in wine (page 258) in Italy and France—quince is poached in a syrup with a strong sweet wine called Mavrodaphne, which is very similar to the Sicilian Marsala and the Portuguese port. You could poach the pears on page 258 in Marsala as well, but I prefer a full-bodied red wine for that. The strong perfume of quince, however, matches Marsala well.

In Turkish pastry shops, they also stuff poached quince halves with jam, but these quartered ones are delicious with whipped cream, ice cream, or even strained yogurt (*labneh*; page 170).

*Serves 4–6*

2 cups (500 ml) Mavrodaphne,
    Marsala, or port wine
2½ cups (500 g) sugar
2–3 cinnamon sticks
juice of 1 lemon
2 large quinces,
    or 3 medium ones
1–2 cloves for each
    quince quarter

In a large pot, bring the wine to a gentle simmer with the sugar, cinnamon sticks, and lemon juice.

Meanwhile, peel the quinces, cut each into quarters, and remove the cores. Stick 1–2 cloves into each quince quarter.

Add the quince quarters to the simmering wine. Put the lid on and poach the quinces in the sweet, spicy wine over low heat for 15–45 minutes, depending on the variety and freshness of the fruit, until they are no longer rock-hard. (Don't be tempted to skip the poaching step, as it infuses the quinces with all the exquisite flavors, and softens them for the baking stage.)

Meanwhile, preheat the oven to 425°F (220°C). Transfer the quince quarters to a baking dish, then pour the poaching liquid over them. Transfer the dish to the oven and bake for about 1 hour, until the quince edges are shriveled and lightly browned.

Cool slightly before serving with ice cream, custard, whipped cream, or *labneh* (page 170).

# Labneh with (rose petal) jam

Whether we call it *labneh* as they do in Arabic, or *suzma* in Central Asia, or *mast-è chekideh* (literally "strained yogurt") in Iran, or simply Greek yogurt, this fermented (and often strained) milk is the glue that connects all of Central Asia, the Middle East, the Eastern Mediterranean, the Levant—and even the Balkans and beyond.

From dressing all sorts of *borani* (pages 66–69), to dumplings and grilled meat, yogurt is omnipresent wherever you go in these regions. True, the former Ottoman Empire and the animal husbandry culture of the Turkic people in Central Asia had much to do with this, but even before that, yogurt had been present in many Persian dishes that then found themselves in medieval Arab cuisine, too.

Something that is remarkable in the Levant is eating *labneh* for breakfast, sprinkled with salt and drizzled with good peppery olive oil, with pita bread, olives, the ripest tomatoes, crunchy and aromatic little cucumbers, and fresh mint or za'atar. Another brunch favorite is *cilbir*, Turkish poached eggs on *labneh*, drizzled with an oil infused with paprika or red pepper flakes.

But I prefer it sweet, which could be as simple as drizzling it with honey and sprinkling it with cinnamon, as is done in Greece—something quite similar to what my mom sometimes made for us as a treat after meals, when she would simply add swirls of jam to yogurt. Not just any jam, though—you want something aromatic and rather thick. My favorite is the unexpectedly chewy rose petal jam, but you could use a thick-cut orange marmalade or quince jam, too. Speaking of quince, the spicy drunken ones on page 168 are also wonderful with *labneh*—as are the pears poached in wine on page 258.

*Makes 1 cup*

generous 2 cups (500 g) plain
    yogurt
a pinch of salt
2 tablespoons rose petal jam,
    marmalade, or quince jam,
    to taste

Mix the yogurt with the salt. (The salt won't actually alter the flavor but will draw the water more easily from the yogurt.)

Line a small colander with a clean cotton tea towel, or two layers of cheesecloth, and place it over a bowl so that it doesn't touch the bottom. Pour the yogurt in, then lightly cover it with the corners of the cloth.

Leave to drain in the fridge for 5–10 hours.

Spoon the *labneh* onto a plate, leaving swirls to hold your favorite jam topping.

Italy

The ache for home lives in all of us. The safe place where we can go as we are and not be questioned.

Maya Angelou, *All God's Children Need Traveling Shoes*


*"Passaporto UE?"* asks the officer when we enter Rome's Fiumicino Airport. No, I don't have an EU passport. So I'm directed to the second hallway, where we get checked for our permissions to enter the other side of the fence. I do have one such permission, my *permesso di soggiorno*, possibly the most prized possession I own, because I know well the hell I'd have to go through if I ever lost it.

The passport control police here are used to us darker-skinned passengers, and we're used to their tendency to rudeness. My officer doesn't answer my greeting, but he's delighted that I speak Italian. He asks me many questions about where I live and what I do, and I answer dutifully. We're also used to the idea of being interrogated by the police at borders. Only when he repeats that we could meet somewhere in Rome do I realize that I'm not being interrogated but hit on.

Blatant discrimination has rarely come my way in Italy. I have the significant privilege of very light skin, indeed much lighter than many Italians. I also have the protection of dark hair and eyes, which, as many Italians are pleased to inform me, make me look "like them."

My name, which is objectively difficult, is troubling to Italians. Often they offer me an Italian nickname. My response to this has always been outrage, but I have seen too many Black and brown workers in Italy who have been rechristened by their employers. My other huge privilege is my virtually perfect Italian, which makes me hard to undermine or talk over.

There's a tinge of English in my Italian accent, a relic of neverending language school in my childhood. It's impressive to speak good English in Italy, although not quite as impressive as being from an English-speaking country. In my first few years in Rome, the woman who gave me an underpaid cash-in-hand job as an English teacher at an afternoon school told the children's parents I was from Canada. It's also a lot easier to be a professional Italophile when you're white, particularly if you work in food and wine, or tourism. Much more *Under the Tuscan Sun*. Much more *Eat, Pray, Love*.

Italians frequently ask me why I have chosen their country. Often they presume it was *per l'amore*, meaning an Italian man. Quite a few ask why anyone would ever come to live in their country. Not in a "go back to your country" way but in a "we want to go away from this country" way. They don't have much confidence in their beautiful country, but boy do they have confidence in their "Latin lovers."

Indeed, many young Italians who seek to excel or create a different life move to Berlin, London, or New York. And no one asks them why, because it's just something you do. They become "expats." Cosmopolitans, citizens of the world. Just like other white people who leave their country for another.

Migration has been a familiar idea to Italians since the nation was first unified in 1861. Many from the southern regions immigrated to the north for work. Until not long ago, Italy was a country to emigrate from (to the UK, the US, Australia, and even North Africa), not a country to immigrate to. For decades, Italians abroad were discriminated against and harassed for their darker skin.

Here, the phenomenon of receiving immigrants is fairly new. Back in the 1990s, the first large waves of immigrants arrived from Balkan countries, but with the arrival of the Bangladeshis and later the boats from Africa, the "problem" of the neighboring white migrants was somehow put aside.

Before catching the train out of the airport, invariably I stop at the bar in need of an espresso, wondering whether I have become a little Italian myself after all. My passport disagrees, and so do the officers at the immigration office, as well as the visa granters of most countries. Sure, my fence is now as large as the Schengen area, thanks to my *permesso di soggiorno*. But if I had stayed *per l'amore* and married an Italian, or if I had a long-forgotten Italian great-great aunt, even if I had earned more money during the years of the pandemic, I would be on my way to being officially Italian now.

*"Un caffè macchiato per favore"*; I watch the hustle and bustle of the bar, transfixed. The familiar bangs and tinkles of making and serving coffee are music to my ears, the speedy and ritualized actions mesmerizing to watch.

I have loved Italy fiercely in these years. Its diverse regional cultures, the simplicity and complexity of its food, its excellence, its warmth of temperatures and of people, its flawed humanity, and the possibility of a less complicated life. Its blue skies that are not quite the color of other blue skies, and the earthy tones, brick reds, ochres, and oranges of its poetically decaying walls with ancient and worn textures. Its beauty: the unpretentious beauty of its charming little angles, and the breathtaking beauty of its many magnificent wonders.

As the train gets close to Termini Station, I notice the iconically graffitied buildings, the rowdy wires of electricity, the unruly and somewhat artistic presence of television antennas on them, against a backdrop of blue skies punctured by the umbrella-like presence of Rome's famous stone pines. I feel these colors as my own. I have grown into an adult woman here. I have lived in Rome for more years than any city in Iran.

This is my stop.

I am home.

# THE ITALIAN PANTRY

Look for a specialty Italian food store in your town. In some, you can find the most peculiar pasta shapes, and some of the shop owners may even have family connections to local Italian producers. Another good idea is to ask your Italian friends for advice on where to buy the best products. It's possible they may also get what you need in their next *pacco da giù*, the goodies package almost all emigrated Italians get from their families.

**Extra virgin olive oil:** A good olive oil, often in abundant measure, is the soul of Italian food. The rule to know is that a good olive oil is not— and should not be—cheap. Don't save your good olive oil for a long time to be served for special occasions, as it goes rancid. Do keep it in a dark bottle, never a transparent colorless one.

**Bread:** The "body" of Italian food, consumed in all forms. From the thinnest Sardinian *pane carasau*, to all the doughs that are topped or stuffed and then baked or fried, and the things that sometimes go by the name of "pizza," to the saltless loaves in central Italy served with extra-salty cured meats, to the simple "little roses" that become panini filled with anything from mortadella to Nutella, it's very hard to imagine an Italian table without good bread.

**Wine and vinegar:** If olive oil is the soul of Italian cooking, and bread its body, wine is undoubtedly its blood. Red or white wine vinegar and balsamic vinegar are also very commonly used, especially for dressing and conserving cooked and raw vegetables.

**Tomato:** Whether you're using them fresh or preserved, as cans of *pelato*, jars of passata (puréed tomatoes), tubes of paste (concentrated purée), or sun-dried and preserved in oil, the miracle of Italian food is its incredible flavor with very few ingredients, so find the best-quality tomatoes you can.

**Pasta:** What Italian pantry would be without pasta, dried or fresh, in different shapes?

**Anchovies:** Either on toasted bread with some butter, or as a foundation of a pasta sauce or soup, anchovies make a difference in Italian cooking. A good canned variety works well.

**Cheese, aged and fresh:** Dry, aged cow's milk cheeses such as Parmigiano Reggiano or Grana Padano, and aged sheep's cheese such as Pecorino Romano, which can be grated, are often used in fillings, as well as on top of pastas and soups. Very fresh cheese such as ricotta and mozzarella are sometimes used in cooking as well. A slab of any cheese, a slice of bread, and a glass of wine is already a meal, or at least an *aperitivo*, in Italy.

**Nuts and dried fruits:** Pine nuts, almonds, hazelnuts, raisins, and candied fruits are mostly used in sweet recipes, although some nuts end up occasionally in savory dishes, too.

**Herbs:** Bay leaves, rosemary, thyme, basil, fennel, and local herbs from the mint family are commonly used.

**Spices:** Cinnamon, nutmeg, and chile flakes— but not too much of any of them.

**Legumes:** Chickpeas, various types of beans, fava beans, and lentils are the backbone of many dishes, especially rural ones.

# The market & the pantry:
# a few simple dishes

It was a revelation to me when, years ago, I learned about the simplicity of everyday Italian cooking. Ingredients are disarmingly few, often both seasonal and local. The cooking, if required at all, is quick. If you have some pasta, good olive oil, garlic, chile, and aromatic herbs in your pantry, or some bread (even if not fresh), and some tomatoes or any other vegetable at the bottom of your fridge, you can make a meal.

The recipes in this chapter represent my favorite kind of cooking. Quick, simple, fuss-free. This is how I cook for myself when alone (which is most of the time). With this in mind, the market comes as an inspiration. Tomatoes, zucchini, and eggplant only in summer; and pumpkin and winter squash, broccoli, and cabbages only in winter. Porcini mushrooms in fall, artichokes in spring. In the pantry, always dried beans, grains, and anchovies.

Some of these dishes can be made as an antipasto for a larger meal, some as a *contorno* (side dish). Most can be prepared in advance.

# A simple salad of grilled zucchini, garlic, mint & (a lot of) olive oil

In the summer of 2008, after having lived in Italy for almost a year, I spent a week or so with my friend Dora and her family in Calabria—a southern region much overshadowed by Sicily and Puglia, with stunning nature and a rich culinary culture, known particularly for the strong hint of chile that lingers in most dishes.

We had arrived in Calabria on the cheapest night train from Bologna, where we had just been to a Metallica concert. Looking back, I wonder whether I was nurturing a secret desire to torture myself. As doe-eyed as I was, getting out alive from amidst an excited throng of hardcore metal music fans had not been a given, especially after spending many hours under Bologna's scorching July sun waiting to be let into the concert venue. But after the 900-kilometer (56-mile) journey on the clanky and distinctly uncomfortable train, Calabria awaited with deep blue waters and green mountains, and many lazy meals by the pool of Dora's parents.

Best made with in-season pale green romanesco zucchini, this salad may rightly remind some of another side dish called *zucchine alla scapece*, or *concia*. A staple of Jewish cuisine in Italy, and much loved in both Naples and Rome, *concia* stars zucchini that has been fried, then marinated in vinegar with some garlic and plenty of mint leaves. Although this salad is grilled as opposed to fried, and there's no vinegar in it (but you could add some if you wanted to), Dora's mom must have been inspired by *concia*.

Enjoying this salad as a light summer meal over the years, often with a piece of fresh cheese, also reminds me of a summer staple my own mother used to prepare—a dish of zucchini, sliced lengthways, then pan-fried and served with copious amounts of garlicky yogurt, and perhaps some golden onion (page 16). Similar flavor palettes, distant memories and places.

*Serves 3–4 as a side*

½ cup (125 ml) extra virgin
　olive oil
2 generous handfuls of mint
4 garlic cloves
4 large zucchini,
　or 7–8 small ones
½ teaspoon salt, or more to taste

Start by flavoring the oil. Pour the oil in a large, quite deep dish. Tear most of the mint leaves into it, saving a few nice-looking ones for garnishing. Put the garlic cloves on a chopping board and bash them once with the flat blade of a knife, or with the bottom of a sturdy mug, which feels less "cheffy." This should remove the skin easily. Slice the garlic lengthways, thinly enough to impart maximum flavor to the oil but not so thinly that it will dissolve when the grilled zucchini is added later—just large enough to spot, if someone wants to skip eating it.

*Continued ›*

«

Heat a grill pan or barbecue grill to high. Rinse the zucchini well with water, trim the stem ends, then slice lengthways, about ¼ inch (5 mm) thick. Working in batches if needed, grill the zucchini on both sides until dark scorch marks appear, but don't let them shrivel up too much. Put the grilled zucchini in the flavored oil, tossing gently and sprinkling with the salt, making sure all parts of the zucchini are coated with the oil.

Let the salad rest for at least 30 minutes before serving; it tastes even better the next day.

Summer days of zucchini galore will find you wanting to make this dish more often than you might imagine. Keep the flavored oil in the fridge after eating the zucchini, and use it over the next few days as a base for encores. Simply "refresh" it with a bit more olive oil, just one chopped fresh garlic clove, and a few more mint leaves if need be.

# Easy, versatile farro salads for all seasons

*Insalata di farro*

The two dishes that follow are more a description of an idea rather than actual recipes. The idea is simple: cook a grain (in this case, farro), add vegetables (raw or cooked, depending on what you have available), then add cheese, if necessary—and you have a quintessentially Mediterranean meal. Farro has been grown on the Italian peninsula since Roman times. Farro and other grains were an essential weapon of the masses in the war for survival. Soups, grains, and porridges were the food of the poor, often flavored with scraps of a slaughtered animal or dried beans, and whatever vegetables were on hand. You can still find farro soups with pig's trotters and pork rinds in some parts of Italy.

In modern times, the principle of a filling dish for those on meager means remains. This made farro salad a favorite of my former roommates on tight student budgets. They would make a whole lot of it that would feed us for days. I have to say I absolutely hated it.

Then something happened. When I was barely 30, I met Alice Adams Carosi in her newly opened, charming food and photography space called Latteria Studio, in the Trastevere neighborhood of

Rome. It was peak summer, and she had made the most delicious farro salad, with roasted tomatoes and zucchini, all properly seasoned and drizzled with generous glugs of olive oil. At the time, I was on the verge of dramatically changing the course of my life, and this dish tasted like the possibility of new horizons. A new space, a new salad. A new life.

Farro salad has since become part of my cooking repertoire, whatever the season, whatever the weather. The trick to a good farro salad is to roast the vegetables properly and to season each element—even the grain—separately. For some reason it's easy to under-salt these dishes, so keep tasting. Acidity is a game changer here—a combo of vinegars, lemon juice, and the freshness of lemon zest. The final secret is not really a secret: olive oil, a good one. Always drizzle on a bit more than you think is enough.

## For summer: cherry tomato, zucchini, basil (& mozzarella)

*Serves 3–4*

10½ oz (300 g) cherry
    tomatoes, halved
½ teaspoon sugar
1¼ teaspoons salt,
    plus extra for seasoning
1⅓ cups (250 g) farro
olive oil, for cooking
    and drizzling
2 garlic cloves, peeled
2 large zucchini, or 4 small
    ones (about 1 lb/450 g), cut
    lengthways into quarters
1 tablespoon white vinegar
zest and juice of ½ lemon
a handful of basil leaves
½–1 red onion (preferably a
    Tropea onion), or a handful
    of scallions, thinly sliced
freshly ground black pepper
fresh cheese, such as mozzarella,
    burrata, or stracciatella
    (optional), sliced or torn

Preheat the oven to 400°F (200°C). Arrange the tomatoes, cut side up, on a baking pan. Sprinkle with the sugar and ¼ teaspoon of the salt. Roast for about 1½ hours, until cooked dry.

Meanwhile, cook the farro in a pot of boiling salted water according to the package instructions; this usually takes about 30 minutes.

While the farro is simmering, heat 2–3 tablespoons olive oil in a large frying pan with the garlic cloves. Add the zucchini and cook over high heat, stirring frequently, for 10–15 minutes, until cooked but not too soft. Season with the remaining 1 teaspoon salt. Transfer to a large bowl and mix in the vinegar.

Drain the farro, then toss it with the zucchini and another 1 tablespoon olive oil. Leave to cool while the tomatoes finish roasting.

Mix the lemon zest and juice through the salad. Tear in most of the basil leaves, leaving some for garnishing. Add the onion and about two-thirds of the roasted tomatoes. Mix well, then season to taste with salt and black pepper.

Pile the salad onto a shallow platter. Top with the remaining roasted tomatoes, basil leaves, and the fresh cheese, if using. Drizzle with more olive oil and serve. This salad (*sans* cheese) keeps in the fridge for a few days.

# For winter: roasted squash & shallots, toasted hazelnuts & soft cheese

*Serves 3–4*

1 lb 9 oz–1 lb 12 oz (700–800 g) butternut, kabocha, or mantovana squash, peeled and chopped into 1¼ inch (3 cm) cubes

3 French shallots, peeled, with the roots left on, then quartered lengthways

1–2 teaspoons salt, plus extra for seasoning

olive oil, for cooking and drizzling

2 rosemary sprigs

1⅓ cups (250 g) farro

⅓ cup (50 g) hazelnuts

zest and juice of ½ lemon

1 teaspoon white vinegar

freshly ground black pepper

7 oz (200 g) soft cheese, such as robiola or goat cheese

1½ teaspoons balsamic vinegar

Preheat the oven to 400°F (200°C). Put the squash and shallots on a large baking pan with ½ teaspoon of the salt, 2 tablespoons olive oil, and the rosemary sprigs. Toss to coat the vegetables, then arrange them on the pan so they're not overlapping. Roast for about 30 minutes, or until the shallots are soft with some brown edges. Remove the shallots and, if necessary, roast the squash for another 10–30 minutes, until soft with some brown edges.

Meanwhile, cook the farro in a saucepan of boiling salted water according to the package instructions; this usually takes about 30 minutes. Drain the farro, place in a large bowl, and toss with about 1 tablespoon olive oil, so it doesn't dry out.

Toast the hazelnuts in a hot frying pan for just a few minutes until lightly browned and fragrant with an earthy aroma. Transfer immediately to a chopping board so the nuts don't burn, leave until cool enough to handle, then coarsely chop.

Add the toasted hazelnuts to the farro with the roasted squash and shallot (discard the rosemary twigs). Toss with the lemon zest and juice, white vinegar, and another 2 tablespoons olive oil, then season to taste with salt and black pepper.

Pile the salad onto a shallow platter. Crumble the cheese into large chunks over the salad and drizzle with the balsamic vinegar; of course, another drizzle of olive oil never hurts.

You can keep this salad in the fridge for a couple of days; save the cheese for serving.

# Pasta & chickpea soup

*Pasta e ceci*

In my small living room in Rome, there's a wall covered with many frames of different things I like.

The two largest frames are black and white. One is a map of Tehran; the other displays just one sentence: "Make it simple, but significant," a motto borrowed from *Mad Men*. There are two of my own photos, one of a wall in Negarestan Palace in Tehran, another of a wall in Puglia iconically covered in prickly pears. And then there's a large frame holding the most gorgeous illustration, by the super-talented Felicita Sala, of a pasta and chickpea soup recipe. That is how much I love this soup, enough to put it next to the map of my natal city and the motto of my life.

Unsurprisingly, a soup (or *minestra*) with chickpeas and pasta is as ancient as recipes can be—mentioned by Horace in first century BC Rome, and found with regional differences across provinces such as Basilicata and Puglia.

The Roman *pasta e ceci* is known to be brothy, and a more comforting pasta soup you couldn't find. Even now, if you walk past a Roman trattoria on a Friday, you may catch a whiff of a pot of chickpeas boiling away, especially during Lent. Although the Catholic Church has loosened its rules of fasting, the tradition of having *pasta e ceci* (and *baccalà*—cod) on Fridays remains.

The Roman version of this soup is known to have salted anchovies that go with the sautéed onion, celery, garlic, and carrot (the *soffritto*); you could replace the anchovies with thinly sliced guanciale or pancetta—or skip them altogether. You should *not* skip the *soffritto*, however, no matter what.

Besides that, you can play with this soup as much as you like. I like mine with an extra pinch of chile and many extra drizzles of olive oil. Don't forget bread for mopping up the juices. Start this recipe the night before you wish to serve.

*Serves 4–6*

1¾ cups (300 g) dried chickpeas
   (see Note)
1 bay leaf
1 large onion
1 carrot
1 celery stalk
1 garlic clove
1 small chile, or chile flakes,
   to taste
⅓ cup (80 ml) olive oil,
   plus extra for serving

Soak the dried chickpeas overnight with the bay leaf in plenty of cold water. Changing the soaking water at least three times will reduce possible problems with a gassy stomach later.

About 2 hours prior to serving, finely dice the onion, carrot, celery, garlic, and chile and place them in a large heavy-based pot with the olive oil. If you're using pancetta or anchovy fillets, also add them now. Sauté over medium-high heat for about 10 minutes, then stir in the tomato paste and cook for a few more minutes, until the color brightens a little.

1 slice of pancetta, lardo, or
   guanciale, chopped, or
   2 anchovy fillets (optional)
1 tablespoon tomato paste, or
   3 tablespoons tomato passata
   (puréed tomatoes)
2 teaspoons salt
1 parmesan rind (optional)
9 oz (250 g) small pasta, such as
   tubetti or ditaloni

Drain the chickpeas, then add them to the pot with the bay leaf, salt, and parmesan rind, if using. Pour in about 6 cups (1.5 liters) water. Bring to a boil, reduce the heat, then cover and simmer for about 1½ hours, or until the chickpeas are quite soft.

Taste and adjust the salt if necessary. Discard the bay leaf and parmesan rind. Depending on how chunky you like your soup, remove about half the chickpeas with a slotted spoon, then use a handheld immersion blender to blend the remaining chickpeas to create a smooth, starchy base. Add the whole chickpeas back into the soup.

We're about to add the pasta now, and it'll need a lot of liquid to cook properly. Only you can tell how much more water you'll need to add; I'd say about 2 cups (500 ml) boiling water.

Add the pasta and boiling water, then be sure to stir every now and then, so it doesn't stick together. A couple of minutes before the total cooking time suggested on the pasta package, turn off the heat and let the soup rest for about 10 minutes; you might find a bit more boiling water is needed at the end, too.

Drizzle each bowl with good olive oil when serving.

**Note:** I recommend using dried chickpeas, because I like their taste better, but if it's more convenient, use three 14 oz (400 g) cans of chickpeas, which will yield 1 lb 5 oz–1 lb 9 oz (600–700 g) when drained, and be sure to rinse them. Cook the *soffritto* with the bay leaf and parmesan rind in 4¼ cups (1 liter) water for about 15 minutes before adding the canned chickpeas, then simmer for another 10–15 minutes. Blend as indicated, then proceed with the recipe as directed.

# Midnight spaghetti with garlic, chile & olive oil

*Ajo, ojo e peperoncino*

Sharing an apartment with a bunch of students, or recently graduated twenty-somethings, leaves you with memories to last a lifetime. There'd be disagreements over whose turn it was to mop the floor, or who hadn't yet paid the electricity bill. But there'd also be ridiculous laughter for no particular reason, and easier solutions to most of life's questions, and these would often involve alcohol and food. Whether we passed an exam with a great grade, or we failed and had to repeat it next term, when someone met a cute new girl, or a boy didn't call back, the answer was the same. Celebration and commiseration came in the form of cheap bottles of beer, then something a bit stronger, sometimes dancing it off, sometimes eating it up.

In Italy, kids take their feelings out with them for a beer and dance. In Iran, culturally introverted and politically bound by tyranny, we partied indoors. Perhaps not as often as kids in Italy, but definitely harder than them. We might've gone out after the party, in search of a late-night sandwich, or for an early-morning *kalleh pache* when feeling particularly audacious. In Italy, the reward for finally coming back home in the early hours of the morning, feeling a bit tipsy and hungry, is conjuring a *spaghettata ajo ojo peperoncino*—a fast, cheap, and easy spaghetti meal, usually just with garlic, olive oil, and chile, but ridiculously delicious.

Originally from Naples, this pasta is a favorite all over Italy for its convenience and speed, and for the nostalgia of having a big pan of pasta at 3 a.m. Curiously, when I was once in Milan, a Neapolitan guy whipped up another *spaghettata* with anchovies, garlic, and walnuts, and said this was what students there made at midnight.

With only garlic, chile, and heaps of olive oil, it might look as if this pasta dish has left a main ingredient behind—but taste it and you'll no longer think this. In the Neapolitan dialect, this dish once went by the name *vermicelli con le vongole fujute*—vermicelli with "escaped clams"; arguably, all you'd need to turn your *ajo ojo peperoncino* into real spaghetti with clams is a cup of wine and the clams themselves. (In Naples, the current version of spaghetti with escaped clams has tomatoes, too—a further step away from *ajo ojo peperoncino*, which is always "white.")

My favorite version of this dish is with breadcrumbs, a celebration of carb on carb that creates the most satisfying sandy texture; they say it's a Sicilian touch. As an extremely "poor" dish, it doesn't even require cheese—and most importantly, cheese is not required flavor-wise. (I am diplomatically trying to tell you to never, ever add cheese to this dish.)

Midnight spaghetti with "escaped clams" is both for those nights when something has escaped us, or to celebrate the things that haven't escaped—all tinted with the intense flavors of garlic and chile.

*Continued ›*

«

*Serves 4–6*

salt, for seasoning
   the pasta water
1 lb 2 oz (500 g) spaghetti
½ cup (125 ml) good-quality
   olive oil, plus extra for serving
3 garlic cloves, finely chopped
¼–½ teaspoon chile flakes, or
   1 red chile, finely chopped,
   seeds included
½ cup (50 g) dry breadcrumbs

Bring a large pot of water to a boil and season generously with salt. Add the spaghetti. We're going to cook it very al dente, only for half the time recommended on the package.

So, you have about 5 minutes to add the oil to a large (but not necessarily very deep) sauté pan with the garlic and chile (but don't turn the heat on yet; just let the oil, garlic, and chile get to know each other). Meanwhile, toast the breadcrumbs in a small frying pan for a minute or two, until fragrant and lightly browned, then tip into a little bowl.

Set the heat under the pan with the oil, garlic, and chile to medium-low. Be very careful not to burn the garlic, as it'll get a nasty aftertaste that will ruin the dish.

When your spaghetti is half cooked, save 3–4¼ cups (750 ml–1 liter) of the cooking water. Drain the spaghetti and immediately add it to the pan of oil on blazing high heat and give it a stir with a wooden spoon (or even better, a pair of kitchen tongs). Add 1 cup (250 ml) of the cooking water and stir vigorously for a minute. Keep stirring for 4–5 minutes, then add the remaining cooking water little by little, until you get a silky, creamy sauce that is still too wet to serve; keep in mind that it'll keep drying up after you take the pan off the heat.

Mix in half the toasted breadcrumbs. Dish up the spaghetti quickly, sprinkle each bowl with more breadcrumbs, drizzle over a bit more oil, and serve immediately. No cheese needed.

# A Tuscan bread salad

*Panzanella*

In the Mediterranean and the Middle East, as in any other culture where bread is the main victual, there are many dishes that give new life to stale bread using frugal but flavorful ingredients—herbs, onions, vegetables, oil, wine, vinegar.

*Panzanella* is one such dish, born of avoiding waste in times when famine and shortage were always around the corner. In the 1800s, Luigi Bicchierai, who ran an *osteria* (inn) near Florence, documented *panzanella* in his diaries as a way to make use of rough crusts of bread. He describes it as "a dish of the poor, but so delicious even gentlemen, priests, and officers like it." He also mentions a recipe for *sugo della miseria*, or "poverty sauce."

*Panzanella* is strikingly similar in idea to the bread salads of the Levant (page 140), especially *fattoush*. This is a manifestation of human beings coming up with similar solutions when faced with the same problem in quite similar conditions. The vegetables in *panzanella* are even similar to those in *salad Shirazi* (page 63), which again has similar versions around the region.

*Continued ›*

«

Very similar to the Tuscan *panzanella*, the lesser known *caponata napoletana* is sometimes made with *fresella* or *frisa*, a twice-baked dry bread that was once the only food of seamen in southern Italy, particularly in Puglia, where it's still very popular. It is said the seamen would "bathe" the dry bread in salty sea water, reviving it and adding flavor in one step, and it is still dunked in water and left to rehydrate to this day.

*Panzanella* is the pride and joy of Tuscans, who cherish their unsalted bread and have come up with several ways to reuse it—such as *pappa al pomodoro*, a very popular bread and tomato soup that is usually served at room temperature on hot summer days (and made with canned tomatoes in winter). You can't help but be reminded of the Spanish *gazpacho*. Again, it doesn't mean one was necessarily inspired by the other, just that the conditions that gave rise to these dishes were similar.

This is how I live in summer: bread, *panzanella*, gazpacho. *Fattoush* is too fancy for the Italian heat, so I keep it for occasions that go beyond mere survival.

For me, the key to a good *panzanella* is fearlessness with salt, vinegar, and olive oil. The latter won't ever be too much. If something is missing in the taste, an extra dash of salt and a splash of vinegar will probably fix it. To this basic recipe, I sometimes add canned chickpeas or tuna. You can play with the vegetables, too; I love thinly sliced fennel in it.

*Serves 4–6*

2 small onions, or 1 large one
¼ cup (60 ml) vinegar, such as white wine vinegar, plus extra for the onions
1 lb 2 oz (500 g) good-quality crusty bread, a few days old
1 lb 2 oz (500 g) tomatoes
2 large cucumbers, peeled and quartered, then deseeded if particularly seedy
2 teaspoons salt, or to taste
⅓ cup (80 ml) olive oil
a large handful of basil leaves
freshly ground black pepper

Thinly slice the onions and leave them to soak in a small bowl with some water and a small splash of the vinegar, just to take the sharpness from the raw onions.

Cut the hard crusts off the bread and place the crusts in a large bowl. Add a splash of water so that the crust starts to soak. Dice the remaining bread and add to the bowl with enough water to soak the bread without losing its consistency; the exact amount of water depends on your type of bread and how old it is. Add 2 tablespoons of the vinegar and leave for 10–20 minutes.

Now slice and quarter the tomatoes directly above the bowl of bread, because we don't want to lose even one drop of the tomato juices. Drain the onion and add to the bowl, together with the cucumbers. Add the salt, olive oil, and remaining vinegar. Tear in the basil leaves.

Give it all a good toss, then season to taste with more salt and some black pepper. The *panzanella* is best served after resting for about 30 minutes. You could serve some milky mozzarella on the side.

# Oniony, garlicky braised bell peppers

*Peperonata*

It's almost unimaginable to think that until as recently as 200 years ago, bell peppers were not much appreciated or commonly used in Italy. In his 1773 cookbook *Il Cuoco Galante*, Neapolitan cook and scholar Vincenzo Corrado considered them "too rustic and vulgar." Barely a century later, they were inseparable from the food of the *osterias*, or inns, where they would often be served in preserved form with vinegar and oil, next to salami, cheese, and wine.

Among the foods that arrived from the "New World" with the colonization of the Americas, corn integrated into Italian cuisine relatively quickly. Other foods such as tomatoes, potatoes, and bell peppers faced resistance. Writing on bell peppers in *Italian Cuisine: A Cultural History*, Massimo Montanari observes: "As it normally happens in the history of culture—therefore also in cooking— what is considered 'different,' in order to be recognized as one's own, is transformed to adapt to the system of values."

The same is true in the Levant and the Middle East, where the famous stuffed bell peppers (page 145) and *muhammara* dip (page 132) with roasted bell peppers, walnuts, and pomegranate molasses are dishes that are about 200 years old.

*Peperonata* is very simple and much appreciated in Rome. A famous variation is served with chicken, with or without tomato sauce—and always at room temperature on Ferragosto, a national public holiday on August 15, at the peak of the summer vacation, that is celebrated with a feast.

Some people roast their bell peppers and peel them before stewing them in a *peperonata*. I don't. I believe when I take the time to roast and peel them, they deserve to be served as silky ribbons with no intervention other than salt and olive oil.

*Peperonata* is a very rewarding dish that pays back for the time it takes. You can toss some pasta in it (don't forget a little of the pasta's cooking water), spoon it on toasted bread, or do as the *osterias* of the nineteenth century did—serve a simple cold supper of *salumi* and/or cheese, maybe a boiled egg or two, with *peperonata* on the side.

*Continued ›*

«

*Serves 4–6 as a side*

3 large bell peppers, about
    2 lb 4 oz (1 kg); use orange,
    red, and/or yellow ones,
    never green
¼–⅓ cup (60–80 ml) olive oil
2 onions, sliced
2 garlic cloves, finely chopped
1 tablespoon tomato paste,
    or 3 tablespoons tomato
    passata (puréed tomatoes),
    or 2 chopped fresh tomatoes
1½ teaspoons salt
2 tablespoons white vinegar
freshly ground black pepper

Slice and discard the tops from the bell peppers, then cut them into long ribbons, about ½ inch (1 cm) thick, removing the seeds and any white inner membranes from the flesh.

Heat the oil with the sliced onion in a large sauté pan over medium heat and cook for 5 minutes, until the onion is translucent. Add the garlic. After a few minutes, when the garlic is fragrant, stir in the tomato paste. After another few minutes, add the bell pepper ribbons, mixing often for about 10 minutes, to let the flavors familiarize. Stir in the salt.

Reduce the heat, then cover and simmer gently for 45 minutes to 1 hour, until the bell peppers are very soft.

Add the vinegar and give it all a good toss. Adjust the salt and add pepper to taste. Simmer, uncovered, for another 10–15 minutes, to cook off a bit more liquid; the *peperonata* will dry out a little more once cooled.

Leave to rest for 15 minutes, then serve with toasted crusty bread or next to any kind of potato dish or grilled sausages.

It will keep well in the fridge for a few days, and can be brought back to room temperature or slightly reheated for serving.

*Pictured opposite*

# A simple artichoke soup

*Vellutata di caciofi e patate*

It was 2012, and I had been living in Italy for five years, when I decided to get an annual public transport ticket. At the time, this ticket was available only from a special office at Termini Station in Rome—where, caught in the labyrinth of some construction work, I took the wrong exit, crossing the turnstile that led to the piazza outside. On the wrong side of the turnstile, I noticed a respectable-looking Italian man in his late forties, wearing a handsome navy suit similar to those worn by railway officials, who opened the little turnstile gate to enter the platform. Thinking he was a railway official, I asked if he could help me, as I'd come out of the wrong exit and was looking for the special ticket office. He curtly told me I couldn't enter the station without a ticket.

*Continued ›*

«

Then it hit me: he was not a railway official, just an Italian man who felt entitled to get on the train without a ticket. As I protested, he turned and shouted, *"Sì, ma almeno questa è casa mia, non la tua"*—"Yes, but at least this is my home, and not yours. Go back to where you've come from."

I stood there, with no air in my lungs, for a moment that seemed to last forever, his horrible sentence pounding in my ears. *Non la tua*, not your home.

I don't know how I got home, but my uncontrollable sobs were loud enough to bring my favorite roommate, Maria Laura, to my room. She then treated me to lunch. But not just any lunch—an artichoke soup made by her grandmother, sent from her family in Puglia.

Every few months, Maria Laura, like all students who have migrated from southern regions, would receive an epic food package from home, containing all the imaginable provisions. Maria Laura's would also contain many jars of different soups made by her mother, grandmother, or an aunt. She would often put torn pieces of bread in the bottom of her bowl, sometimes with a few chunks of local cheese and olive oil, then pour the hot soup on top and drizzle on more oil.

The recipe that follows is just an imitation of that rustic artichoke soup that helped me feel at home on a day when home was nowhere to be found.

*Serves 4–6 as an appetizer, 2–3 as a main*

¼ cup (60 ml) olive oil
1 onion, diced
2 lb 4 oz (1 kg) potatoes, peeled and diced
1 lb 2 oz (500 g) fresh or frozen Roman or globe artichoke hearts, halved (or any leftover artichoke stalks from the salad on page 199)
2 teaspoons salt, plus more to taste
1 cup (250 ml) boiling water
freshly ground black pepper

For serving
a few cubes of semi-hard cheese such as asiago, provolone, or gouda, for each bowl
a small slice of crusty bread for each bowl, roughly torn
olive oil, for drizzling
finely chopped parsley, to garnish

Heat 2 tablespoons of the olive oil in a pot and sauté the onion over medium heat for about 10 minutes, until translucent. If needed, add a splash of water, as we want the onion to be nicely cooked before other ingredients are added.

Add the potatoes, artichokes, and 1 teaspoon of the salt. Pour in the boiling water, then cover and simmer gently for 1 hour.

When the potatoes and artichokes are very tender, blend the soup with a handheld immersion blender. You can decide how fine you want the texture; I like to leave some chunks of potato.

Add the remaining oil and salt. Check the seasoning, adding black pepper and more salt to taste.

For serving the Maria Laura way, put some cheese and bits of torn crusty bread (preferably stale) in the bottom of each bowl. Drizzle the bread with a little olive oil, then ladle the soup over the top. Drizzle with more olive oil, sprinkle with parsley, and serve immediately.

# Artichoke & potato salad

*Insalata di carciofi crudi e patate bollite*

The best artichokes—the romanesco type in Rome, and the globe variety in Tuscany—are at their prime in spring. They're also a favorite food during Lent. One well-known salad is simply raw sliced artichokes with shavings of parmesan, olive oil, and pepper. Add some boiled potatoes, as in the recipe below, and you have a weekday lunch or a weekend side dish that is especially popular for Sunday meals in the Italian countryside.

In summer, when artichokes are long gone, try the same recipe using blanched green beans instead, throwing in some black olives as well.

*Serves 4–6 as a side*

5–6 small potatoes, about
   1 lb 9 oz (700 g)
3 large fresh Roman or globe
   artichokes, or 5–6 small ones
juice of 1 lemon
2 pinches of salt
shaved parmesan or pecorino,
   to serve
3 tablespoons olive oil,
   for drizzling
freshly ground black pepper

Wash the potatoes well, leaving the skin on. Add the whole potatoes to a pot with enough water to cover them well. Bring to a boil, then cook until just tender but not collapsing; the time will vary based on the size and type of your potatoes. A toothpick should pierce them easily. Drain and leave to cool.

Meanwhile, trim the artichokes. Pull off all the hard external "petals," until you reach tender, soft petals. Using a sharp knife, chop and discard ¾–1¼ inches (2–3 cm) off the tip of each artichoke "flower." Cut the artichokes in half lengthways. Use a teaspoon to enlarge the inner heart of each artichoke and to scoop out and discard any hairy bits—a good, fresh, perfectly in-season artichoke won't have much. (You could trim off and very finely chop the fibrous external part of the stalk, too, but I suggest you keep the stalks for a soup, such as the one on page 195, or a risotto or pasta sauce.)

Now thinly slice each artichoke in half crossways. Gently open out the petals with your fingers and sprinkle the lemon juice on them, as well as a good pinch of salt.

Peel and dice the potatoes. Arrange them on a platter and sprinkle with another good pinch of salt. Arrange the artichokes on top, drizzling with any juices left in the bowl.

Scatter with parmesan or pecorino, drizzle with the olive oil, sprinkle with black pepper to taste, and serve.

# An appreciation
# of *aperitivo*

More than a drink, and the food next to it, *aperitivo* is a state of mind. Once, long ago, its whole purpose was to "open" the appetite for the main course by serving bitter and herby liquors, vegetables preserved in vinegar, cheeses, and sometimes charcuterie. You may wonder whether that crosses the borders of what we know today as *antipasto*. It does.

The modern *aperitivo* is much about the end of a workday, but not quite as late as dinner. You can have it at sophisticated places in office-dense neighborhoods of Milan and Rome, and you can have it at any small bar. Perhaps not as elaborately, and maybe even with something nonalcoholic, like a Crodino or a Sanbitter—the famous bitter, colorful drinks in iconic little bottles that have become known as the quintessential Italian touch at the table.

The recipes for this chapter are a little more playful, but remember, you can just uncork a bottle of wine (even around noon, as quite frequently happens in the region of Veneto, for example) and that would be a great *aperitivo*, too. Put a bowl of olives or chips next to it. The key to *aperitivo* is taking it with *leggerezza*, lightness. *Salute!*

# Timeless & easy: my three favorite aperitivo cocktails

## Spritz, the Classic

There has been a lot of inadequate enthusiasm, followed by an unfair backlash, toward spritz, but the truth is, a spritz is not really a cocktail. Rather than being a "serious" drink that relaxes you, or makes you light-headed in a sophisticated or over-joyous way, a spritz simply celebrates the end of the working day and the beginning of the *aperitivo* hour. It's a promise of what the coming evening can bring. That's why it is "watered down" and light. Austrian soldiers stationed in the Veneto region in the 1800s found the local wines too strong, so they would *spritzen* them—which means "to splash"—with sparkling water. Later, Aperol and another red bitters called Select were drunk the same way, becoming popular in the early twentieth century and giving birth to spritz.

A spritz should be an orange accessory you wear in your hand that doesn't leave a mark, other than enticing your appetite a bit. Whether you're chilling after work in a busy bar in Rome or in a neighborhood office in Milan, or on a beach getting ready for sundown, you don't order a spritz when you want to drink. You order a spritz when you want to nibble on something, or to signal it's time for relaxation to begin. *Leggerezza*, or lightness, is essential to a spritz—the mood, the alcohol level, the setting. As a personal preference, I always choose Campari over Aperol, but the world of ruby red bitters is vast and fabulous for you to select from.

Serve this classic spritz with any of the nibbles and small bites on page 207, or any recipe from this chapter. For a small crowd, multiply the measurements of the bitters and the sparkling wine in a pitcher at the moment of serving. Have glasses filled with ice on hand and fill them when ready to serve, topping each with sparkling water. Don't keep this mixture in the fridge, as the wine will lose its bubbles.

*Serves 1; multiply for more*

ice cubes
2 fl oz (60 ml/2 parts) Campari, Aperol, or other red-orange bitters of your choice
3 fl oz (90 ml/3 parts) prosecco or sparkling white wine, chilled
a splash of sparkling water
a slice of orange

Fill a large wine glass with ice cubes. Pour in the bitters, then the wine, and top with a splash of sparkling water. Slide the orange slice in and serve immediately.

*Pictured opposite, center*

# Negroni, the Bold

You either love negroni or hate it, but for me, a negroni is the drink of choice for both before and after dinner. There's no denying it is a strong drink; the sum of alcohol in it is outstanding, and the flavor profile is distinctly bitter with herby notes. Gin is my favorite spirit (see what I've done to a classic Iranian *sharbat* with vinegar syrup on page 120) and as someone who dislikes fruity, citrusy, egg-whitey cocktails, a negroni is always a safe choice. Since it only uses equal amounts of each ingredient, even the most inexpert bar attendant is unlikely to get it wrong.

Legend says the cocktail was born when Count Camillo Negroni wanted his Americano (vermouth, Campari, soda) to be stronger, and a barman swapped the soda water with gin—as you do! As cultures and recipes change over the years, variations have been spun on the negroni as well. *Negroni sbagliato*—the "wrong" negroni—uses prosecco instead of gin, and in a negroski, the gin is swapped for vodka.

Unlike a spritz, which you will barely notice you're drinking, a negroni asks for your full attention. Whenever an evening of casual *aperitivo* drags into dinner, or a long evening, I like to start with a good negroni, and then drink something lighter for the rest of the night, but in the same flavor profile—usually a spritz, as it hardly counts as a drink. If I'm feeling particularly in a drinking mood, I'll continue with a *negroni sbagliato* instead of a spritz.

A negroni needs to be sipped slowly, because it's strong, so it is best enjoyed with a substantial choice of *aperitivos* from this chapter, such as the crostini with lardo and figs on page 221 or the polenta bites with porcini on page 216.

It's unlikely that you will serve a negroni to an entire crowd (in my experience only a few say yes as it's so high in alcohol), but you can multiply the ingredients in a small pitcher and chill it in the fridge; just fill your glasses with ice and pour the cocktail over as needed.

*Serves 1; multiply for more*

ice cubes
1 fl oz (30 ml/1 part) gin
1 fl oz (30 ml/1 part) red
  vermouth
1 fl oz (30 ml/1 part) bitters,
  such as Campari
a slice of orange

First, chill an old-fashioned glass with ice cubes. Discard any excess water. Pour in the gin, vermouth, and bitters and stir. Garnish with a slice of orange and serve.

*Pictured on page 202, right*

# Bellini, the Peachy

A bellini is "simply" crushed-down peaches topped with prosecco. The fact that you can mix peach pulp with sparkling wine and call it a cocktail with its own name must be one of the best things about life—something straight out of that scene in *Fantasia*, with Bacchus drinking and making wine with satyrs and centaurs and centaurettes. In reality, however, the cocktail was famously created at Henry's Bar in Venice by Giuseppe Cipriani in 1948.

And yet it reminds me of those times in Iran when we would inject a huge watermelon with almost an entire bottle of precious vodka, smuggled from the black market, and then eat the watermelon slice by slice—sometimes by a pool in the countryside.

The bellini has some variations too; replace the peaches with strawberries and you have a *rossini*. The famous mimosa is of course another variation that substitutes peaches for fresh orange juice— giving a whole new meaning to our Sunday mornings when we're allowed to drink at 11 a.m. in the name of brunch—and if you make it with pomegranates, it's called a *tintoretto*.

Basically, add prosecco or sparkling wine to fruit pulp or juice and you'll have a fantastic drink. As Italians say, it's like "inventing hot water"—meaning it's too obvious. But while the principle may be elementary, the result is undeniably delectable.

Serve for a small crowd with something light and delicate for an early *aperitivo*, possibly followed by a summer dinner. You can make the peach purée a day or two ahead and keep it in the fridge. If you're making the peach purée close to serving time, cool it briefly in the freezer so it's properly chilled.

*Serves 6–8*

4 white peaches
750 ml (25 fl oz) bottle of
 prosecco or other white
 sparkling wine, chilled

Start by preparing the peach purée. Using a sharp knife, score a cross on the bottom of each peach. Dunk them in a bowl or pot of boiling water for just 20 seconds, then immediately pass them under cold running water.

Peel the peaches by simply pulling off the skin from the incision. Remove the pits, then purée the flesh in a blender or food processor. If you're not making it in advance, freeze the purée for 10–20 minutes to ensure it's properly chilled, as the bellini needs to be cold.

Pour some peach purée into each champagne flute to one-third full, then fill the glass up to half with sparkling wine and stir to mix well. Top up with more wine to the brim, being careful not to spill. Serve immediately.

*Pictured on page 202, left*

# Nibbles & small bites next to those cocktails

There are no specific rules about what to munch on while enjoying an *aperitivo* cocktail. The general idea is that you can serve any small thing with your drink, but below is a list of nibbles and bites that you're most likely to find in Italy. To serve your own *aperitivo*, choose any of the suggestions below, or any of the recipes in this chapter.

A small bowl of potato chips—yes, banal, you might say. But would you really claim you wouldn't enjoy that next to your spritz (page 203)?

A small bowl of salted peanuts—okay, this is by no means fancy, but it's still quite frequent. For a more sophisticated option, make the saffron-toasted pistachios and almonds on pages 111–112.

Olives—any kind. Serve with toothpicks on the side, with an extra little bowl for the pits.

Taralli (page 210) and other wonderful baked Italian snacks.

Pizzette and little squares of *pizza bianca* and/or *pizza rossa*. Sourced from a *forno* (bakery), these delicious bakes—which are good even when a bit stale, as they often are in unpretentious neighborhood bars—are favorites at both children's birthday parties and adult *aperitivos*.

Any pickles or *sotto aceti*. Whether it's tiny pickled onions, or little bell peppers stuffed with tuna, or delicate artichoke hearts preserved in olive oil, those beauties stored in jars are always welcome at an *aperitivo* table.

All the glorious cheeses—from little mozzarella bites, or *bocconcini*, to tiny cubes of parmesan, slices of taleggio, and chunks of the local pecorino. Unsurprisingly, a variety of cheeses can even be the star of an *aperitivo* table, especially when the drink of choice is wine. It is always a thrill to go to a small Italian town and find the words *selezione dei formaggi locali* ("selection of local cheeses") written in chalk outside a bar, next to their *aperitivo* offer. Some of these cheeses are accompanied with fruit preserves. I must say, this, with a glass of wine, is my favorite type of *aperitivo*.

All the *salumi*—prosciutto, salame, capocollo, salsiccette, speck, cured meats, and charcuterie—are naturally welcome at the *aperitivo* table, as well as the famous chicken liver pâté in Tuscany. As with the cheeses, local varieties are praised and are a point of discovery in each town.

Fresh fruit—pears with cheese, melon pieces with slices of prosciutto, fresh figs, grapes, and even peaches—especially when cheese and/or cold meats are present.

# Deep-fried artichoke wedges

*Frittura di carciofi*

As often mentioned in this chapter, the origin of several beloved Italian dishes lies in Jewish culinary traditions. These recipes were born not only out of observing the rules of *kashrut* (being kosher) but also from the discrimination Jewish people faced as outcasts in a Christian society that limited their access to ingredients and forced them to use those that were considered "low" (as explained in the eggplant parmigiana recipe on page 243). Not everyone knows that dishes like fried zucchini blossoms, fried zucchini in the *concia* style, *caponata* with eggplant, and even the original version of the Tuscan *cacciucco* fish soup—which used only cheap, small fish and no shellfish—sprang from Jewish tradition but are now loved as quintessentials of Italian cuisine.

One dish that has never forgotten its Jewish ties is the deliciously famous *carciofo alla giudia*—literally "Jewish-style artichoke"—which has been served on the streets of Rome since at least the 1500s and consists simply of twice-fried whole artichokes. While arguably the recipe that follows has little to do with that, the tradition of frying vegetables—especially zucchini and artichokes—is quintessentially (Roman) Jewish as well.

Of the many fried things that can appear next to an effervescent drink at sunset hour, fried artichokes are probably my favorite—but please don't make me choose between them and fried anchovies, or zucchini, or homemade fries.

*Serves 4–6 as an aperitivo*

1 lemon, cut into wedges
6 fresh artichokes (see Note)
1 cup (250 ml) oil, for frying
scant 1 cup (100 g) all-purpose flour
scant 1 cup (200 ml) chilled water
a good pinch of salt, plus extra for sprinkling
grated parmesan or pecorino, for sprinkling (optional)

Rub the lemon wedges over your fingers, then squeeze the juice into a bowl of water, tossing the lemon wedges in as well. Remove the fibrous outer bits from the artichoke stems, and where the "petals" meet the stem, pull off the hard petals until you reach tender, soft petals. Cut away the fibrous outer parts of the stalks too. Using a sharp knife, cut off and discard 1¼–1½ inches (3–4 cm) from the top of each "flower." Cut each artichoke in half and run the knife around it to remove the hairy center. Cut each artichoke half into two or more wedges and keep them in the bowl of water with the lemon to avoid oxidation and browning.

Heat the oil over high heat in a small, deep pot in which the artichoke wedges can be completely submerged in hot oil.

While the oil heats, make a batter by mixing together the flour, cold water, and a pinch of salt.

Line a dish with paper towels. (At this point you could also open a bottle of sparkling wine, so you can fry and drink—but carefully. It's best to have this *aperitivo* right next to the stove, company included.)

Working in batches, completely dry the artichoke wedges with a clean tea towel, as any water in them will make the hot oil spit. Dip each wedge into the batter, letting any excess batter drip away before carefully adding to the hot oil. When the artichokes rise to the top of the oil and the batter is pale golden—which shouldn't take more than a minute—fish them out with a slotted spoon. Drain briefly on paper towels and serve immediately, sprinkled with more salt and perhaps some grated parmesan.

**Note:** Instead of fresh artichokes, you can use frozen artichoke wedges. Working in batches, briefly submerge them directly into the batter, allow the extra batter to drip off, then gently drop into the hot oil. They might take slightly more time to fry.

*Pictured on page 213, center*

# Taralli with chile flakes or fennel seeds

From mid-Italy southward, whenever a glass of something a bit bitter or boozy is offered, it's quite probable that a small bowl of taralli pops out of a cabinet to go with your drink. It's such a merry duo that there's even a proverb about it: *finire a tarallucci e vino*—"ending up with taralli and wine," which means that a dispute has ended amiably.

Nowadays, few people make their own taralli, as it requires a patience that rarely matches our time. Essentially, taralli are a form of bread, kneaded with wine and olive oil, and mixed with seeds or spices. Taralli come in all sizes, but my friend Fiammetta from Puglia, where the best taralli can be found, says they should be as large as the diameter of a small wineglass. Fiammetta, who just turned 80, told me that, as a reward for being a good girl, her grandmother would give her one *tarallo*—sometimes even two—from a terracotta container that was locked in a closet.

The process of boiling and baking them is similar to making bagels, but unlike bagels, the whole point of boiling the taralli, drying them completely, and then baking them is to get a perfectly crunchy and friable result.

*Makes 1 big jar*

2 cups (250 g) all-purpose flour
5 tablespoons olive oil
1 teaspoon salt, plus extra for
    seasoning the cooking water
scant ½ cup (100 ml) white wine
1 tablespoon chile flakes or
    fennel seeds (or a mix of both)

In a stand mixer (or alternatively, in a large bowl) combine the flour, oil, salt, and half the wine. When the mixture kind of comes together, add the remaining wine, and the fennel seeds or chile flakes. Knead the dough for 5–10 minutes, either in the mixer or by hand, until it all comes together.

Bring a large pot of water to a boil, and line two trays with clean tea towels.

Meanwhile, take small pieces of the dough, about the size of a hazelnut. With the palm of your hand, roll each out on a work surface into a thin sausage about 3¼ inches (8 cm) long and less than ½ inch (1 cm) thick. Roll each sausage around your pinky finger, and pinch one end on top of the other, into a circle. (I like small taralli, aka *tarallucci*; you can make them larger, which will take less time.) Continue with all the dough and arrange on a platter.

Season the boiling water with salt. Working in batches, so the taralli don't stick to each other, gently lower them into the water a few at a time. When they come to the surface (it shouldn't take more than a few minutes), fish them out with a slotted spoon and leave to drain on the lined trays.

Leave the taralli to dry uncovered at room temperature for at least 5 hours, ideally overnight. This resting time is the secret to friable taralli, which is their characteristic feature. For best results, turn the taralli around about halfway through, so both sides dry in equal measure.

Preheat the oven to 450°F (230°C). Line one or two baking sheets with parchment paper, and arrange the taralli on them; you can fit them quite snugly as they won't rise. Bake for 30–35 minutes, until golden, then turn the oven off and leave to rest in the oven for another 10 minutes.

Once cooled down, the taralli will keep for days (but I bet you'll see to that). It's better not to store them in an airtight container, as they might become soft.

*Pictured on page 212, center*

# Batter-fried pears & pecorino

Serving cheese with pears is such a classic combination in Italy that no one stops to wonder how this came to be. Its real origin, as explained extensively in the pears poached in wine recipe on page 258, is an ancient medical belief that raw fruits are too "moist and cold," so they should be consumed with something "dry and warm"—such as cheese.

Fascinatingly, serving cheese with pears even has its own proverb: *Al contadino non far sapere, quanto è buono il cacio con le pere*—"Don't let the peasants know how good cheese with pears is." Frankly, I have always found the attempt in this proverb to keep knowledge, and therefore power, from poor farmers disturbing. And given that cheese has been the food of villagers for centuries, it is hard to believe farmers were not aware that cheese and pears are great together.

Setting considerations of social and economic class aside, we can now do a little experiment, by frying the cheese and pears—a combo I tasted in Florence. For this to work, you need Pecorino Toscano or a similar semi-hard cheese that hasn't been aged for long. It shouldn't be too salty or too hard. In Rome they sometimes serve fried pieces of apple or pear topped with shaved Pecorino Romano. The concept is the same, but the result is drastically different.

The different coatings for the pears and cheese is fundamental here. You need the batter on the pears to be light, and the crumbing to be consistent all over the cheese, otherwise it will ooze in the hot oil—and trust me, this is the last thing you want. Remember that all things taste better when fried, "even shoe soles," as Romans say. As usual with fried things, I suggest a bubbly beverage alongside.

*Serves 4–6 as an aperitivo*

oil, for frying

### For the cheese
9 oz (250 g) Pecorino Toscano, or other semi-hard, not too sharp cheese, such as gouda or fontina (but not Pecorino Romano)
1 egg
½ cup (50 g) dry breadcrumbs
salt and freshly ground black pepper

Cut the cheese into 1½ inch (4 cm) squares, about ½ inch (1 cm) thick. Beat the egg in a bowl with 1 tablespoon water. Put the breadcrumbs on a plate and season with salt and black pepper. Coat each cheese slice generously in the egg mixture, then the breadcrumbs, making sure all parts are coated. Pass the cheese once more into the beaten egg, then the breadcrumbs.

In a small pan deep enough for the cheese pieces to be completely submerged, heat the oil over high heat. Line a dish with paper towels, and have a pair of tongs ready.

Once the oil is hot, carefully dunk the cheese pieces into the hot oil, and be ready to fish them straight out again after a few seconds, as soon as they rise to the top. Drain in the lined dish, but DO NOT eat straight away, as the melted cheese will be very hot and can burn you.

**For the pears**
scant ½ cup (50 g) all-purpose
    flour
scant ½ cup (100 ml) water
a pinch of salt
2 pears, cored, halved, and cut
    into ¼ inch (5 mm) thick slices

Next, prepare the pears. Make a loose batter with the flour, water, and salt and drop in several pear slices, making sure they're well coated but letting the excess batter drip off into the bowl before carefully easing them into the hot oil. The pears will take a bit more time to fry, but you'll know they're ready when they rise to the surface; they will only ever turn a very pale shade of gold. Fish out the fried pears.

Once you've finished all the frying, there shouldn't be any risk of burning anyone's mouth, so place one piece of fried pear on top of a piece of fried cheese and serve immediately, possibly with a negroni (page 204), a spritz (page 203), or sparkling wine.

*Pictured on page 213, bottom*

# Fried polenta bites with porcini mushrooms

*Polenta fritta con i funghi porcini*

Polenta is a fascinating food that has fed humans since at least ancient Roman times. The concept was simple—grains of cereal pounded and refined almost to a dust (in Latin, *pollen*—"fine flour"—and *pulvis*, "dust" or "powder"), then cooked with water to form a thick porridge that went by the name of *puls* or *pulentum*. Back then, this peasant dish was made mostly with farro, and later with rye and other less-refined grains. Modern polenta, which is predominantly made with corn, is, of course, the result of the colonization of the Americas and the introduction of corn to the Old World.

Polenta is now mostly consumed in the northern parts of Italy, especially the mountain areas, and it is classically served with *ragù*, sausages, or a selection of mushrooms. It's a hearty dish that warms up crowds, as it's often served on a large board in the middle of the table. Quite a treat to come back home to on cold winter days.

I am not the biggest fan of polenta served that way, but I could eat a million of these little deep-fried polenta bites. What's more, they somehow taste like my favorite corn-puff snack from my childhood, called *pofak namaki*.

For this recipe, look for quick-cooking fine polenta. Or, if you can get your hands on it, you can use ready-made polenta that is sold in little blocks and used for grilling, in which case just cut them into small pieces for deep-frying.

You can top these polenta bites with anything you like, but they work particularly well with ingredients polenta is traditionally served with—hence the mushrooms here. This version is completely plant-based, but gorgonzola or other types of blue cheese would taste wonderful with this combo as well.

As with most fried things, these snacks are a joy when served with chilled bubbles. They're also great with a nice white wine, possibly from Alto Adige or other parts of northern Italy.

*Makes about 8 canapés*

## For the mushroom topping
¾–1 oz (20–30 g) dried porcini
    mushrooms, approximately
1 tablespoon olive oil
1 garlic clove, peeled
a handful of good fresh
    mushrooms (such as fresh
    porcini, or even buttons),
    cleaned and sliced thinly
a splash of white vinegar
salt and freshly ground black
    pepper

## For the fried polenta
1 teaspoon salt
⅔ cup (100 g) quick-cooking
    fine polenta cornmeal
oil, for frying

Soak the porcini mushrooms in warm water for 10–15 minutes to rehydrate them.

For the polenta, bring about 1½ cups (350 ml) water to a boil in a small saucepan (check the package instructions for the precise ratio of water needed). Add the salt. Slowly pour in the polenta ("rain" it in, as Italians say), while stirring vigorously all the time. Cook according to the package instructions (usually 8–10 minutes for this quantity), until nice and thick; a bit thicker than usual is okay, since we won't be serving it hot with a sauce. Spread the polenta on a plate in a single ¾ inch (2 cm) layer and let it cool completely.

For the topping, heat the olive oil in a small sauté pan with the garlic clove over medium-high heat. Drain the porcini and roughly chop, then add to the hot pan with the fresh mushrooms. Cook for 2–3 minutes, or until the liquid is absorbed, then add the vinegar and cook a little more. Set aside, discarding the garlic clove. Season with salt and black pepper.

Heat the oil for frying over high heat. (I like to use a small pot for these bites to use less oil, but it needs to be deep enough to completely submerge the polenta pieces.)

Using a sharp knife, slice the polenta into 1½ inch (4 cm) squares. Fry each polenta bite for 1½–2 minutes, until golden and crispy on both sides. Set on a dish lined with paper towels to absorb the excess oil.

Spoon some of the mushrooms on top of each polenta bite. Arrange on a nice plate, and serve immediately, with something boozy and possibly bubbly.

*Pictured on page 212, top*

# Oranges & anchovies

Food has traveled whenever people have, conquering or being conquered. The south of Italy and Spain are home to citrus fruits galore due to the Arabs, who brought them in the Middle Ages, together with cane sugar, eggplant, and other foods. Centuries later, it's impossible to imagine Sicily or Andalusia without oranges, or the Amalfi coast without lemons—but these foods were once culinary aliens.

The little dish that follows is not really a recipe; I could be melodramatic (it's a tendency of mine) and call it a love letter to Sicily. To me it's a jubilation of flavors—sweet and acidic orange, the explosive saltiness and fishiness of anchovies, and the pungent pepperiness of extra virgin olive oil. It's also exactly the kind of intense combination that tickles the appetite with an *aperitivo* drink. Naturally, with only three ingredients, one of them being anchovies, this dish is a delight for anchovy lovers only. When I was first served it many years ago, I was a long way away from being an anchovy lover, but good anchovies from Sicily helped completely transform me. Now I could live off toasted bread with butter and anchovies. Imagine a hot sunset by the Mediterranean, sipping on something chilled and boozy. With these colors and flavors, it's hard not to. This dish also works well as an appetizer for a nice seafood dinner, and looks even more stunning when made using one regular orange and one blood orange.

*Serves 4–6 as an aperitivo*

3 salted anchovies or
   6 anchovy fillets in oil
2 oranges
1–2 tablespoons good-quality
   olive oil

If you're using salted anchovies, clean them under cold running water, rubbing off the silver scales. Remove the spine, then discard the tail and other bits, to be left with two fillets. Leave them on a dish lined with paper towels and pat dry.

Cut the tops and the bottoms off the oranges, then sit them upright on a chopping board. Run a sharp knife around the outside from top to bottom, in a slightly curved motion, to completely remove the orange peel and pith and only be left with the flesh. Remove any white bits that may be left. Now cut the oranges crossways into nice discs. Arrange them on a large plate or a platter.

Arrange the anchovy fillets nicely on top. You could halve each fillet for practicality, but it's prettier if they're whole. Drizzle with the olive oil. Serve with toasted bread, with a drink for *aperitivo*, or as an *amuse-bouche* for a nice dinner.

# Crostini with lardo, figs & honey

*Crostini di lardo, fichi e miele*

*Aprire* means to open; *aperitivo* is something that opens. For many centuries, the idea of "opening" meals with *salumi*, bread, dried fruit (especially figs), and wine belonged to the peasants. This habit was later adopted by restaurants in the form of antipasto, when the new bourgeoisie could afford to dine out. This simple dish of crostini with lardo and dried figs looks quite medieval, from a time when the Germanic culture of pork products fused with those iconic symbols of Mediterranean agriculture—bread, olive oil, and wine.

The first thing to say about this delight is that you shouldn't confuse *lardo* with lard. *Lardo* is pork back fat, cured with herbs and spices (especially pepper). One of the most highly prized is from the town of Colonnata in Tuscany, which enjoys Protected Geographical Indication status and is registered on the Ark of Taste heritage foods catalog. The next thing to say is that *lardo* is a treat, so don't fear the fat.

*Lardo* has long been enjoyed with figs and honey. If using fresh figs, squash them and drizzle them with honey. If using dried figs, you will only need a little honey.

You can have these crostini at any time of the day as a *merenda* (midday snack), preferably with red wine—perhaps a fruity new one in late summer or early fall, when using fresh figs. Or sip a deep, rich red when using dried figs in the heart of winter

*Serves 4–6 as an aperitivo*

6 small slices of bread, about
   1¼ inches (4 cm) across and
   ½ inch (1 cm) thick
3 slices of lardo (about
   1½ oz/40 g), cut in half
2 fresh figs, quartered, or
   3–4 dried figs, cut in half
honey, for drizzling
thyme leaves, to garnish

Preheat the oven to 425°F (220°C) and toast the bread slices for 3–5 minutes to get them hot. Remove from the oven and immediately top each with half a slice of lardo, then the figs.

Drizzle a little honey on top; I use a lot less honey when using dried figs, as they're very sweet.

Sprinkle with thyme and serve immediately.

# Il pranzo della domenica
# & other celebrations

The recipes in this chapter are meant to feed a small crowd on a special occasion. The structure of a traditional celebratory feast in Italy is a five-course meal consisting of *antipasto, primo, secondo, contro*, and *dolce*—and can take hours, turning events such as weddings, where different types of each dish are served, into a long, slow torture.

There's truth to that endearing yet slightly clichéd image of a *nonna* making thousands of tortellini by hand to be cooked in *brodo* (broth) for Christmas lunch. Usually women work for days to put the perfect lunch on the table.

I have intentionally avoided this model. I prefer to serve two side dishes and one substantial main dish. Appetizers could be cheese (and fresh fruit), with a simple dessert at the end. I think the celebration should be fun and easy for the host, too.

Until not long ago, serving a large piece of meat such as an *arrosto* or entire bird was something reserved only for Sundays and special occasions. This is a sustainable model we should consider as well, given the state of our planet.

# Rustic savory pies, two ways

*Torta rustica / salata*

Like most of my other Italian home-cooking experiences, I first discovered the world of savory pies—*torta rustica*—when I was sharing an apartment with other students, most of whom were from southern Italy. I soon learned that a savory pie is a cheap and easy way of preparing food for a small crowd, an excellent way to consume all the odd bits of vegetables and cheese remaining in the fridge, and a great dish to bring to a picnic or a party. We always used the ready-made puff pastry from the supermarket, and I still do sometimes—but these days I search for one containing only butter and no funny vegetable fats. The rustic pies, like the homemade *ragùs* or lasagnes, were of course the best when the parents of said roommates would visit and bring us all food.

There are many, many versions and regional varieties of savory pies, going by the names of *torte salate*, *torte rustiche,* or even *pizza ripiena*, depending on where you are in the *bel paese*.

In Italy, it's traditional to make these pies around Lent and Easter, when fresh spring vegetables abound, in particular spinach and artichokes, but you could use any greens in your *torta rustica*, as it's a celebration of spring—in the same way that the herby frittata *kuku sabzi* and other herb-laden dishes in Iran are made for Norouz and the arrival of spring.

Some of these rustic pies are crustless, such as the potato one that follows. There are also cakes that look like sweet bundt cake but are made with cheese and stuffed with more cheese and eggs. These are popular in parts of central Italy, such as Le Marche. The crustless potato pie was one that the mother of a particularly tedious roommate once brought him. This (and the fact that he opened a jar of preserved mushrooms with a slab of cheese every afternoon, announcing "*Facciamo aperitivo!*") is the only way I got through the trauma of sharing an apartment with this epitome of a bad roommate. While his mother didn't quite teach me the recipe, she did give me an oral account of it—among many praises for her beloved son, whom she declared had always loved this cake and needed its health-giving energy for the studying he never did.

For the spinach pie, I use a classic *pasta brisée* (shortcrust) pastry, which sounds and tastes like many other French influences on Neapolitan cuisine.

*Continued ›*

## The crustless one with potato, eggs & cheese

*Makes an 8–8½ inch*
*(20–22 cm) pie;*
*serves 4–6*

2 lb 4 oz (1 kg) potatoes
3½ oz (100 g) pecorino or
　parmesan, grated
2 tablespoons finely
　chopped parsley
½ teaspoon salt, plus extra
　for sprinkling
freshly ground black pepper
3 tablespoons butter, softened
2 tablespoons dry breadcrumbs
4 hard-boiled eggs, peeled and
　cut in half lengthways
3½–5½ oz (100–150 g) dry, spicy
　salami, diced
3½ oz (100 g) provolone, fontina,
　or cheddar, diced

Wash the potatoes well, leaving the skin on. Place the whole potatoes in a pot with enough water to cover them well. Bring to a boil, then cook until a toothpick can spear them easily. Drain, then leave until just cool enough to handle.

Meanwhile, preheat the oven to 350°F (180°C).

Peel the potatoes, then mash them in a bowl. Mix in the pecorino, parsley, salt, and a few generous sprinkles of black pepper.

Use half the butter to generously grease the bottom and sides of an 8–8½ inch (20–22 cm) pie dish. Dust the dish with half the breadcrumbs, swirling them all around and tapping underneath to make sure it's all well coated, so the pie doesn't stick.

Spread half the mashed potatoes in the bottom of the dish, evening it out. With the back of a spoon, push eight regularly spaced indents into the mash, around the dish, to make spaces for the eggs.

Sprinkle the eggs with salt and place one half, cut side down, into each indent. It should look like a simple daisy flower now. Evenly scatter the diced salami and cheese around, pushing them lightly into the mash. Cover with the remaining mash, using your hands to make an even surface and filling out the edges.

Dust the surface with the remaining breadcrumbs, then dot the remaining butter around. Bake for 20 minutes, then cook for another 10 minutes under the broiler for a golden crust.

Remove from the oven and let the pie cool in the pie dish for at least 30 minutes, before carefully transferring to a chopping board and slicing.

Serve simply with a green salad or spring vegetables; the pie is also incredibly good with *peperonata* (page 193), and is also exquisite cold the next day, perhaps for a picnic.

*Pictured on page 225*

# The one with shortcrust pastry, spinach & ricotta

*Makes a 9½–10½ inch
(24–26 cm) pie;
serves 6–8*

**For the filling**
1½ cups (350 g) ricotta
1–2 tablespoons olive oil
2 garlic cloves, peeled
approximately 14 oz (400 g)
    spinach leaves, or 7 oz
    (200 g) frozen spinach
1 egg
⅓ cup (30 g) grated parmesan
zest of ½ lemon
¼ a whole nutmeg, grated
1 teaspoon salt
freshly ground black pepper

**For the pastry**
3 cups (350 g) all-purpose flour
a pinch of salt
¾ cup (175 g) very cold butter,
    diced
½ cup (120 ml) very cold water

**For the egg wash**
1 egg, well beaten with a splash
    of water

Start with the filling. Place the ricotta in a small colander perched over a bowl and set aside for at least 30 minutes, to drain its excess water. Don't skip this step; a soggy filling will make the bottom crust gummy.

For the pastry, toss the flour in a large bowl with the salt and butter, pinching each piece of butter between your thumbs and index fingers, until you get a sandy texture. (Alternatively, you can pulse the butter and flour in a food processor—but don't over-blend.) Gradually add the ice-cold water and bring the dough together. Do not overwork the dough; there is no need for kneading.

Shape the dough into two unequal balls, using about one-third for one piece and two-thirds for the other. Flatten each one into a ¾ inch (2 cm) thick disc. Cover with plastic wrap and rest in the fridge for 30–60 minutes.

When ready to start baking, preheat the oven to 400°F (200°C).

Meanwhile, continue with the filling. Heat the oil in a pot over medium heat and add the garlic cloves. When fragrant, add the spinach. Cover and cook fresh spinach for 5–7 minutes, until wilted; give frozen spinach more time to fully cook. Discard the garlic and squeeze the spinach over a bowl to get rid of the excess water. (You can keep the spinach water to use in cooking within the day, or drink it right away. It's packed with the good stuff!) Chop the spinach, place it in a large bowl, and mix it thoroughly with the drained ricotta. Add the remaining filling ingredients, mixing until well combined. Season to taste with black pepper and set aside.

Roll out the larger disc of dough between two sheets of parchment paper, so it is slightly larger than the diameter of a 9½–10½ inch (24–26 cm) pie dish. Leaving it sandwiched between the two sheets, ease the dough into the pie dish. Peel away and keep the top paper sheet. Push the dough into the dish, filling out any gaps at the side with any overhanging pieces of dough. Cut off the overhanging parchment paper from around the rim.

*Continued ›*

«

Poke holes into the bottom of the crust with a fork. Ideally, chill the pie dish with the crust in the fridge for 10 minutes, before adding the filling to the dish.

Meanwhile, roll out the remaining piece of dough between two sheets of parchment paper (including the one you saved earlier). When the dough is just as large as the top of the dish, peel off the top paper sheet and invert the dough over the filling. Peel off the second sheet of paper, too. Pinch the bottom and top pastry edges together to seal them. Close any gaps with bits of dough.

Brush the top of the pie with the egg wash. Bake for 40–45 minutes, or until dark golden on top.

Remove from the oven and let the pie rest in the dish for at least 20 minutes before cutting. I always leave it in the pie dish (a nice one), but you can transfer the pie to a serving plate if you prefer.

This pie tastes even more marvelous the next day.

**Note:** You can make the pastry ahead and rest it in the fridge for several hours, or even overnight. Let it sit at room temperature for 5 minutes before rolling it out for assembling the pie.

# Stuffed artichokes, Sicilian style

*Carciofi ripieni alla siciliana*

Stuffed vegetables—*dolmeh, dolma, mehshi, gemista, ripieni,* and so on—are testimony to the undeniable culinary connection that pervades the vast region spanning Central Asia, the Middle East and the Levant, through to the Mediterranean and the gates of Europe. Claudia Roden, in her *New Book of Middle Eastern Food,* calls stuffed artichokes "an old Arab dish." Like most of the stuffed vegetables of the Middle East, Roden's stuffed artichokes speak of abundance: her recipe uses lamb in the stuffing, and Turks call meatless stuffed vegetables (like the stuffed bell peppers on pages 145–148) not *dolma,* but *yalanchi*—meaning "liar," a fake *dolma*!

*Continued ›*

«

In the Mediterranean, the fillings in stuffed vegetables are a lot simpler than in the East. In Italy, stuffed artichokes and eggplant were historically associated with poverty, looked down upon as the food of the Jewish community and the lower classes. In the last few centuries, artichokes have become more mainstream, with Pellegrino Artusi in his 1891 cookbook writing of the Tuscan bourgeoisie enjoying artichokes stuffed with fatty ham, garlic, and herbs.

These artichokes are stuffed essentially with stale bread reduced to crumbs. Additional elements are sought to give the bread flavor—anchovies, garlic, butter—but the heart of the stuffing is truly the bread. Combining these flavors with pine nuts and raisins is typically Sicilian, with nudges toward the flavors of nearby North Africa and Tripoline Jewish cuisine.

*Serves 4–6 as a main,*
*8–10 as an appetizer*

8 large fresh globe artichokes
juice of 1 lemon
chopped parsley, to garnish
 (optional)

## For the filling
7 tablespoons (100 g) butter
5–6 anchovy fillets, chopped
1¾ cups (200 g) dry
 breadcrumbs
zest of 1 lemon
1 large garlic clove, finely
 chopped or grated
1 tablespoon olive oil
½ teaspoon salt, plus extra
 for sprinkling
¼ cup (40 g) pine nuts
¼ cup (50 g) raisins
1 small potato, peeled (optional)

## For the poaching water
1½ teaspoons salt
1 cup (250 ml) water
1 cup (250 ml) white wine
 (or water)
2 tablespoons olive oil

Start by cleaning the artichokes. Remove the woody outer "petals," until you get to the tender, soft ones. Cut off the stems (you can trim these, then finely slice and use in risottos and pasta sauces, or the soup on page 195). Chop off and discard the tip of the artichokes' "flower" as well. Lightly bash them on a chopping board so that the "flower" opens out a bit, then prize it open further with your hands. Squeeze the lemon juice into a large bowl of water and let the artichokes soak in the acidulated water until you're ready to cook, so they don't discolor.

To make the filling, mash the butter and anchovy fillets in a bowl, into a soft paste. Mix in the breadcrumbs, lemon zest, garlic, olive oil, salt, pine nuts, and raisins.

Find a heavy-based pot or Dutch oven in which all the artichokes will fit snugly. Remove the artichokes from the lemony water, lightly pat them dry, and gently prize the petals open without breaking them. Sprinkle the insides with some extra salt, then spoon in some of the filling, not just into the center but also between some of the petals. Gently squeeze the artichokes between the palms of both hands to close them a little.

Arrange the artichokes upright in the pot. If there's any space left between the artichokes, you can fit in a small peeled potato to make sure they stay upright.

For the poaching water, dissolve the salt in the water, in a large bowl. Mix in the wine (or extra water) and olive oil. Very gently pour this into the cooking pot, from the side.

Put the lid on and bring to a boil. Reduce the heat and simmer, covered, for 45 minutes to 1 hour, until the artichokes are very tender.

Serve at room temperature, garnished with parsley if desired.

*Pictured on page 229*

# (An ode to) *Pasta al pomodoro*: bucatini "marinated" in tomatoes

*Pasta al pomodoro*—pasta with tomatoes—is so deeply rooted in the imagery and identity of Italy that it's difficult to imagine how relatively "new" this simple dish truly is.

In his delightful book *A Short History of Spaghetti with Tomato Sauce*, Massimo Montanari, an Italian historian specializing in food and medieval agriculture, tells us the thrilling tale of how what we currently know as spaghetti finds its roots in a Sicily dominated by Arabs in the eleventh century; how that whole story about Marco Polo bringing back noodles from his travels to China is "fake news"; how the dawn of industrialization transformed Neapolitans from *mangiafoglie* ("leaf eaters") into *mangiamaccheroni* ("macaroni eaters"); how not until the early 1800s was pasta ever dressed with tomato sauce; and how it is due to the Tuscan Pellegrino Artusi and his celebrated cookbook, *Science in the Kitchen and the Art of Eating Well*, published only a few short decades after the unification of Italy, that tomato sauce found its way into all Italian kitchens in the twentieth century.

Today, there's another side to the story of tomatoes. In all the years that I have lived here, not one summer has gone by without the news of a day laborer dying under the scorching sun of the south while picking tomatoes. In fact, according to a 2020 report, in six years 1,500 workers died while picking tomatoes and other produce in Italian fields. These seasonal workers (*braccianti*) are often immigrants, invisible in a system that seems designed to keep them vulnerable, making them easy prey for local organized crime and the *caporalato* mob that recruits them. These *braccianti* are paid as little as €1–3 per hour, and live in undignified camps (sometimes even called "ghettos") unfit for human habitation, where they risk being mugged, assaulted, and even murdered, ironically often by the same local mob that recruits human flesh in exchange for crates of produce.

Tomatoes, these miraculous balls of sunshine come at a high price, often paid in modern slavery, organized crime, and even blood. This story needs to change.

This recipe is from my dear friend Fiammetta, a true *nonna* from the south of Italy, who first cooked this dish for me with tomatoes from her garden in Puglia many years ago. The dish is unusual in several ways. Perhaps the most remarkable is that the pasta—and it must be bucatini—is never cooked. Instead, it is left to "marinate" between layers of sliced tomatoes before being baked— hence the name *bucatini alla crudaiola*, or "raw bucatini." Those of us not blessed with sun-ripened tomatoes from the garden should aim for the best-quality tomatoes at the peak of summer, as this dish sings with the essence of tomatoes. It's also a convenient and cheerful way to feed a crowd.

*Continued ›*

«

*Makes a 9 x 13 inch*
*(23 x 33 cm) pan; serves 4–6*

approximately 2 lb 12 oz
   (1.25 kg) tomatoes, the best
   quality you can get
⅔ cup (80 g) dry breadcrumbs
½ cup (125 ml) extra virgin
   olive oil, plus an extra
   2 tablespoons for drizzling
½ large onion (about
   2¾ oz/80 g), or a few
   scallions, sliced
a handful of basil leaves
   and/or other fresh herbs
3 teaspoons salt
9–12 oz (250–350 g) bucatini,
   depending on the size of
   your pan

Using a serrated knife, and taking care to retain as much of the tomato juice as possible (as this is the main flavor of the dish), slice each tomato lengthways, less than ½ inch (1 cm) thick.

Sprinkle most of the breadcrumbs into a 9 x 13 inch (23 x 33 cm) roasting pan. (These breadcrumbs will absorb any extra liquid from the "marinating" process.) Pour in a splash of the measured olive oil. Cover the entire roasting pan with a layer of tomatoes, cut side up, fitting them snugly, and even overlapping slightly. Scatter with some of the onion slices, and tear some basil leaves over. Sprinkle generously with some of the salt and more breadcrumbs, then splash more of the olive oil over it all.

Now spread a single layer of bucatini over the tomatoes. Make sure nowhere is left uncovered by pasta, but more importantly, that the pasta pieces are not overlapping. Add more of the olive oil and sprinkle more of the salt on the pasta.

Repeat this process until you run out of ingredients; the top layer, however, should be tomatoes, this time cut side down. Drizzle with whatever olive oil is left from the original ½ cup (125 ml).

Cover with foil and rest in the fridge for at least 3 hours—ideally 7–8 hours, but no longer than that, or the pasta will become oversoaked and soggy. Also, the last hour of marinating should be at room temperature.

When you're ready to serve, preheat the oven to 350°F (180°C).

Bake the foil-covered pasta for about 1 hour, then remove the foil. Drizzle with the extra 2 tablespoons olive oil and bake for another 10–20 minutes. You can add another 10 minutes under the broiler if the tomatoes don't seem too shriveled to you.

Remove from the oven and let the pasta rest for at least 10 minutes before serving. Cut and serve as you would a lasagne.

# The majestic rice timbale from Naples

*Sartù di riso*

They call this magnificent dish a triumph of rice, the pride and glory of high-end Neapolitan cooking. It looks like something out of a medieval painting, but in fact it is more modern than that. The legend goes that the queen of Naples and Sicily in the late eighteenth and early nineteenth century, Queen Maria Carolina of Austria, was not a huge fan of Neapolitan cuisine, so she hired French cooks, who created this dish as a way to make rice appealing to the court.

Rice came to Italy with the Arabs in the Middle Ages, together with many other foods, including cane sugar, eggplant, and spinach from Persia. For centuries, rice was regarded as something exotic, found in spice shops where precious and rare goods were sold. Then it changed status and became something to feed the poor and the ill—mostly in flour form, and as a form of *blancmange* (*biancomangiare*). In the eighteenth century, the fate of rice changed again, as the grain made its way to the tables of the rich as refined risottos in the north and majestic *sartùs* in the south.

Now that you have reached this point in the book, can you spot the visual similarities between *sartù*, *tahchin* (page 72), and *maqluba* (page 158)? The paths that led to these rice recipes are very different, but one cannot deny the similarities. The Neapolitan *sartù* is closely related to *timballo*, a dish with a crust of dough, filled with *maccheroni* and *ragù*, while *timballo di melanze*, a version covered with slices of fried eggplant, looks staggeringly like the Palestinian *maqluba al badinjan*. The resemblance between the Iranian *tahchin* and *sartù* is equally striking. Even the concept is similar: in *tahchin* the rice is bound together with yogurt and eggs; in *sartù*, with cheese and eggs (and sometimes tomato sauce).

The original *sartù* of Queen Maria Carolina's court had meatballs, chicken liver, mozzarella, boiled eggs, sausages, mushrooms, and peas. The archaic versions of *tahchin* served in Persian royal courts also had a ludicrous number of ingredients, enough to put the *sartù* to shame.

This recipe is slightly lighter. I learned it from my friend Fiammetta, who won a competition in Naples in 1969 for her *sartù*. It's a complicated dish, and a project to dedicate a day to when you want to impress a crowd, but oh so worth it.

This is a traditional version, from which meat is ineradicable, but you could also play with vegetarian ingredients. The important thing is to serve it with a lot of extra tomato sauce to pour on each slice.

To guarantee success when unmolding the *sartù*, make sure you use a good pan, as much butter as physically possible, and heaps of breadcrumbs to cover it all. Let the *sartù* rest before attempting the unmolding.

*Continued ›*

«

*Makes a tall 8 inch (20 cm)*
*cake pan; serves 8–10*

### For the *ragù*
a handful of dried porcini
    mushrooms
3 tablespoons olive oil
1 small onion, diced
1–2 bay leaves
1 clove
1 slice of lardo, pancetta,
    or rindless bacon, sliced
10½ oz (300 g) beef, such
    as brisket or shin, diced
1 sausage, skin removed,
    meat crumbled
2 tablespoons sweet Marsala
    or port wine
¼ cup (60 ml) red wine
4¼ cups (1 liter) tomato passata
    (puréed tomatoes)
2 teaspoons salt
freshly grated nutmeg

### For the rice
1 tablespoon salt
3 cups (700 g) risotto rice,
    such as arborio, carnaroli,
    or vialone nano
7 tablespoons (100 g) butter
3 eggs
¾ cup (70 g) grated parmesan
freshly grated nutmeg, to taste

### For the meatballs
10½ oz (300 g) ground meat;
    beef is traditional, but you
    could also use pork
3 tablespoons dry breadcrumbs
2 tablespoons grated parmesan
1 egg
½ teaspoon salt
freshly ground black pepper
3 tablespoons olive oil,
    for pan-frying

### FOR THE RAGÙ, RICE & MEATBALLS

Start with the *ragù*. Soak the dried porcini in a small bowl of hot water. Meanwhile, heat the oil in a large pot over medium heat. Add the onion, bay leaves, clove, and lardo. After a couple of minutes, mix in the beef and crumbled sausage. Cook for about 10 minutes, until the meat is no longer pinkish. Turn up the heat, then stir in the Marsala and red wine and let it simmer to reduce a bit.

Drain the porcini, chop them, and add to the pot, along with the tomato passata. Pour ½ cup (125 ml) water into the passata cans/bottles to loosen any remaining sauce, then add this to the pot as well. Bring to a gentle simmer over medium-high heat, then reduce the heat and simmer, covered, for 1 hour. Check on it midway and season with salt and nutmeg to taste.

Now start on the rice. Bring a pot of water to a boil and season with the salt. Add the rice and boil for slightly less time than indicated on the package. Drain the rice, place it in a large bowl, then immediately mix in the butter and set aside to cool completely.

While the rice is cooling, make the meatballs. Mix the meat, breadcrumbs, parmesan, egg, salt, and some black pepper in a bowl and knead to get a smooth paste. Shape into tiny meatballs the size of an unshelled hazelnut. Heat the olive oil in a large pan and cook the meatballs for about a minute on each side to sear them. Set aside.

Now that the rice has cooled, add the eggs, parmesan, and nutmeg. To give the rice a pinkish orange color, mix in about ½ cup (125 ml) of the sauce from the *ragù* (but try not to get any meat chunks in it). Season lightly with salt.

Remove the bay leaves from the *ragù*. Set aside about 2 cups (500 ml) of the sauce (again, minus the meaty bits) to serve alongside the *sartù*.

## To assemble

3½ tablespoons butter, for greasing, plus an extra 1½ tablespoons chopped butter, to finish

3 tablespoons dry breadcrumbs

7 oz (200 g) mozzarella, drained and cut into small pieces

generous 1 cup (200 g) frozen peas, cooked and drained

### ASSEMBLING THE SARTÙ

Preheat the oven to 400°F (200°C). Generously grease a deep 8 inch (20 cm) round cake pan (mine is 4 inches/10 cm deep) with the 3½ tablespoons butter, then coat it with about 2 tablespoons of the breadcrumbs, making sure the pan is well coated with both butter and breadcrumbs. (If your pan size is different, you may need less or more of each.)

Now you want to start building a rice crust on the bottom and sides of the pan, to hold the *ragù* and filling. First, set aside about 2 ladlefuls of the rice as a "lid" to close the *sartù* at the very end.

Start by adding several ladlefuls of rice to the pan, pressing the rice down with the back of the ladle. You want to have 1¼–1½ inches (3–4 cm) of rice at the bottom. Then build a ¾ inch (2 cm) thick "wall" of rice all around the sides of the pan, starting at the bottom, pressing up with the back of the spoon or ladle. Toward the end, you will need to use your hands to shape the top of the wall.

Fill the crust, first with a scattered layer of mozzarella, then some spoonfuls of *ragù*, then some peas, then some meatballs. Repeat until you run out or the pan is full. Remember that the "virtue" of a good *sartù* is to have a *cuore umido*, a wet heart, which should spill out when you cut into it, so be generous with the sauce.

Lastly, enclose the filling with the remaining rice you set aside, pushing down gently with your palms. If there's a little eruption of sauce, patch it up with rice.

Sprinkle the top with the remaining breadcrumbs, and add the remaining butter in tiny pieces.

Bake for about 1 hour, or until the top is golden. Remove from the oven, and prepare to be patient—the *sartù* MUST rest for an hour before serving.

*Continued ›*

«

**SERVING THE SARTÙ**

Once your *sartù* has rested, run a knife gently around the inside edge of the pan. Put a serving dish on top. With the help of tea towels or oven mitts (the pan might still be too hot to hold), invert the pan onto the dish. You should hear the *sartù* sliding down. Do not rush to remove the pan; do this very gently and slowly. (If you've used the right pan with enough butter and breadcrumbs, the *sartù* should slide out easily.)

Heat the reserved *ragù* sauce and pour it into a gravy boat, then take it to the table with your masterpiece. The first cut is a triumph, the saucy heart of gooey cheese, peas, and meatballs spilling out of its elegant shell of rice. Serve drizzled with the sauce.

# Guinea hen with pomegranate

*Faraona alla melagrana*

Guinea hen in Italian is called *faraona*, which is almost the same word used for "pharaoh." This, plus the supposedly exotic pomegranates, makes the dish sound and look extravagant and luxurious.

I first heard about this dish from my friend Valentina, whose family has peasant roots in the Le Marche and Romagna regions. She mentioned it in passing as something her mom would cook, and I was immediately reminded of chicken with pomegranate sauce (*nārdoon*, page 86) from northern Iran. Although very distant geographically, they're basically the same dish: poultry with pomegranate seeds and juice. Only the aromatics are different: in Iran turmeric and saffron are used; in Italy, local herbs such as rosemary and thyme. Both dishes are born out of a peasant lifestyle.

"Romanìa and Other Arabic Words in Italian," a paper that historian Maxime Rodinson published in *Medieval Arab Cookery*, is about another similar dish called *romanìa*. It is a recipe for chicken with pomegranate juice mentioned in a nineteenth-century Italian manuscript about the food of the fourteenth and fifteenth centuries. There's a similar recipe with the same name in Arabic medieval manuscripts. Here's the riddle: was the dish called *romanìa* in Arabic because it was originally from the Byzantine Empire—which in Arabic was called *Romanìa*? Or was it named after *rumman*, "pomegranate" in Arabic, which means the dish in fact traveled from the Middle East and found itself in an Italian cooking manuscript centuries later?

*Continued ›*

«

Ugo Tognazzi, the celebrated actor who appeared in Italian movies in the second half of the twentieth century, had a lot to say about *faraona alla melagrana*. Tognazzi was a true gourmand with an undying love for cooking. He had a little farm where he raised chickens and pigs, and even made some *salumi* from scratch. His recipe for guinea hen with pomegranates appears in his delightful cookbook, *Il Rigettario*. The title plays with the word *ricettario*, which means a recipe collection, whereas a *rigettario* would be a collection of "rejections." It's an entertaining book in which Tognazzi shares his memories, and of course menus, as megalomaniacally as only a rich and powerful man can. His recipe for *faraona alla melagrana* is disappointing, however. I only borrow the idea of dried porcini mushrooms from him to give this autumnal dish depth of flavor. The rest of this recipe is inspired by Valentina's mom.

Guinea hen is less wild and gamey than I imagined, and works just as well cooked in a Mediterranean style with citrus and local woody herbs such as rosemary, thyme, and bay leaves. If you can't find guinea hen, use a good-quality free-range chicken. Make sure you crisp up the skin first.

*Serves 2–4 (depending on the size of the bird)*

a handful of dried porcini
   mushrooms
3 tablespoons olive oil
a handful of thyme sprigs
2 rosemary sprigs
2 bay leaves
3–4 garlic cloves, skin on,
   lightly bashed
1 guinea hen, cleaned, skin on,
   cut into 6 pieces; my bird
   weighed a bit more than
   2 lb 4 oz (1 kg)
1 cup (250 ml) unsweetened
   pomegranate juice, or the
   juice of 2 pomegranates
1 teaspoon salt
freshly ground black pepper
seeds of 1 pomegranate

Soak the porcini in a small bowl of hot water for 10–15 minutes.

In a large heavy-based pot, heat the olive oil with all the herbs and garlic cloves over medium-high heat. When hot and fragrant, add the bird pieces, skin down. Brown them for about 5 minutes, turning them over around midway.

Drain the mushrooms and add them to the pot, then pour in the pomegranate juice. Bring to a simmer, then reduce the heat, cover, and cook for 15–20 minutes.

Add the salt and some black pepper and turn the bird pieces over in the juice. (If your bird is larger, you probably need to cook the pieces a bit longer with the lid on at this point.)

Add half the pomegranate seeds and cook, uncovered, for about 10 minutes, so some of the excess liquid can evaporate. Check whether the meat easily falls from the bone; if it doesn't, cook for another 10 minutes.

Remove the rosemary and thyme (and garlic, if you like), but keep the bay leaves because they look nice. Arrange the guinea hen pieces nicely on a platter. Pour the juices and cooked pomegranate seeds over the meat. Sprinkle the remaining pomegranate seeds on top and serve with crusty bread (and red wine).

# The beloved eggplant bake

*Parmigiana di melanzane*

*Melanzana*, the Italian word for eggplant, was once *mela insana*, meaning "insane/unhealthy apple." In the past it was also known as *pomo sdegnoso*, "disdained apple." Many Italian words for fruits and vegetables have the word *mela* (apple) or *pomo* (pome) in them. Indeed, *melagrana* (pomegranate) is made of *mela* and *grana* (apple and grains), just as the English version combines *pome* (apple/pome) and *granate*, meaning an apple with many seeds. In Italy, the original name for tomatoes was *pomi d'oro* (golden pomes), later changed to *pomodoro*.

From the early Middle Ages until the nineteenth century, several written accounts refer to eggplant as vulgar and vile—food for the "low people and the Jews." In fact, as with tomatoes centuries later, it was the Jews in Italy who first used these new foods, because the Christians were wary of them. Amusingly, Pellegrino Artusi turned the tables around on this fact in his nineteenth-century classic *Science in the Kitchen and the Art of Eating Well*, where he wrote that if eggplant were considered vile because Jewish people ate them, it only shows that, "as with other significant things, they have a better nose than us Christians."

Made with layers of sliced eggplant, laced with tomato sauce, mozzarella, and sometimes fried or boiled eggs—or even ham if you're in Naples—eggplant parmigiana has become a symbol of the "heaviness" of Italian cooking but also its ridiculous deliciousness. Unless you're an innate eggplant hater (and if you're an adult, you've got to do something about that), a parmigiana is just about the tastiest thing on the planet. It's the combination of fried eggplant with tomato, just as *mirza ghasemi* (page 57) is the combo of charred eggplant and tomato. Only a few short years ago, parmigiana would be served as a *contorno* (side) between the *primo* (pasta or soup) and the *secondo* (main dish). Hardly anyone would be able to digest that now. It shines alone on the stage as the star of the show—as it should.

So much guilt surrounds parmigiana, just because the eggplant is fried; it shouldn't be a source of torture but joy! What also makes parmigiana truly special is time, not just in the oven, but preparing all the bits, slicing, frying the eggplant, making the sauce, waiting for the cooked dish to rest, and then all the cleaning up. A token to the eggplant gods, gracing us with insanely good flavor *only* after we have paid the price in proper labor.

You could of course consider grilling or even baking the eggplant slices, rather than frying them, but as food writer Rachel Roddy says, "Fry, fry, fry is almost always my answer." The Middle Eastern woman in me rejoices at this, as it is also my answer, even to questions not concerned with eggplant, *la mela insana*.

*Continued on page 246 ›*

«

*Makes a 9 x 13 inch
(23 x 33 cm) dish;
serves 6–8*

2 large or 3 medium eggplant,
 about 2 lb 4 oz (1 kg), sliced
 ¼ inch (5 mm) thick
salt, for sprinkling
10½ oz (300 g) mozzarella
vegetable oil, for pan-frying
2–3 tablespoons all-purpose
 flour
1 cup (100 g) grated parmesan

For the tomato sauce
2 tablespoons olive oil
1 garlic clove, peeled
2½ cups (600 ml) tomato passata
 (puréed tomatoes)
a handful of basil leaves

To rid the eggplant of their water, sprinkle the slices generously with salt, then place in a colander with a tray beneath, to catch the bitter juices. Ideally, weigh them down with something heavy, like a pile of plates. Leave for at least 30 minutes, and up to 2 hours.

Meanwhile, make the tomato sauce. In a pot, heat the olive oil with the garlic clove. As soon as it's fragrant, add the passata. Clean out the passata jar with a little water and stir that in, too. Drop in the basil leaves. Partially cover with a lid (or ideally a splatter screen) and leave to simmer gently over low heat for 15–30 minutes. I don't add salt, because the eggplant will be salty, and the parmesan is also quite flavorful. Set aside.

Preheat the oven to 350°F (180°C). Slice the mozzarella and squeeze the pieces to lose the excess liquid. Leave them in a strainer to drain. Rinse the eggplant slices and pat them dry.

Heat the frying oil in a large deep-sided frying pan over high heat. Meanwhile, line a platter or two with paper towels, and spread the flour on a plate. Coat each eggplant slice on both sides with flour, gently shaking off any excess flour over the plate.

Working in batches, fry several eggplant slices at a time until golden brown on both sides; this is a messy step but only takes a few minutes. Remove immediately and drain on the lined platters.

Discard the basil leaves and garlic clove from the sauce. Spread some sauce over the base of a 9 x 13 inch (23 x 33 cm) baking dish, then cover with a layer of eggplant slices; it's fine if they slightly overlap. Add another few spoonfuls of sauce and spread around, top with some mozzarella slices, and sprinkle generously with parmesan. Add another layer of eggplant and repeat, spreading all the remaining sauce and parmesan over the final layer.

Bake for about 30 minutes, or until the sauce is bubbly and less watery, and most importantly, the top is golden and crisp.

Remove from the oven and rest for at least 30 minutes before serving. In my opinion, parmigiana is best at room temperature.

# Pork roast with pears & chestnuts

*Arrosto di maiale con pere e castagne*

The match of savory pork meat with sweet fruit is one made in heaven, as is lamb and fruit, which is quite common in the Middle East, Iran, and even the Balkans. Apicius, the legendary ancient Roman gourmand who lived in the first century AD, has a recipe for Parthian (Persian) lamb in his celebrated cookbook *De Re Coquinaria*. There's debate on whether it was actually a Persian recipe or he was referring to a particular spice that was originally from what was then Persia, but what interests me most is the use of prunes in that lamb recipe. The same book also has recipes for wild boar with fruit, and mentions prunes as a main condiment for poultry—which to this day is very common in Iran, as seen in the saffron roast chicken recipe on page 83.

Our pork roast, or *arista*, which is exceptionally popular in Tuscany, goes well with many fruits, from apples and pears in fall, to prunes and apricots in summer, and even pomegranates and blueberries. It's a much simpler recipe than it appears, making it a suitable choice for gatherings and holiday meals. Some twigs of bay leaves or thyme add a festive touch.

*Serves 4–6*

10½ oz (300 g) fresh chestnuts (see Note)
1¾–3½ oz (50–100 g) pancetta or bacon, thinly sliced
2 lb 4 oz (1 kg) pork loin, with some fat on
3 large beurre bosc or kaiser pears (or any type suitable for baking)
2 French shallots
2 rosemary sprigs
¼ cup (60 ml) white wine
2 tablespoons olive oil
1 teaspoon salt
freshly ground black pepper

Using a sharp knife, carve an incision in the skin of the chestnuts. Cook them in boiling water for 20–30 minutes. Drain them in a colander, then run them under cold water until cool enough to handle. Peel the chestnuts, discarding the skin, and set aside.

Meanwhile, preheat the oven to 425°F (220°C). Neatly arrange the pancetta slices crossways over the lean side of the pork loin, so they overlap a bit. Press the pancetta onto the meat; this is where the pork will get its seasoning from. Now carefully tie the meat with butcher's twine, several times crossways and twice lengthways, to secure the pancetta slices and to keep the roast nice and snug so it will cook evenly. (You may also ask your butcher to prepare the loin for you in this way.)

Core the pears (I like to leave the skin on) and cut each into four wedges. Peel the shallots, leaving the roots intact, and cut each into four wedges as well. In a roasting pan, toss the pear and shallot wedges with the rosemary sprigs, wine, olive oil, salt, and black pepper to taste. Gently roll the pork loin over all the seasonings in the pan, rubbing them into the pork to take up the flavors. Make space for the pork in the middle of the pan,

*Continued ›*

«

then nestle it into the wedges, pancetta side up. Rub some of the seasoned oil from the pan all over it.

Roast for 30 minutes, then turn the oven down to 350°F (180°C). Baste the pork with the pan juices, toss in the chestnuts, and roast for another 35–45 minutes. Remember that the roasting time here is for a 2 lb 4 oz (1 kg) pork loin, so adjust the time based on the weight of your pork.

Remove the roast from the oven. Cover with foil and leave to rest for 30 minutes before very thinly slicing and serving with the chestnuts, pears, and shallots. Crusty bread to mop up the juices is a must—and so is red wine to sip alongside.

**Note:** If fresh chestnuts aren't available, use 7 oz (200 g) frozen or parboiled chestnuts.

*Pictured opposite*

# Tomatoes stuffed with rice

*Pomodori al riso*

The beach at Ostia Lido, barely 19 miles from the center of Rome, is considered a rather ugly one—but we would take the *trenino* (little train) there anyway. Apart from us Iranians on that train, I noticed many blondes from the eastern gates of Europe, dark men with large eyes from the Middle East, as well as Filipinos and South Americans. In short, we were united on that *trenino* by not being able to afford to travel to better beaches. There were also Black and Bangladeshi vendors, sweating under the weight of heavy bags of shawls, accessories, coconuts, and fresh drinks that they'd sell to the beachgoers. Occasionally they would be harassed or even assaulted by some far-right thugs from Forza Nuova or CasaPound, who would "police" the beach. Sometimes someone went to their rescue. I was always grateful to these people, knowing very well that with my foreign accent, I too would be a target for them if I went to protest.

It was on this beach that I first spotted, but did not taste, *pomodori al riso*—tomatoes stuffed with rice, marinated in tomato juice. Some loud teenagers leapt out of the water and came running to their mom, who was sitting under a huge umbrella. She opened a plastic lunchbox and passed them

*Continued ›*

«

each a tomato, into which they bit enthusiastically—because everything tastes better when you're 13 and you've just emerged happy, exhausted, and hungry after having thrashed around for an hour or so in the sea.

With an uncanny resemblance to the Iranian *dolmeh*, the *dolmas* of Turkey and the Balkans, and the Greek *gemista*, the Italian *pomodori al riso* are the simplest of them all. My theory is that the further west you travel, the fewer ingredients are used in stuffed vegetables—in this case only rice soaked in the juice of the tomatoes, salt, olive oil, and basil. Ada Boni, the legendary Roman cookbook writer and author of *The Talisman of Happiness*, first published in the late 1920s, has a surprising ingredient in her *pomodori al riso*—cinnamon, which is unusual to find in modern savory dishes from central Italy southward. But in Ada Boni's recipe, it's as though a whiff of warmth from the East lingers on the shores of Italy where these stuffed tomatoes are often eaten.

Choose tomatoes that are perfectly in season but a tiny bit on the harder side; you don't want them to split in the oven. As with the Greek *gemista* (stuffed tomatoes or bell peppers/eggplant), these tomatoes are baked on a bed of potatoes, giving soft-textured bits of potato when hidden under a tomato, crispy bits when exposed. You don't want to miss those crunchy bits of potato stuck to the side of your pan, lightly flavored with tomato and garlic, drunk on olive oil.

*Serves 4–5 as a light main, or more as a side*

8–10 large tomatoes,
    ripe but not too soft
salt, for sprinkling
a few pinches of sugar
a pinch of ground cinnamon
2 tablespoons olive oil,
    for drizzling

## For the filling
½–⅔ cup (120–150 g) raw risotto
    rice (or more precisely,
    1 tablespoon for each tomato)
a handful of basil leaves
1 garlic clove, lightly bashed
2 tablespoons olive oil
1½ teaspoons salt

## For the potatoes
2–3 potatoes, 7–10½ oz
    (200–300 g)
2 tablespoons olive oil
1 teaspoon salt

Start by cutting ½–¾ inch (1–2 cm) off the top of each tomato, to make "lids"; set these aside. Leaving a thick shell, scoop the flesh, core, seeds, and juices into a bowl and blend together with a handheld immersion blender.

Add the filling ingredients to the tomato pulp and mix together. (If you don't want to have to fish out the garlic clove later, you can finely chop it.) Cover and set aside to marinate for at least 30 minutes; an hour or two is better. Meanwhile, season the cavity of the hollowed-out tomatoes and the inside of the lids with salt, and sprinkle with sugar and cinnamon. Leave them upside down on a tray lined with paper towels.

If you're making these tomatoes for the next day (great idea), possibly during one of the hottest days of summer, now would be a good time to go out and have dinner and come back after an hour or two.

Presumably it's evening now and you can brave turning on the oven; preheat it to 375°F (190°C).

Peel the potatoes (or don't, if they're organic and well scrubbed). Slice them into sticks larger than chunky fries, or dice them—however you like roast potatoes best. Toss them in a large baking dish or roasting pan with the olive oil and salt to make sure the potatoes are well seasoned; I like to use my hands for this.

Discard the garlic clove from the marinating rice. Fill each tomato a little more than halfway with the rice, then add a generous tablespoon of marinating liquid. Place the tomatoes on the nest of potatoes in the dish or pan and put their lids back on. Drizzle them all with about 2 tablespoons of olive oil.

Roast until the tomatoes are shriveled and wrinkly. The baking time depends on your tomatoes and your oven, but start checking after about 45 minutes; normally it takes 1–1¼ hours. I like to turn the broiler on for the last 10 minutes to lightly char the tomatoes.

These tomatoes are better served cold the next day (at the beach, or at least alfresco), but if you must eat them today, let them rest for at least 30 minutes before serving.

*Pictured opposite*

# Coffee, *merenda* & other indulgences

Patience Gray in her *Honey from a Weed* describes *merenda* as something associated with wine and conviviality, beyond an ordinary snack. Her *merenda* is savory: a slice of good bread with some mortadella or salame.

*Merenda* as I have come to know it, however, is indeed a snack. Something you have mid-morning or mid-afternoon. The best-loved Italian *merendas* are very simple and close to Patience's vision: *pane e olio*, bread drizzled with olive oil and sprinkled with salt, or *pane e pomodoro*, bread rubbed with tomato, or bread with hazelnut cocoa cream.

The recipes of this chapter are sweet. They can be made for dessert, breakfast, or *merenda*, because I like my midday snacks to be sweet.

Italian baking is often rustic and simple, albeit regionally diverse. It's quite common for a cookie or fritter to have different names in different regions, with the recipe remaining almost the same. The baking tradition is closely entangled with religious and folkloric rituals, with sweets for Christmas, Easter, Carnival, Lent, and the day dedicated to the patron saint of each town being the most popular.

# Tiramisu, two ways

Embarrassingly, for too many years I was convinced tiramisu was a Roman dessert—a belief that was shattered when I visited Padua in the Veneto region and was told of its origin there. I excitedly shared this on social media—to the immediate outrage of the Friuliani (from the Friuli–Venezia Giulia region), who also claim to have invented this beloved dessert.

Although its recipe didn't appear in cookbooks until the 1960s, the wordplay on *tirami su*—"pick me up"—slightly reminds us of the experiments of Filippo Tommaso Marinetti, the poet and founder of the Futurist movement. In the early twentieth century, he made some unfortunate attempts to Italianize the names of some foods, coming up with words such as *pranzoalsole* for picnic (lunch in the sun), or *traidue* for sandwich (between two).

To completely enjoy tiramisu, you have to be at peace with the possibility of salmonella infection, and in Italy we are—at least with the homemade version. We are blessed with good eggs, pasteurized when bought in supermarkets, but we long to use the freshly laid eggs from the countryside that always result in the best creams. All this to say, the following recipes use raw eggs, so you need to be sure about them.

I must confess I like the strawberry tiramisu better than the classic one because it has a hint of acidity. The classic coffee tiramisu shouldn't be too wet and soggy, so make sure you dip only the sugary sides of the cookies in the coffee, then lay them down on the smooth sides, so that the coffee slowly bathes all the cookies with a little help from gravity.

The paradox is that the strawberry one is nicer when the cookies are properly wet.

If you feel creative, you could substitute the cookies with sponge cake, or other spongy, cookie-like things that would suck up liquid. Some even substitute mascarpone with other creamy cheeses or ricotta—but for me, honestly, the whole point of tiramisu is to have an excuse to eat mascarpone cream by the spoonful, with some other nice bits in between.

# Classic tiramisu with espresso

*Makes an 8 x 12 inch
(20 x 30 cm) dish;
serves 6–8*

5 fresh organic eggs, separated
5 tablespoons sugar (see Note)
1 lb 2 oz (500 g) mascarpone
1 tablespoon lemon juice
    (optional)
1¼ cups (300 ml) freshly brewed
    espresso, cooled to lukewarm
30 savoiardi (ladyfinger cookies),
    approximately
unsweetened cocoa powder,
    for dusting

Whisk the egg yolks with the sugar using an electric mixer (or by hand) until pale and fluffy. You should not be able to feel sugar grains if you rub the creamy mixture between your fingers. Gently mix in the mascarpone until smooth.

Using a clean whisk or beaters and a very clean bowl, whip the egg whites until white and stiff; adding a tablespoon of something acidic like lemon juice helps. In a circular movement, very delicately fold the egg whites into the mascarpone cream.

Pour the lukewarm espresso into a small dish or a wide, shallow bowl in which a savoiardi will fit easily. Spoon a bit of the mascarpone cream into an 8 x 12 inch (20 x 30 cm) serving dish, and spread well until the bottom is coated.

Dip one cookie, sugary side down, into the espresso, but only halfway through, then place the cookie smooth side down in the serving dish. (The coffee will gravitate downward and soak the whole cookie with time; if you fully dip the cookies in the coffee to begin with, they will get too soggy and the excess coffee will run into the dessert.)

Repeat until you have covered the bottom of the dish, breaking the cookies where they don't fit whole. Cover with a thick layer of the mascarpone cream. Repeat with another layer of cookies, and finish with another layer of mascarpone cream. (If you use a deeper but smaller dish, you might end up with three layers of cookies, which is why the number of cookies is approximate. Some people add a layer of chopped dark chocolate in the middle, but I honestly find it too sweet. )

Heavily dust the final layer of mascarpone cream with cocoa powder. Cover loosely with foil and leave in the fridge for 4–8 hours, to allow the mascarpone to thicken again and for the cookies to soak. It is then best enjoyed straight away. Enjoy as a dessert, midnight snack, or lavish breakfast.

**Note:** An easy ratio to remember is 5 eggs, 5 tablespoons sugar, and 500 g (1 lb 2 oz) mascarpone.

# Strawberry tiramisu with Marsala

*Serves 6–8*

4 eggs, separated
4 tablespoons (50 g) sugar
   (see Note)
zest of 1 lemon
14 oz (400 g) mascarpone
1 tablespoon lemon juice,
   optional
16 savoiardi (ladyfinger cookies),
   approximately

For the strawberries
1 lb 2 oz (500 g) strawberries
juice of 1 lemon
3 tablespoons sweet Marsala
3 tablespoons sugar

Hull the strawberries, then cut into quarters and place in a bowl. Dress with the lemon juice, Marsala, and sugar. Cover and leave to macerate for at least 2 hours—or better still, overnight in the fridge—until the strawberries are sitting in a pool of sweet, slightly tangy crimson liquid. Strain the strawberry liquid into a deep dish large enough to roll the cookies in, and set the strawberries aside.

Whisk the egg yolks with the sugar and lemon zest using an electric mixer until pale and fluffy. No sugar grains should be felt if you rub the creamy mixture between your fingers. Gently mix in the mascarpone until smooth.

Using a clean whisk and a very clean bowl, whip the egg whites until white and stiff; adding a tablespoon of something acidic like lemon juice helps. In a circular movement, very delicately fold the egg whites into the mascarpone cream.

Set out six to eight nice-looking cups or fancy little glasses. Add a dollop of the mascarpone cream into the bottom of each cup, then spoon in some strawberries. Roll a cookie a few times in the strawberry juice and let it suck in the liquid at its leisure (unlike the method used with the coffee in the classic tiramisu on page 255). Break the cookie into pieces so that it fits in the cup, pushing down a bit to fill any gaps. Add more strawberries, then a good dollop of mascarpone cream, and repeat. Before finishing with one last layer of mascarpone cream, gently tap each cup on your work surface to settle the ingredients, so that empty spaces are not left in the middle.

Cover each cup loosely with foil and chill in the fridge for about 4 hours before serving, so that the mascarpone cream sets. They are then best served straight away.

**Note:** The simple ratio to remember for this recipe is 4 eggs, 4 tablespoons sugar, and 400 g (14 oz) mascarpone.

# Plain gelato drizzled with olive oil & flaky salt

You might wrinkle your nose at this idea, but please stay with me. I was once invited to an olive oil mill in Umbria to taste the new oil of the season. Our visit ended with a rather fancy lunch, with different types of olive oil per dish, and for dessert we were offered simple *fior di latte* gelato. To our astonishment, the chef drizzled each cup with the new olive oil, peppery and green, then sprinkled on some flakes of sea salt. It was unexpectedly wonderful. Try it! This is not really a recipe but more an invitation to a seemingly outrageous culinary move; all you need is good-quality plain tasting ice cream (possibly from your favorite ice cream place), good-quality extra virgin olive oil (preferably new season), and good salt. Fleur de sel is a fancy expensive salt that tastes great, but crushed pink Himalayan salt would look nice, too—just don't sprinkle on too much.

*Serves 1*

2 scoops of good milk flavored
   ice cream or fior di latte gelato
1 teaspoon good-quality
   extra virgin olive oil
a tiny pinch of your best salt

Scoop the ice cream into a cup. Drizzle with the olive oil and very lightly sprinkle with salt.

Serve immediately, preferably with a dessert wine such as Passito.

# Pears poached in wine with mascarpone cream

Like many Iranians before me, I was raised with the idea that certain foods are "cold" and "moist" and need to be accompanied by "warm" and "dry" foods, and vice versa. For example, we wouldn't serve fish with yogurt on the side—indispensable as yogurt is on the Iranian table—because they are both "cold." This is also why we add the "dry" and "warm" mint and walnuts to the "cold" and "moist" yogurt and cucumber dip, *mast-o khiar* (page 68)—and why "warm" and "dry" spices such as cinnamon and ginger are added to "cold" vegetables to balance them.

These unwritten rules that we know by heart and apply to our cooking as part of our culinary identity are relics of traditional medicine from the Middle Ages, practiced by Persian physicians such as Avicenna—who in turn drew on the teachings of the ancient Greek physician Galen,

*Continued ›*

«

who categorized nature, people, food, and plants into the four "humors" of cold, warm, moist, and dry. In pre-modern Europe too, these same medical principles were applied to diet and food combinations. The idea was to "correct" each food with cooking and pairings so that they would be balanced. For example, fruits, being "cold" and "moist," had to be consumed with "warm" and "dry" things: melons were to be eaten with prosciutto; pears, peaches, and cherries with cheese. Cooking fruit in wine, although more of a French custom, had the same notion behind it, as both cheese and wine were considered "warm" and "dry."

And that's how we got these pears, looking sexy and French in their flamboyant and glossy red wine sauce, with a luscious mascarpone cream on the side. Admittedly, the medieval ones couldn't have been this extravagant.

Italian pears in wine are barely poached with a variety of different warm spices. I use a cinnamon stick, which I just love too much to leave behind, but as Italian cookbook legend Marcella Hazan says, bay leaves are essential for poaching pears in wine.

Make sure you use pears that are suitable for cooking. The Marsala can be replaced with port. If you don't have mascarpone, any sort of cream, ice cream, custard, or even whipped cream could work, as the pears do need something to tame them down. There might be some culinary objections to this, but I admit to eating these pears with Greek yogurt for breakfast, too.

*Serves 8*

4 beurre bosc or kaiser pears,
   or other pears suitable
   for cooking
1 cup (250 ml) red wine
⅔ cup (120 g) sugar
2 bay leaves
1 cinnamon stick

For the mascarpone cream
14 oz (400 g) mascarpone
2 tablespoons sugar
¼ cup (60 ml) Marsala

Peel the pears and cut them in half. Use a teaspoon to remove the seeds and core from each pear half, leaving a nice round hollow.

In a pot wide enough to fit all the pear halves, heat the wine with the sugar, bay leaves, and cinnamon stick, stirring to dissolve the sugar. When it comes to a gentle simmer, add the pears, rolling them in the wine so that all parts are tinged with the wine.

Cover and cook over medium heat for 10 minutes. Remove the lid and simmer, uncovered, for another 20–30 minutes, until the wine has reduced and is a bit syrupy. Leave to cool.

Before serving, whip or mix the mascarpone cream ingredients together until smooth.

Serve the pears with a generous dollop of mascarpone cream, drizzled with the syrupy wine.

# Chestnut flour pancakes with ricotta & honey

*Necci*

These incredibly simple chestnut flour pancakes are from the mountainous parts of Tuscany and Emilia, and are so rustic that they remained hidden and forgotten in those mountains for many decades. But now you can find them in the local markets in Tuscany, mostly in fall.

Chestnut flour, now considered a refined and "special" ingredient, was once dubbed *pane dei poveri*, the bread of the poor. These pancakes were used as bread for sausages, pancetta, stracchino cheese, or ricotta, or were eaten plain. Knowing how much water is needed for the batter requires a bit of practice. The batter needs to be fluid enough so that it spreads in the hot pan, but it won't spread like a normal crepe or pancake batter; the cooking time is also longer than for the average pancake.

*Makes 6–8 large pancakes*

olive oil, for greasing
2¼ cups (200 g) chestnut flour
a pinch of salt
honey, for drizzling (preferably
  chestnut honey)

For the ricotta cream
⅔ cup (150 g) good ricotta
  (preferably made from
  sheep's milk)
1 tablespoon brown sugar
zest of ½ orange
a pinch of ground cinnamon
  (optional)

Preheat a cast-iron or heavy-based nonstick frying pan with a little olive oil, using paper towel to grease the pan well. You don't need a lot of oil, but you might need to repeat this step for each pancake.

Meanwhile, put the chestnut flour in a bowl. Gradually pour in about 2 cups (450 ml) water, whisking well the whole time; you might not need the full amount of water at all. The final batter must be fairly thin, with a consistency not unlike a crepe batter; the amount of water you need depends on how absorbent your chestnut flour is. Add the salt and whisk until smooth.

With the heat on medium-high, pour a ladleful of the batter into the hot pan and swirl the pan around so that the pancake spreads. You'll notice it doesn't spread as widely as regular crepes, nor will it cook as quickly. Cook for 4–6 minutes on the first side before carefully flipping it over (the pancake is delicate). Cook for another 2–3 minutes, then remove from the pan. Repeat with the remaining batter.

Mix the ricotta cream ingredients together until smooth. If your ricotta is too thick, add a tiny splash of water.

To serve, place a dollop of ricotta cream in the middle of each pancake, spread it, then roll the pancake up into a cylinder. Drizzle with honey, but not too much. Serve immediately.

# An easy Italian ring cake

*Ciambellone*

When I was studying Italian in Iran, one of the most memorable conversations that I had to study from my textbook began with the following question: *Fai colazione al bar o a casa?* Do you have breakfast in a bar (café) or at home? To me, back then, this was such an absurd question to ask someone. Months later, I had my first breakfast at a bar, *caffè latte e cornetto* (a latte and an Italian croissant)—a culinary epiphany I won't ever forget.

Apart from *cornettos*, bars also serve simple ring cakes called *ciambellone*—literally meaning a big doughnut. This cake is also often baked at home. It's extremely rustic, and a bit more bready than a batter-based cake, which is why you'll see a lot of flour in the recipe. According to my friend Giulia, a *ciambellone* must be dry, yet light, with a deep crack on top. To get this result it is essential to use liquid oil, as melted butter won't have the same effect.

Serve the cake for breakfast or *merenda*, to dunk in warm milk with coffee, or something stronger; as Marcella Hazan says, peasants would dunk their ciambellone in a glass of wine.

*Makes a 9½ inch (24 cm) cake*

butter, for greasing
3⅓ cups (400 g) all-purpose flour, plus extra for dusting
4 eggs
1 cup (200 g) sugar
zest of 1 lemon
scant 1 cup (220 ml) milk
⅓ cup (80 ml) neutral-flavored oil, such as sunflower
½ teaspoon salt
1½ teaspoons baking powder
confectioners' sugar, for dusting (optional)

Preheat the oven to 350°F (180°C). Grease a 9½ inch (24 cm) ring cake pan with butter, dust with flour, and set aside.

Using an electric mixer, whisk the eggs with the sugar and lemon zest until the mixture is pale and airy and the sugar has dissolved. Gradually pour in the milk and oil, whisking all the while.

In a separate bowl, combine the flour, salt, and baking powder, then gradually sift it into the egg mixture, folding until just combined. Pour the batter into the cake pan.

Bake for about 50 minutes, until the cake is golden, with a deep crack on top, and a toothpick comes out clean.

Remove from the oven and leave to cool in the pan for about 10 minutes, then transfer to a rack to cool completely. Once cooled, you can sprinkle it with confectioners' sugar. Ideally, serve with big mugs of *caffè latte*, though tea is good, too.

The cake will keep on the counter for a few days. After that, it will be a bit stale but still good to dunk in a *caffè latte*.

# An orange-scented rice cake

*Torta di riso al profumo d'arancio*

There is something universal about cooking rice in milk that translates to instant comfort—a soothing embrace that goes beyond borders and cultures and unifies them in silky sweetness. People everywhere make some form of rice pudding. Some more runny, some more dense. Some served cold or at room temperature, some warm. Rice pudding goes by a literal name almost everywhere: *shir berenj* in Persian, *riz bel halib* in Arabic, *sultac* in Turkish, *rizogalo* in Greek, and *budino di riso* in Italian.

More than the density or the temperature it's served at, what makes the rice pudding of each region distinct are the aromatics and spices used. In Iran, rosewater is often used; and when made with saffron, the rice pudding is cooked in water rather than milk and becomes the *sholeh zard* on page 101. Sometimes a few cardamom pods are added too; my mother would use only cardamom and almost no sugar, and serve the pudding cold with sour cherry jam. In Lebanon, Syria, and other parts of the Levant, rosewater, orange blossom water, or both are used. Orange zest, a continuation of orange blossom water, also starts appearing here, with citrus coming forth more often in southern Italy and Spain, as a souvenir of the Arabs who first brought them here. The more we travel west, the more present vanilla becomes.

The following recipe is, by all accounts, just another rice pudding, with an addition of eggs, then baked. I am not sure about its origins, but I have eaten similar cakes both in Bologna and in the region of Campania.

When it comes to orange-flavored cakes that lie halfway between cake and pudding, I can't not think of the famous almond and orange cake of the legendary Claudia Roden. She first wrote about it in *A Book of Middle Eastern Food*, and it has inspired and obsessed many home bakers and food writers alike—including me. In that recipe, two oranges are boiled whole, then blended with ground almonds, eggs, and sugar, then baked for about an hour. The cake is an absolute delight that I bake several times each winter in peak citrus season.

More fascinating still is the journey of that cake, which Roden calls a "Judeo-Spanish cake." Roden, a Jewish Egyptian, says she was given the recipe by her sister-in-law, who in turn learned it from her grandmother—who grew up in Aleppo, Syria, in a family of Sephardic Jews who had emigrated from Spain to avoid persecution.

I would not be surprised if this orange-scented rice pudding cake had a similar journey, traveling full circle, coming back home after a long time away.

*Makes a 10½ inch
(26 cm) cake*

7 cups (1.7 liters) whole milk
scant 1 cup (180 g) sugar
zest of ½ lemon, cut into large
    strips with a vegetable peeler
1⅓ cups (300 g) risotto rice,
    such as arborio, carnaroli,
    or vialone nano
½ teaspoon salt
butter, for greasing
5 eggs, separated
3½ tablespoons orange liqueur
    (I use Cointreau)
3 teaspoons vanilla extract
    or paste
zest of 1 orange, plus extra
    to garnish
¼ cup (40 g) candied orange
    peel, diced
confectioners' sugar, for dusting

In a large pot, bring the milk, sugar, and lemon zest to a moderate boil. Stir in the rice and salt. Cook over medium heat for 30–40 minutes, until the liquid is absorbed and the rice is sticky and creamy, stirring occasionally so the rice doesn't stick. Remember that the mixture will become thicker as it cools. If it looks like the liquid is being absorbed before the rice is completely cooked through, reduce the heat. Transfer to a large bowl and leave to cool completely.

Preheat the oven to 350°F (180°C). Lightly grease a 10½ inch (26 cm) round cake pan with butter. Line the bottom and sides with parchment paper, then rub a bit more butter onto the paper.

Remove as many lemon zest pieces from the cooled rice as you can find.

Using a hand whisk, beat the egg yolks with the liqueur, vanilla, and orange zest, then add to the rice with the candied orange peel and mix well.

Using a clean whisk and a very clean bowl, whisk the egg whites until stiff and smooth, then gently fold them through the batter.

Carefully pour the mixture into the cake pan and smooth the top with a knife.

Bake for about 1 hour, or until the top is golden.

Remove from the oven, then leave to cool completely in the pan for about an hour before unmolding.

Before serving, dust with confectioners' sugar and garnish with extra orange zest. The cake will keep in an airtight container for a few days, refrigerated if the weather is hot.

*Pictured on page 266*

# Ricotta & wild cherry pie

*Crostata di ricotta e visciole*

The Jewish Ghetto in Rome is one of the city's most fascinating neighborhoods for many reasons. One of them is that it's impossible to speak of food in Rome without running into Jewish traditions that are still palpably present in this part of the city. As is the long history of atrocious injustices against the Jewish community.

The Catholic Church officially confined the Jewish population to the ghetto in the 1500s, where Jews were effectively consigned to live as second-class citizens. These systematic discriminations eventually led to the raid by the Gestapo in 1943, which saw 1,023 Jews deported to Auschwitz from those very same streets where artichokes are still fried and kosher trattorias abound. Only 16 of those people survived.

In the eighteenth century, a papal edict forbade Jews to trade dairy products. Legend says that to hide the ricotta filling in the pies from the papal guards, they would cover the pies with another shell—as opposed to a lattice top—and hence the famous *crostata di ricotta e visciole* was born in the ghetto. Whether this legend is true or not, a little bakery in the current neighborhood, called Boccione, has gained fame for just such a pie, heavily stuffed with ricotta and *visciole* jam, and covered with an almost burned top. Their recipe is jealously guarded and hard to replicate, especially that burnished top.

The *visciole* are wild cherries. They have a brief season, and their flavor is somewhere between classic cherries and sour cherries. As an Iranian obsessed with sour cherries, I suggest that in the absence of *visciole* jam, you use sour cherry jam; otherwise, regular cherry jam will do.

*Makes an 8–8½ inch (20–22 cm) pie*

2⅔ cups (600 g) good-quality ricotta
¼ cup (50 g) sugar
scant 1 cup (300 g) sour cherry jam, or *visciole* preserve

Drain the ricotta in a fine-meshed sieve placed over a bowl for at least 4 hours. (You could leave it overnight in the fridge, too.) Don't skip this step, or the pie will be watery.

To make the crust, toss the flour in a bowl with the chilled butter, then pinch the butter between your thumbs and index fingers until the texture looks sandy. (You could do this with a few pulses in a food processor if you prefer.)

In a separate bowl, beat the egg yolks and sugar until well combined, then add to the flour mixture, along with baking powder and salt. Bring the dough together, but do not overwork it.

*Continued ›*

《

### For the crust
3 cups plus 2 tablespoons
  (375 g) all-purpose flour
13½ tablespoons (200 g) very
  cold butter, cut into cubes
4 egg yolks
¾ cup (150 g) sugar
½ teaspoon baking powder
a pinch of salt

### For the egg wash
1 egg, beaten with a splash
  of water

Divide the dough into two portions, one-third and two-thirds. Flatten each into a disc, wrap with plastic, and chill in the fridge for 30 minutes. (You can refrigerate the pastry overnight, just leave it at room temperature for 5 minutes before rolling out.)

Once the ricotta has fully drained, add the sugar and whisk very well, using an electric mixer or by hand, until the sugar has dissolved and the batter is smooth. For an even smoother result, push the mixture through a fine-meshed sieve with the help of a spatula. Refrigerate while you work with the dough.

Preheat the oven to 400°F (200°C).

Roll out the larger pastry portion between two sheets of parchment paper, until it's barely thicker than ¼ inch (5 mm). With the help of the parchment paper, transfer the pastry to an 8–8½ inch (20–22 cm) springform cake pan, then peel off the top layer (save this for later). Leaving the bottom sheet of paper on the pastry, use it to line the bottom of the cake pan, making sure the pastry comes at least 2 inches (5 cm) up the side. The pastry is very flexible, so you can just tear off excess bits and stick them in where needed.

Spread the jam over the bottom, then smooth the ricotta cream over the top. Leave in the fridge while you proceed.

Roll out the remaining pastry portion between two sheets of parchment paper (including the piece you saved earlier), making it a bit smaller than the cake pan. Remove one sheet of paper and flip the dough on top of the pie with the help of the other sheet, then peel it off. I then like to fold the sides up and over the top sheet of pastry, but choose how you'd prefer to seal and pinch all the pastry edges together.

Chill for another 10 minutes in the fridge; the chilling helps immensely with the pastry's friability.

Brush the egg wash all over the pie, then bake for 45–50 minutes, or until the pastry is deep golden on top.

Remove from the oven and leave to rest in the pan for at least 1 hour. I prefer to slice the pie in the pan, as it's tall and heavy. It will keep in an airtight container in the fridge for a few days.

# Little "chestnuts" that are really almond cookies

*Castagnelle*

Mariangela and I first met on Instagram through a discussion of wonderful travel experiences to Iran. She had been there a few years previously and had returned to Rome laden with goodies (many of which ended up as props for the photos in this book), bagfuls of barberries, Iranian black pepper (don't ask me why; I've never known Iranian black pepper to be special in any way), and even the seeds of a Persian melon (Odessa melon), now planted in her lush organic garden.

This recipe for simple almond cookies, known as *castagnelle*, was first passed on to me by Mariangela in a video of her mother making heaps of them for Christmas. Her family is from Puglia, a region famous for white stone villages and crystal-blue seas, thousands of acres of ancient olive groves rooted in rust-colored soil, and amazing food—including almonds.

Not to be confused with *castagnole*—which are fried balls of dough rolled in sugar, a classic festive sweet known by many other names throughout Italy—*castagnelle* has its etymological roots in *castagna*, which literally means "chestnut". In other words, these almond cookies flavored with cocoa powder and lemon zest are "little chestnuts."

They remind me of another almond cookie named after a totally different fruit. *Toot*, the name of an Iranian marzipan cookie, literally means "white mulberry" in Persian. Both *toot* and *castagnelle* have disarmingly few ingredients: the first uses ground blanched almonds and sugar, flavored with rosewater and sometimes saffron and almond extract; the latter has ground toasted almonds and sugar, a dash of flour, lemon zest, and cocoa powder (or espresso, depending on which town in Puglia you're from). Both are named after an ingredient that they do not contain.

*Toot*, being a marzipan, does not require cooking, and is often served during Norouz (Persian New Year) or at weddings. *Castagnelle* should spend only a few minutes in the oven, and is often baked for Christmas.

*Continued ›*

《

*Makes 1 big cookie jar full*

1½ cups (200 g) raw almonds
  (with the skin on)
1⅔ cups (200 g) all-purpose flour
a pinch of baking powder
1 cup (200 g) sugar
1½ teaspoons unsweetened
  cocoa powder
zest of 1 lemon

Preheat the oven to 350°F (180°C). Spread the almonds on a baking sheet and toast them for about 5 minutes, or until they smell fragrant and some of them are cracked, but be careful not to burn them. Remove from the oven and let them cool, then chop them finely on a chopping board, leaving some texture. It's perfectly fine if the result is coarse and uneven.

In a bowl, mix the almonds with the remaining ingredients. Very gradually add very small amounts of water, working it in until you have a thick dough. The total amount of water will be 2–3 tablespoons, depending on your flour.

On a work surface, roll small pieces of the dough into sausage shapes, about ¾ inch (2 cm) thick, then slightly flatten them with your fingers. Using a sharp knife, cut the dough on the diagonal, into diamond shapes.

Carefully transfer to a baking sheet lined with parchment paper, leaving some space in between, as the cookies will rise a bit.

Bake for 5–8 minutes; don't be tempted to overbake. The cookies will become slightly whiter and sometimes a bit cracked, and might look uncooked when hot, but will harden as they cool.

Leave to cool completely before serving. They will keep in an airtight container for a few weeks.

# SUGGESTED MENUS

## Christmas Eve

Oranges & anchovies (page 218)
Stuffed artichokes, Sicilian style (page 228)
Trout stuffed with herbs, barberries & walnuts (page 88)
Syrupy baked quince, spicy & drunken (page 168)

## Christmas

Crostini with lardo, figs & honey (page 221)
Savory stuffed apples (page 95)
Pork roast with pears & chestnuts (page 247)
*OR*
Saffron roast chicken stuffed with dried fruit (page 83)
Pears poached in wine with mascarpone cream (page 258)

## Plant-based Christmas

Fried polenta bites with porcini mushrooms (page 216)
Iranian jeweled rice (page 78)
Artichoke & potato salad (page 199)
Little "chestnuts" that are really almond cookies (page 271)

## Easter

Date & onion frittata (page 40)
Italian rustic pie with potato, eggs & cheese (page 226)
Italian rustic pie with spinach & ricotta (page 227)
Strawberry tiramisu with Marsala (page 257)

## Eid

Fattah bread salad from the Levant (page 141)
The Palestinian upside-down triumph of rice (page 158)
Meatballs with sour cherries from Aleppo (page 161)
Baklava beyond borders (page 162)

# Norouz (Iranian New Year)

*The national dish in Iran for Norouz is sabzi polo, a herb*
*pilaf served with fish. While there's no recipe for it in this book,*
*you can enjoy these other dishes during this spring holiday.*
Balls of herbs & flatbread (page 54)
Trout stuffed with herbs, barberries & walnuts (page 88)
Tiny coconut cookies (page 113) and Tiny walnut cookies (page 114)
Saffron & lemon toasted almonds & pistachios (page 111)

# Yalda (winter solstice)

A simple Iranian salad for winter (page 63)
Iranian rice (page 22)
Chicken braised with pomegranate (page 86)
Milky, silky tricolor pudding (page 165)

# Summer mezze feast

Sharbat with vinegar & mint syrup, cucumber (& gin) (page 120)
Iranian yogurt with cucumber (page 68)
Creamy eggplant & tahini dip (page 130)
Oniony, garlicky braised bell peppers (page 193)
Fattoush bread salad (page 144) or A Tuscan bread salad (page 191)
Zucchini patties with feta & dill (page 137)
Labneh with (rose petal) jam (page 170)

# BBQ party

A simple salad of grilled zucchini, garlic, mint & (a lot of) olive oil (page 180)
Charred eggplant with egg & tomato (page 57)
Scarlet spread of bell peppers, pomegranate molasses & walnuts (page 132)
Lamb kebabs with tomato sauce & yogurt (page 154)
Plain gelato drizzled with olive oil & flaky salt (page 258)

# ACKNOWLEDGMENTS

The long process of making this book coincided with the most challenging physical and mental state I have ever been in in my life, as well as a catastrophic global pandemic, and a brutal war. It is therefore not a cheesy exaggeration to say that without the help of many talented and kind people this book would not be in your hands now. It really did take a village to make *Pomegranates & Artichokes*.

First of all, to my Murdoch Books family, thank you for being the most perfect home I could have wished for this book. Thank you Corinne Roberts for falling in love with it, and for the generous support and immeasurable kindness you have shown me at every stage of the process, despite the distance and opposite seasons and time zones, encouraging me constantly to trust my instincts and voice my wishes for the book.

Thank you Céline Hughes for gently accompanying me on the remaining path of bringing this book to the world. Thank you Virginia Birch for masterfully keeping us all on track. Thank you Katri Hilden for patiently making sense of my entangled words. Thank you Vivien Valk, Megan Pigott, and Madeleine Kane for making this book as stunningly beautiful as it is, accommodating every single one of my many visual whims.

A great thank-you also goes to the people in the publicity, marketing, and rights teams, busy making *Pomegranates & Artichokes* reach as many readers as possible all around the world, and to anyone else who has worked on this book without me knowing their name.

My immense gratitude goes to my agent, Victoria Hobbs, for taking a chance on me despite all odds. Thank you for the patience and wisdom with which you've always been very generous. Thank you Jessica Lee, and Jessica Sinyor before her, and the other lovely people at A.M. Heath who have taken care of me.

Thank you Giulia Picardo for bringing your brightness, enthusiasm, and open heart to the long winter of lockdowns, and for testing each recipe in this book with me while wearing a mask. Your friendship has been one of the best gifts this book has given me.

Thank you Alice Adams Carosi for the phenomenal work you put into getting the right ingredients and cooking the beautiful food for the photos, and for mastering the art of Iranian *tahdig* by the second day of the photo shoot. Thank you also for getting me the ingredients to test and shoot a recipe for the proposal, before we even knew whether there would be a book at all, when the pandemic and a broken knee made it impossible for me to get them.

Thank you Valentina Solfrini for having been a second pair of eyes and hands to me during the photo shoot, for lending your remarkable finesse at photography and styling to this book, and for being tirelessly helpful at every moment, effectively being the only person who never lost her cool during the shoot. Thank you also for the lovely portraits you've taken of me.

Thank you Mariangela Ascatigno and Giulio Rigoni for welcoming me into your beautiful Madonnella farmhouse, for your enthusiasm and your support, and for lending me the relics of your travels to Iran that shine in these photos. Thank you Elisabetta Busini for your helping hands in the kitchen.

A huge thank-you to Hellen Almoustafa, Rania Hammad, Josephine Abou Abdo, and Eleni Vonissakou, my sisters from "In Between" for the long, heart-to-heart chats about Syria, Palestine, Lebanon, Turkey, Greece, and beyond, as well as the many people who helped and advised me during my research travels.

To friends, old and new, who went above and beyond to get me the books I needed for research, either by scanning them page by page, or mailing them to me from across oceans. Thank you Behnaz Motarjem, Zary Hashemi, Mahyar Mahmoudi, and Sepideh Zarrinkelk.

Thank you my dear Fiammetta Greco, the closest thing to a family I have here in Rome, for everything. For your precious friendship, your infinite love for Iran, and your impressive wealth of knowledge and expertise in cooking. Thank you for sharing your cherished family recipes and sublime life stories with me.

I am very grateful to the amazing and big-hearted community of food and wine women (and men) that I have met almost exclusively online. To Emiko Davies, Naz Deravian, Eleanor Ford, Olia Hercules, Mimi Thorisson, Kamin Mohammadi, Tessa Kiros, Saba Parsa, Tannaz Sassooni, Betty Liu, and many others, thank you for the friendship, support, and kindness.

My sincere gratitude also goes to every person who has followed my work during these years, attended my cooking classes and photography workshops, cooked my recipes, and read my articles. I would not be here now without your support.

To my friends near and far, the occasional odd acquaintances, my Buddhist community, my therapist, and anyone who's listened to my rants and put up with my tantrums, thank you for helping me navigate these strange times, battling lockdowns and imposter syndrome while giving birth to my first baby (this book). I know I haven't said it nearly enough, but I am very grateful to you all. I hope you know who you are.

I'm grateful to the kind staff of Palazzo Merulana (which I call my "office"), where I've written this book, from the proposal to these acknowledgments.

My last thank-you inevitably goes to my parents in Iran. I hope I've made you proud, as I know there's not much else I could do for you. Hope you like the book.

# BIBLIOGRAPHY

آشپزی دورهی صفوی *Ashpazie Doreye Safavi
(A Safavid Period Cookbook)* by Iraj Afshar,
Soroush Press, Tehran, 2nd edition, 2011

هنر آشپزی *Honare Ashpazi (The Art of Cooking)* by
Rosa Montazami, Ketabe Iran, 51st edition, 2013

کارنامهٔ خورش *Karnameye Khoresh (The Recipes
of Nader Mirza Qajar, 1884)* edited by Nazila
Nazemi, Atraf Publications, Tehran, 2nd edition,
2020

کتاب مستطاب آشپزی، از سیر تا پیاز *Ketabe Mostatabe
Ashpazi, Az Sir ta Piaz (The Rt. Honorable
Cookbook: From Soup to Nuts)* by Najaf
Daryabandari and Fahimeh Rastkar, Karnameh
Publishing House, 7th edition, 2006

سفره اطمعه *Sofreye Atma'eh (The Cooking
Manuscript of the Cook of the Court of Naser
Al-Din Shah Qajar, 1880)* edited by Ali Akbar
Kashani and Mohammad Mirkazemi, Safir Ardehal
Publications, Tehran, 2013

---

*De re Coquinaria, La Cucina Dell'antica Roma
(On the Subject of Cooking: The Cuisine of
Ancient Rome)* by Apicio, Newton Compton
Editori, Kindle edition, 2012

*Il Mito Delle Origini: Breve Storia Degli Spaghetti
al Pomodoro (The Myth of the Origins: A Brief
History of Spaghetti with Tomato Sauce)* by
Massimo Montanari, Il Mito Delle Origini, Editori
Laterza, 2019

*Il Mondo in Cucina: Storia, Identità, Scambi (The
World in Cuisine: History, Identity, Exchanges)* by
Massimo Montanari, Editori Laterza, 2006

*Il Rigettario (The Collection of Rejections)* by Ugo
Tognazzi, Fabbri, Milan, 1977

*Il Talismano Della Felicità (The Talisman of
Happiness)* by Ada Boni, Editori Colombo, Rome,
1965

*L'identità Italiana in Cucina (Italian Identity in Its
Cuisine)* by Massimo Montanari, Editori Laterza,
2013

*La Cucina Italiana: Storia di Una Cultura (Italian
Cuisine: A Cultural History)* by Massimo
Montanari, Capatti, Alberto, Editori Laterza, 2005

*La Scienza in Cucina e L'arte di Mangiar Bene
(Science in the Kitchen and the Art of Eating Well)*
by Pellegrino Artusi, Einaudi, 1970

*La Tavola e La Cucina Nei Secoli Xiv e Xv (The
Food and Cuisine of the 14th and 15th Century)*
by Lorenzo Stecchetti, Dott. O. Guerrini, and
G. Barbera, Editore, Florence, 1884

*Racconti Di Cucina (Stories of the Kitchen)* by
Angela Frenda, Rizzoli, 2015

*Vincenzo Corrado, Il Cuoco Galante (Vincenzo
Corrado, The Gallant Cook)* by Giorgia Chiatto,
Mavarosa Edizioni, 2011

---

*A New Book of Middle Eastern Food* by Claudia
Roden, Penguin Books, 1968

*Bountiful Empire: A History of Ottoman Cuisine*
by Priscilla Mary Isin, Reaktion Books, 2018

*Delizia! The Epic History of the Italians and Their
Food* by John Dickie, Hodder & Stoughton, Kindle
edition, 2009

*Essentials of Classic Italian Cooking* by Marcella
Hazan, Knopf Doubleday Publishing Group, 1992

*Feast* by Anissa Helou, Ecco Press, 2018

*Five Quarters: Recipes and Notes from a Kitchen
in Rome* by Rachel Roddy, Headline Home, 2015

*Go, Went, Gone* by Jenny Erpenbeck, Granta Publications, Kindle edition, 2017

*Honey from a Weed* by Patience Gray, Prospect Books, 2001

*Italian Food* by Elizabeth David, Barrie & Jenkins, 1990

*Orientalism* by Edward W. Said, Knopf Doubleday Publishing Group, 1978

*Kaukasis the Cookbook: The Culinary Journey Through Georgia, Azerbaijan & Beyond* by Olia Hercules, Mitchell Beazley, 2017

*La Cucina, The Regional Cooking of Italy* by Accademia Italiana Della Cucina (The Italian Academy of Cuisine), Rizzoli International Publications, 2009

*Medieval Arab Cookery: Essays and Translations* by Maxime Rodinson, A. J. Arberry, and Charles Perry, Prospect Books, 2006

*Scents and Flavors: A Syrian Cookbook*, edited and translated by Charles Perry, NYU Press, 2017

*Taste Makers: Seven Immigrant Women Who Revolutionized Food in America* by Mayukh Sen, W. W. Norton & Company, 2021

*Tasting Rome: Fresh Flavors and Forgotten Recipes from an Ancient City* by Katie Parla and Kristina Gill, Clarkson Potter, 2016

*The Ethnic Restaurateur* by Ray Krishnendu, Bloomsbury Academic, 1st edition, 2016

*The Good Immigrant*, edited by Nikesh Shukla, Unbound, 2016

*The Good Immigrant USA* by Nikesh Shukla and Chimene Suleyman, Little Brown Book Group, 2019

*The Greek Slow Cooker* by Eleni Vonissakou, Page Street Publishing, 2019

*The Language of Food: A Linguist Reads the Menu* by Dan Jurafsky, W. W. Norton & Company, 2014

*The Oxford Companion to Food* by Alan Davidson, Oxford University Press, Kindle edition, 2014

*The Turkish Cookbook* by Musa Dagdeviren, Phaidon, 2019

*Samarkand: Recipes and Stories from Central Asia and the Caucasus* by Caroline Eden and Eleanor Ford, Octopus Publishing, 2016

"Trembling Before Blancmange" by Tamar Adler, *The New York Times Magazine*, 26 May 2016; nytimes.com/2016/05/29/magazine/trembling-before-blancmange.html

"A History of Börek" by Alexander Lee, *History Today*, volume 69, issue 9, September 2019; historytoday.com/archive/historians-cookbook/history-borek

# INDEX

First published in 2023 by

Interlink Books
An imprint of Interlink Publishing Group, Inc.
46 Crosby Street
Northampton, Massachusetts 01060
www.interlinkbooks.com

Published simultaneously in the United Kingdom
and Australia by Murdoch Books, an imprint of
Allen & Unwin

Publisher: Corinne Roberts/Céline Hughes
Editorial Manager: Virginia Birch
Design Manager: Vivien Valk
Editor: Katri Hilden
American edition editor: Leyla Moushabeck
Proofreader: Rachel Markowitz
Map illustrator: Rose Russell
Recipe development assistant: Giulia Picardo
Photography and styling: Saghar Setareh
Photography and styling assistant: Valentina Solfrini
Home economist: Alice Adams Carosi
Assistant home economist: Elisabetta Busini
Production Director: Lou Playfair

Cover illustrations Background images: Shutterstock/
Viacheslav Lopatin and ilolab. Other elements: Artichoke
leaves, Creative Market/ Patterns for Dessert; whole
artichoke, iStock/Azurhino; bird, iStock/Andrew_Howe;
all other images from rawpixel.

Library of Congress Cataloging-in-Publication
Data available

ISBN 978-1-62371-740-7

Color reproduction by Splitting Image Color
Studio Pty Ltd, Clayton, Victoria
Printed by C&C Offset Printing Co. Ltd., China

OVEN GUIDE: You may find cooking times vary
depending on the oven you are using. For convection
ovens, consult the manufacturer's instructions or, as a
general rule, reduce the oven temperature by about 25°.

IMPORTANT: Those who might be at risk from the
effects of salmonella poisoning (the elderly, pregnant
women, young children, and those suffering from immune
deficiency diseases) should consult their doctor with any
concerns about eating raw eggs.

10 9 8 7 6 5 4 3 2 1